BEGINNING NOW

JOHN D. DAVIES

BEGINNING NOW

*A Christian Exploration of
the First Three Chapters
of Genesis*

FORTRESS PRESS

PHILADELPHIA

Library of Congress Catalog Card Number 70-157535

ISBN 0-8006-0037-1

Printed in Great Britain

*To the Christian Institute of
Southern Africa and the Anglican Students'
Federation of South Africa*

Contents

Preface   9

1. CHRIST THE BEGINNING   13

2. THE ORDERED UNIVERSE   22

3. MAN AND ME   66

4. FIRST INTERVAL   117

5. THE EXPERIMENTERS   129

6. SECOND INTERVAL   179

7. TRAGEDY   186

8. CURSE AND BLESSING   226

Notes   259

Acknowledgments   273

Index of Names and Subjects   275

Index of Scriptural References   281

'I believe in life after birth.'

Preface

THIS book began as a series of Bible Studies which I led at the 1964 national conference of the South African Anglican Students' Federation. The original studies were distributed under the imprint of 'The Doormat of Godot'; the present book represents the development of those studies during my subsequent six years as Anglican chaplain at the University of the Witwatersrand and the Johannesburg College of Education. It has grown almost uncontrollably, and it would go on growing if I had not decided, almost arbitrarily, to call a halt at the point of the study's present condition. I have a great deal of sympathy for Professor Ian Barbour's remark, in the preface to his book which is immeasurably more complete and systematic than mine: 'One never finishes a book – one simply abandons it eventually.'[1]

One reason for the undisciplined growth of this book is that the subject-matter of the first three chapters of Genesis is virtually the sum of all things; hardly a day can pass without some event or reflection which could be relevant to this material: this is presumably true for anyone, anywhere in the world. But another reason has become apparent to me only in the last few years, in which the Christian Institute of Southern Africa and the South African Council of Churches have been exerting significant leadership, and which have seen the publication of the 'Message to the People of South Africa' and a good deal of subsequent material. This second reason for the character of this book is the development of the ideological conflict in South Africa. To an increasing extent, the Church in South Africa is called not only to state the truth, not only even to try to live the truth, in the midst of all its own compromise and separatedness; it is called also to an intellectual and spiritual wrestling with all sorts of false gospels, distorted understandings of

1. Ian G. Barbour, *Issues in Science and Religion* (SCM Press, London, 1968), p. iii.

9

human identity, and tragic deceptions concerning the nature of human security. As well as being the scene of grotesque suffering and day-to-day frustration, South Africa is a uniquely instructive theological laboratory. I wish that I could make this aspect rather more explicit in the following pages; but my specific references to our South African context are far from being the only points where this Genesis material has sharp local significance.

This study, therefore, is not offered as a systematic, universal commentary; it starts with *me*, with my situation, my awareness and my blindness. There are whole worlds of interest which it does not touch. Alongside the work of the systematic scholars, I believe that the word of God is also communicated through situational, non-systematic perceptions. Certainly, in the context which lies behind the writing of this book, we urgently need a truly situational theology. I hope that this book may be seen to some extent as an experiment in this direction, on the understanding that error and failure are inevitable in any experimental discipline.

My main thanks are due to the members of the Anglican Students' Federation, especially those of our Johannesburg student parish, for their stimulus and encouragement over the past seven years. It must be obvious that at a great number of points in the book I am following ideas borrowed from many previous writers: for their general approach and for providing starting-points for my own thought, I am most conscious of my indebtedness to Bishop J. E. Fison and Fr Harry Williams, C.R. Another very basic starting-point was provided by Joseph Haydn; his study *The Creation* is, I believe, a work of profound theological validity; it offers an essential critique of my own work, for it exposes the inevitable feebleness of any theological study which attempts to communicate through words alone.

The New English Bible version of The Old Testament appeared when I had completed much of the writing of this book. I quickly realized that there were several points at which it represents the views of scholars which I had already incorporated into my comments. I therefore made a detailed revision of the book, taking the New English Bible as a working text.

For their encouragement and suggestions, I am grateful to Beyers Naudé of the Christian Institute, Stephen Hayes of Windhoek (the original 'Doormat of Godot'), John Fenton of St Chad's, Durham, Leonard Cutts and David Edwards in London. For their patient and generous help in typing I am grateful to Merle Stoltenkamp of the Christian Institute and Snoeks Maclagan of the Study Project on Christianity in Apartheid Society. The help of my wife Shirley has been the most valuable throughout; not only has she supplied both typing and encouragement in large quantities when they were most urgently required; she has also been the most thorough critic and improver of the work as a whole; and as a wife and mother she has, consciously or unconsciously, offered me the most wonderful material and data from which to make a study of creation.

For the introductory quotation, 'I believe in life after birth', I am grateful to Canon Eric James of Southwark: he saw these words on a button worn by some prophetic character in America. I believe that this credo sums up the biblical affirmations about creation: it sums up God's mandates to man which find expression in medicine, education and politics, in the struggle against injustice and isolation, in the concern to overthrow ideologies of death and superstition: it sums up the splendid surprise of the gospel of Jesus Christ. If there is anything valid in this book, it will be at points where the truth of this belief may succeed in breaking through the confusion of my own perceptions. To believe in God is to believe in life, in the most passionate and crucial sense. This is all that I am really wishing to say.

Johannesburg, July 1970   J. D. D.

Christ the Beginning

I WAS once asked to give a lecture on the first three chapters of Genesis to a university rationalist society. Bearing in mind that the audience would not share my Christian beliefs, I thought that it would be best to confine myself to an account of the universal human significance of these chapters, particularly of the story of Adam and Eve, leaving out any Christian slant. So I was a little taken aback when the first questioner after the exposition blamed me quite vigorously for depriving him of the expected ammunition, saying, 'It seems to me extraordinary that you can talk for an hour about Adam and Eve without once mentioning St Paul'. After which he proceeded very competently to give the said Apostle a thorough hammering.

The first three chapters of Genesis were written long before Christ or St Paul, and they can stand on their own as valid documents; but my disarming questioner did have a genuine point. Until the Christian preachers started work, surprisingly little attention was paid to these chapters, which are hardly anywhere referred to in the rest of the Old Testament. Adam comes into his own as a counterpart or foil to Christ. Those who are aware of the unity of mankind in Christ are enabled to perceive a unity of mankind in Adam as well. Those who are aware of salvation in Christ have the freedom and courage to look squarely at Adam and not be horrified by the image of their own doom. For the men of the old covenant, the Bible began with Abraham or the Exodus, and the creation stories were a preface to complete the picture; for Christians, it could be said that the whole Bible is to be found in these three chapters, and that the rest of the Scripture is response, expansion and commentary.

This study is not meant to be a technical working-out of the original significance of the words for the people who first heard them; it is an attempt to see what these words can mean for people who approach them in this age with the pre-

13

supposition of Christian faith. We shall be closer in spirit to the studies of St Augustine[1] and of Bonhoeffer[2] than to any more academic commentary on the text.

The Old Testament was not written with Genesis first and everything else progressively deriving from it; the Old Testament is a series of climaxes and covenants, of which the most formative is the Exodus and law-giving under Moses; history works backwards or forwards from that extended event. Abraham, though important in himself, is a preparation for Moses; in turn, the earlier chapters of Genesis work backwards from Abraham to creation. The character of God is known primarily not from creation but from Exodus. The character of the God of Exodus, the God of the covenants, is read back into the creation stories. It would be perfectly possible to have a creator-god quite unlike the God of Genesis 1–3.

Christians also work backwards from a covenant event which determines our knowledge of God's nature. For us, God is known as the God and Father of our Lord Jesus Christ; Jesus Christ is the means by which the character of God is known – 'He who has seen me has seen the Father'.[3] For us, therefore, creation is an activity of this God who is Father of our Lord Jesus Christ; we read Genesis not as a record of what God was like before he became Father, but with Christian presuppositions. This is, maybe, not the usual method of technical critical scholarship, but this study is not scholarly in that sense – it aims to be an exploration of the text in the light of Christian theology. And Christian theology begins and ends with Christ. Christ is not a further factor introduced when the creation section has been dealt with, nor is he an optional extra for those who want a fancier religion for themselves; Christ, the same yesterday, today and forever, is the clue to creation; because he is always contemporary, he ensures that we see creation as a contemporary event and not merely as something in the distant past. The Hebrew text of Genesis speaks to us of the Creator under the titles of Yahweh and Elohim; but, in the context of Christian faith, these chapters speak to us of the one God and Father of our Lord Jesus Christ, the one God of the whole Scripture. So the Revised Standard Version forsakes the translation 'Jehovah' – 'the use of any proper name for the one and only God, as though there were other gods from whom He had to be distinguished, was discontinued in Judaism before the Christian era and is entirely inappropriate for the universal faith of the Christian Church'.[4]

Christians, like the Hebrews of old, look at creation in the light of the covenant events by which we live. Our Creator is known to us first as our Saviour. The old Israel knew itself as a community that had been created by the act of God in the Exodus; God was known to them as Creator and covenant-maker; and they saw him then not only as their own Creator but as Creator of everything. For Christians, God is known in the same manner, as the maker of the risen Christ, as the maker of the individual Christian, who is risen with Christ. The covenant story of the Exodus starts with the saving of the individual child Moses through water; it takes effect for the whole community of Israel in their passing-over the water of the Red Sea and in the protection of their houses by the sprinkling of the Passover blood. The covenant story of the Christian Exodus, the effective beginning of the gospel and appearing of the Kingdom of God, starts with the baptism of the individual man Jesus in the water of Jordan; it takes effect for the whole community of the disciple-Church in his death and the releasing of water and blood on the cross. The covenant story of the individual Christian starts in his baptism in water and is continued in his sharing of the community action of the eucharist, the sacrament of the body and blood of Christ. Like the old Israelites, we see this same God of the covenants active in the first creation, active in the element of water. We see this same God as Lord of the end of history also; the blood of the Lamb is a cleanser, a whitener more effective than water, for the members of the new community of God's design, the community that shall overcome and put into the past all barriers of race and language and culture;[5] through the blood of the cross God is reconciling to himself the whole universe, the whole scheme of things which was inaugurated in the Genesis activity.[6]

As it was for the people of the old Israel, so for Christians history is not a repetition of events or patterns endlessly going round in circles; it is a line, a movement from a beginning to an end. This picture of history has taken such a strong hold on us who share 'Western' presuppositions that we may not feel how widely acceptable the cyclical picture can be. Few academic historians follow Toynbee in plotting regular patterns, but many less sophisticated people find security in a cyclical image, represented by proverbs like 'history repeats itself' and beliefs associated with reincarnation. A linear view of history which offered certainties concerning the beginning and the end of the line would also offer a satisfying security; but neither secular history nor biblical history can do this, although several Christian traditions have failed to resist the temptation to develop the hints of the New Testament into something like a railway timetable of the hereafter. For us, the line of history is determined not by its extremities but by its middle; it is an event in the centre of history which indicates the character of both the beginning and the end.

For people who neither have hope nor want hope, things go round and round in circles, getting nowhere. Things may seem to follow each other; but, in reality, nothing really changes. For such people, God is the one who keeps things in order, who can be appealed to for deliverance from the threat of change; and the recognized agents of God are paid and expected to be representatives of the past; the Church is valued as a guardian and preserver, rather than as an explorer or pathfinder. This conservatism cannot be wholly wrong; for the dispossessed, for people who are being continually shifted around by arbitrary legislation and are losing landmarks of geography and community, the Church should stand for the utter reliability of God, and may be serving a real human need by being conservative in its liturgy and symbolism. Nonetheless, both Old and New Testaments proclaim that God is the one who changes things, that he acts in and through the great changes in history, most typically in that change which started in a bricklayers' strike and ended in a mass migration, which we call the Exodus. Whatever we may think in detail of the doctrine of transubstantiation, it stands squarely for the belief that at the heart of our religion things get changed. Because of this, the Bible sees history not as a circle, nor as a series of circles, but as a line stretched out from a beginning to an end. The Bible does not in itself work out a theory of evolution: but it does give a linear view of history and a positive valuation of change, both of which are essential for the development of an evolutionary understanding of the world. The Bible has, therefore, provided a context in which such an understanding could be apprehended.

So, the God of the Scriptures is not presented as a guarantee against change; he is the master of the process by which change takes place. He cannot be relied on to bring us back to the old securities in a time of disorder; he can be relied on to give a new experience of order on the far side of our disorder – if we are prepared to accept the new thing which he gives us and not to hanker after the old. He does not promise preservation; he does promise resurrection. After the Crucifixion, both the friends and the enemies of Jesus found themselves in a conspiracy to ensure that his body should be preserved, trapped in a hole in the ground. Faithless disciple shared one aim with diligent policeman, that of keeping the past in the past. Resurrection comes to upset the plans of Church and State. The deadness of Christ passes out of him into the guards, the preservers, the men who aim to keep him dead. The messenger of the new creation comes saying: 'Why do you look for the living among the dead? Why do you look for Christ only in the places where he cannot disturb you, in the places where there can be no change? Come,' he says, 'look at the grave, the place of the past where you expect to find him, and see that it is the one place on earth where he is not to be found.'[7]

This is the nature of the Creator. The great event of Easter is needed to make this clear, but it does not present a doctrine which is basically different from that of these chapters in Genesis. To say that God the Father of Jesus Christ is the main actor in creation does not seriously disturb the theology of Genesis. The vital theological changes have already been made by the authors of Genesis themselves. They took the basic outline of Genesis chapter 1 from a creation epic current in Babylonia at the time when the Hebrews were in exile and captivity there. The similarity between Genesis 1 and the Babylonian story has been widely noticed since the latter was discovered almost a century ago; but the real genius of the Hebrews is to be seen in the radical differences which they introduced. They took many of the details of the Babylonian account and used them as an outer frame; but in the centre they put the utterly different and revolutionary figure of the one Creator-God. They took over much of the Babylonian cosmology – a chaos of darkness and water, a first creation of light, a structure of waters divided by a firmament. But, in the Babylonian account, heaven and earth, the abyss and chaos, have existence from the first; and *then* gods are created; and one of them, Marduk, arises as champion and defeats Chaos and divides her up into firmaments. There is a world of difference between this and the Hebrew picture, in spite of so many words and ideas being transferred from one to the other. It is not merely that the Hebrew version is more intellectual than the Babylonian; it is not merely that it gives a story about one god instead of a story about many gods. 'The great contribution of the priestly writer . . . was nothing less than to remove the whole conception of creation out of the realm, not only of myth, but also from the concepts of space and time, and to tell the mighty story of the beginning of all things in terms, not of time, but of purpose.'[8]

The Hebrews were not interested in developing myths, nor in the kind of questions which man now asks in the name of natural science. It was into theology, not into cosmology, that they put their primary energies of intellect and imagination.

But they were not uninterested in the study of things: there would be something wrong if people could have a passionate interest in the Creator and be indifferent to the Creation. The ideas of the Hebrews released them and their successors to study phenomena of nature without either being inhibited by religious sanctions or being discouraged at the outset by the common belief that matter is unreal. It would be appropriate, therefore, that a treatise on the activity of the Creator (e.g. Genesis 1) should be inspired by an interest in what we should call scientific study, as well as by theological motives. 'In the scientific ideas of the time', says Professor von Rad, 'theology had found an instrument which suited it perfectly.'[9] Theology and science could be expounded with equal enthusiasm; but this is not 'science without pre-suppositions'. It is not a study of 'things' but an interpretation of events. The world itself is known only as a series of events, not as a thing-in-itself. An essential factor among these events is, as we shall see, the arrival of a mind to know them and to formulate words about them: without this, things scarcely are. 'The world', says von Rad again, 'does not have unity in itself, and certainly not in any "principle"; it has unity solely in its relationship to God, in its origin in his creative will, in his continual sustaining of it, and in the goal he appointed it.'[10] Beyond the interest in things, therefore, is a greater interest in the Maker of the things. In Genesis 1, the great majority of sentences have 'God' as their subject, and the real events are in God's mind.

The fact that things are is one thing; the question of their attitude to me, and my attitude to them, is quite another. The repeated statement in Genesis 1 is that God not only made things but that he found them good. He loved what he had made. It is not necessarily so. If we feel, deep down, that our own presence in this world, and the presence of the world around us, are essentially devoid of value, that we are the product of an irresponsible fancy, we shall prefer the old Egyptian interpretation, that the whole created order is simply the effect of a casual act of divine masturbation. But casual creation is impossible to attribute to the God of the Scriptures. There is no creation without love, according to Professor van der Leeuw, who compares the biblical view of creation to the attitude of an artist towards his painting: 'Creation is not a stationary bringing-into-being, but the pledging of one's life for what is created. . . . God created the world, not in the sense of an arbitrary act which he might just as well have left unperformed, but out of love, which is confirmed and revealed in Christ, the Mediator of creation.'[11]

The theology of the Babylonian account of creation, as well as that of many other legends and traditions, is that the material universe has come into being through conflict, through murder, outrage, fragmentation and curse. Such a theology has always been attractive; it has made its way into some Christian theology. It gives good religious sanction for my own self-rejection. It allows me to feel that I have reached a satisfactory conclusion, when I can simply feel that it is wicked to be me. Because the basic stuff of me is founded in conflict and curse, I do not need to grow into maturity, I can rest in the belief that I am bound to my nature, my fate. Further, I can rest in the easy assumption that the faults in my fellow-men are really the most characteristic aspects of them, and therefore I can, without disturbing my conscience, reject the person in rejecting his faults. Or, I can set up a specimen of what a person ought to be and demand from the person behaviour of which he is not yet capable, so as to give myself good reason for rejecting him. I do this because deep down I believe that for both of us the main character of our existence is this condition of having been determined by a curse. Both of us are what we are, and that's that. There seems to be a great deal of this in our church attitudes, in both education and discipline. It is alarming that some African groups find it easier than Europeans, with their many generations of Christianity, to accept a person as a person without accepting all the bad aspects of that person. And yet, such acceptance is the only way of helping a person to be free to become. In its gospel and in its sacraments, Christianity is overwhelmingly committed to a theology of becoming; this is what is implied in the theology of Genesis. But in our practice, we often seem to have committed ourselves to a Babylonian kind of fatalism.

We have to insist that creation is good, and that the Creator is good. Our Saviour does not come to save us *from* creation, for he who creates us is not to be separated from him who saves us. It is wrong to teach that loving Son delivers us from angry Father; equally it is wrong to think that spiritual Saviour delivers us from the traps of physical Creator. The Creation is emphatically not the same as the Fall. The story of creation is not a lament. On the contrary, it is a hymn of praise. It does not deplore the material world and man's place in it; it expresses a wonder at the fact that things are. Before anything is said about evil and disorder, this must be said. And this is why Genesis I must come as the Scripture's opening announcement. Once we have made this amazing and revolutionary basic statement, that things are good, everything else can find its place.

Although the whole of the first chapter of the Bible is cast in the form of a narrative about the past, its basic dynamic is hope. History is not a movement away from God; there is no justification here for the lament 'that there hath past away a glory from the earth'.[12] Nor is there any suggestion that man may find his way back to God through nature. On the contrary: the development of things in nature and history is a gradual working-out of God's purpose: man is at the end of this system, himself the closest to God and the only being with a conscious responsibility to God. At a time of national tragedy and disillusionment, Hebrew faith asserted that, if God is to be found at all, this can happen only in the determined facing of human history at a national and personal level, and any reversion to the surrounding mythologies, fertility cults and nature-worship could lead only to deeper loss.

So, even when it would seem that Scripture is speaking to us of our origin, it is really speaking to us of our destiny. Certainly it is speaking to us of where we have come *from*; but it speaks more strongly of where we are going *to*. This is the direction of faith rather than of knowledge. Both '*nature*' and '*nation*' speak to us about the past, about the situation into which we had our natal birth. They can be known and valued, for they are what we are coming *from*; but the faith of the Scripture urges us to find our most significant identity in terms of the community *into* which we are moving and to think of this as our 'homeland'.[13] Man keeps on devising ideologies which will give him security in terms of the past, in terms of his nationality or ancestral group. There is, in principle, no difference between such ideology and nature-worship; they are both substitutes for faith in the living God who is our destiny. If we despair of seeing God in the human brother, if we seek God instead in nature or ideology, any god that we do find there cannot be the Creator-God of Genesis; still less can it be the God and Father of our Lord Jesus Christ.

CHAPTER TWO

The Ordered Universe

GENESIS I: 1–2

In the beginning of creation, when God made heaven and earth,ᵃ the earth was without form and void, with darkness over the face of the abyss, and a mighty wind that sweptᵇ over the surface of the waters.

a) Or *In the beginning God created heaven and earth.*

b) Or *and the spirit of God hovering.*

GENESIS states that God was in the beginning and his activity *is* the beginning.

Christians do not say that this is wrong, but they go one stage further back. As St John Chrysostom pointed out, the Old Testament says that in the beginning God *made*, but the New Testament says that in the beginning the Word *was*; and what God was, the Word was; and the Word was made flesh and dwelt among us.[1] Action has a beginning, but the being of God, the being of the Word, does not have a beginning; it is simply in the beginning. Of this, we can know nothing; if we did know of it, this knowledge would merely push the frontier one stage further away. To ask what is in the beginning is like asking what is beyond space – if we had access to it it would cease to be 'beyond'. The beginning is 'beyond' in this sense.

'Luther was once asked what God was doing before the creation of the world. His answer was that he was cutting canes for people who ask such useless questions.'[2] This answer was apparently well known long before Luther, however, for St Augustine strongly disapproves of it. 'This frivolous retort', he says, 'has been made before now in order to avoid the point of the question. But it is one thing to make fun of the questioner and another to find the answer. So I shall refrain from giving this reply. For in matters in which I am ignorant I would rather admit the fact than gain credit by giving the wrong answer and making a laughing-stock of a man who asks a serious question.'[3]

Augustine can answer only that before he made heaven and earth, God made nothing, because time is part of the created order and there could be nothing *before* the Creation started. 'It is therefore true to say that when you [i.e. God] had not made anything, there was no time, because time itself was of your making. And no time is co-eternal with you, because you never change; whereas, if time never changed, it would not be time.'[4]

In other words, there was no *before* creation; there was only eternity, in which the direct rule of the mind of God has control instead of the most rigid rule known to us in time, namely the rule of sequence. Eternity is characterized by what would seem to us to be the most incomprehensible disorder, namely genuine freedom, a freedom conditioned by no previous factor, not even a previous freedom; in eternity there is no previousness, and therefore no repetition; freedom does not repeat itself. From time to time we may experience something like this unconditioned freedom, and we would say that at that point eternity broke into time; Big Brother, outside us or inside, will object: 'What would happen if everyone behaved like that?' And the only free answer is: 'Don't worry – they won't.' The characteristic and normative specimen of such an invasion of eternity into time is in the event of the gospel, represented in the virgin conception of Christ; here was the unconditioned breaking into time, upsetting all the ordinary sequences and ordered character of society; the *Magnificat* is the 'Red Flag' of eternity's revolution – the song of the new beginning. It is perhaps unfortunate that we have become so accustomed to using the *Magnificat* as an evening canticle; as Michael Tippett's setting suggests, it is more truly a dawn-song, an anthem of cockcrow.

To the question, 'What was in the beginning?', it is easy enough to answer 'God'. To the questions, 'Who made potatoes?', 'Where do babies come from?', 'From where do ducks get webbed feet?', and so on, it is easy enough to answer 'God'. But does this pious word help at all? Is it anything more than a cipher, an 'x', a noise to make when we are unwilling or unable to make a more specific answer? Is there any way of checking whether such an answer is true or false, or indeed whether it has any meaning at all? Does such an answer *do* anything at all, does it supply any knowledge not previously known? Does it indicate anything except the fact that the answerer has a preference for active rather than passive verbs, or that he has not the courage to say 'I don't know'?

The word 'God' is completely useless as an answer to this kind of question unless it has previously acquired meaning from elsewhere. And biblical teaching never attempts to begin at the beginning in this way. The idea of 'God' is not constructed as an abstract component of a metaphysical argument, and then applied to creation; the Hebrews used this term 'God' to express something which had met them in their contemporary experience, something for which no lesser term was adequate. From this experience, they worked back to the belief that the same God was in charge of things in the beginning. It is only by editorial arrangement that the Bible begins with Genesis 1; this is logical enough when one is faced with the very necessary task of bringing the learnings of experience into something like a co-ordinated form; but, unless we do have some idea of what we are talking about, some idea derived from the contemporary setting, it is intellectual arrogance and escapism to presume that one can begin at the beginning. It is wiser, therefore, to make our *beginning now*.

This was the judgement and hope of both the Old Testament prophets and Jesus. Even the people who had been born out of the Exodus experience could find themselves relying overmuch on the God who was known in that 'beginning' and not 'now'. So Jeremiah foretells that people will stop talking about the Exodus event and will characterize God in terms of his deliverance of them from their immediate situation of political fragmentation.[5] The last Old Testament prophet, John the Baptist, gives the same kind of warning to the Jews not to be satisfied with the character of their 'beginning' in Abraham; what is important is the present character of the God who was made known in Abraham.[6] And the characteristic action by which Christians remember

24

their 'beginning' – the eucharist – is essentially a preliminary activity; always it looks forward to the one who is to come. Memory, therefore, is a talent given to God's people only in order to enable them to expect, to see the activity of God in the present and in what is coming to us. Christians are in a situation of greater danger than Jews at this point; our historical exodus is an even more powerful factor than that which took place under Moses; it is in more danger of holding our minds towards the past and locking them there. We maintain that Messiah has come, that what was future is now present, and maybe is even past. Our 'beginning' may so fascinate us that we forget what it was for. We can make an idol out of the Christ of the past, and then we have only ourselves to blame if other Christians overcompensate for this by living in a fantasy world in their enthusiasm concerning the future. The only reason for teaching what Christ *was* like is so that we may see what Christ *is* like; the only reason for teaching about what Christ *did* is so that we can see more clearly what Christ *does*. Our church teaching can so satisfy us with our 'beginning' that we ignore the Christ who is 'now'; in fact, the whole failure of the Church can be summarized by the statement that it fails to enable us to go out prepared for the surprise of meeting Christ in today's history and in the man next to us. Time and again, especially in Southern Africa, we hear the request for a statement of 'Christian principles', for yet another repetition of the abstractions which we derive from our 'beginning'. But, in principle, there are no such principles; our commitment is to watch for the acts of God in the present, to hear his word of 'Thus says the Lord' in the immediate situation, which in politics as in everything else is continually changing. This is the biblical understanding of our response to God, who is not the God of the dead but of the living. And every encounter with this God that we experience is a further addition to the content which we can give to this term 'God'.

GOD

'God' is the subject of the first verb. The Scripture is not an account of man's speculation; it is the record of God's action. It speaks of the one God who is the origin and destiny of the universe, the master and critic of all that is. It speaks of his purpose in creating the universe and bringing it into relationship with himself. It speaks of his power over the earth;[7] it witnesses to his authority over history, for he can use even the authorities of the heathen for his purposes.[8] This is not a truth which we can easily gain from experience; experience rather suggests that we are caught up in a muddle of conflicting authorities, rivalling and falling over each other in their attempts to catch us. Experience suggests something much more like the multiplicity of gods in a heathen pantheon. Experience suggests that each group has its god, its ideology, its form of justice which happens to suit its interests, in the manner of the heathen tribes which lived around the Israelites. But here in the Scripture, from beginning to end, is the uncompromising statement that there is one God, and therefore one justice, one righteousness and one purpose. If we give our primary obedience and commitment, which is due to this one God alone, to something else, to some sectional idol, we are not merely being disobedient to the words of the commandment; we are defying the central truth about ourselves and our universe.

The commandment to worship God alone is not a command to *make* God God; our good behaviour is not intended to bring about a desirable state of things; it is intended to acknowledge a state of things which already exists. The first Christian preaching was not 'Repent, so that the Kingdom of God may come', but 'Repent, *because* the Kingdom of God has arrived'. The initiatives, therefore, are with God.

God's opening initiative is in creating. But there is very little difference between God's work in creating and his work in bringing in the Kingdom. God's creative work is not a mere demonstration of power; it is not a great impressive display which is designed to make everything feel very small and ineffective in comparison. Creation is a working out of God's righteousness; it is not intended to enslave everything else but to release all things to be effectively, to the fullness of their potential. The development of creation is the development of an orderly situation in which all things can be, in this way; like the Kingdom, the Creation is the appearance of true and universal justice. And this justice depends, in the first instance, on a recognition of the one source and designer of this justice. Where men claim an autonomy for their idea of justice, it nearly always means that a subsection of man is wanting to by-pass the norms of justice in order to sanction its unjust treatment of another subsection. For such men it would be a great blessing to be liberated from the domination of God. Christ comes to liberate mankind from the threat of such a false liberation; he comes to assert that the Kingdom is God's alone, and that he alone has the right to make decisions concerning it.

God is on the scene before there is a scene. He is there before there is anything else which could perceive him. He is the one who is unpreceded and unprecedented. 'God' stands for the sense that there is always something before us, something anticipating us, something over which we have no control or power. The ultimate initiatives lie in an area beyond ourselves. This is most deeply true of our interpersonal relationships; in this area the most valuable skill lies not in being able to control what is going on but in being able to perceive what is going on; and those who are most keen on control are likely to be deficient in the skill of perception. The same applies at the public level, in politics. And religion often confirms, reinforces and articulates our weaknesses. Man prefers to have a god whom he *can* control, whom he can anticipate, for whom he can take responsibility. Man prefers a god who will minister to his need for sectional security, who stands or falls with his particular group, and whether the result is an idol or an ideology is immaterial. We shall note later the importance of light and visibility; in order to approach man fully, God had to be revealed in a visible manner and be made in the likeness of men. But the fact remains that God is heard before he is seen; he speaks before there is any light to see by. Man prefers a god who can be seen and not heard, a god who can be visibly checked and acknowledged but who does not come with any inconvenient demands. Man prefers a god who will not condemn what we condone and who will not forgive where we condemn – and, again, whether you call such a god an idol or an ideology is immaterial. Religion can be a powerful agency for the production of such gods; the more highly a man is placed in religion, the greater his investment in it, the greater his danger. It was the archbishop Aaron who produced the golden calf.[9] It was that old man of religion, Uzzah, who felt it necessary to stretch out his hand to prevent God from the disgrace of falling off a cart.[10] And when we consider it necessary to bring in the force of human law to protect our God from blasphemy, we ought to ask just who it is that is being threatened by these vicious artists and these abominable journalists; can they damage the Creator of the heavens and the earth? Or is it we ourselves who feel insecure, because we have attached ourselves to a little local god, and therefore we must cry out 'blasphemy' in self-defence?

HEAVEN AND EARTH

God made all that is. The Hebrews did not have a term to express what we mean by 'the universe'. To speak of the sum total of everything, they used this phrase 'the heaven and the earth'. We shall consider the variety of factors included in this phrase when we meet it again at the end of this chapter, when we have been faced with the variousness of the created order. At present, let us consider the unity which this phrase implies.

There is no sense in which one sector of the universe is any more the creation of God than the other. By the deliberate choice of God, there may be, temporarily, places on earth which have particular sanctity; these will be the places which he chooses as his meeting-places with man. They are not chosen by man or 'consecrated' by any action of man. Examples are the place of Jacob's sleep,[11] and the place of the Burning Bush.[12] And, most particularly, there was the place which the Lord was to choose, to make his name dwell there – the temple at Jerusalem.[13] The highest heaven was unable to contain God, but he chose to work through a particular people centred on a particular place. Even this was a very conditional arrangement; as it became clear to the men of God that the temple was highly inadequate as a guarantee of God's presence, due to the disobedience of the human communities associated with the temple, so the way came more and more open for the teaching of the New Testament, that the dwelling-place of God is primarily man, and that no particular spot on earth should have special privileges.[14] Sacredness, therefore, does not attach to any one point in spacial extension rather than another. Sacredness belongs to all space in virtue of its createdness and is to be worked out in obedience by man.

The New Testament asserts that this obedience was to be seen completely in the one man Jesus Christ, and that in him the whole habit of splitting apart into sacred and non-sacred was overcome. All sectors of the universe which had become or were in danger of becoming alienated from God were reconciled to God through the blood of the cross of Christ.[15] Further, he is the reconciling principle not only across space and mankind but also across cosmic history. Christ who is the agent of the new creation is not different from the agent of the old creation, for, now that we have seen him, we know him as the one in whom all things originally took their being; he is not a new invention, brought into existence by the emergency situation of the times of Herod the Great and Pontius Pilate. He is the 'firstborn of all creation'[16] – 'firstborn in relation to every creature in all senses of "before"'.[17] He reasserts the unity of all things, 'whether on earth or in heaven',[18] not just as a static eternal fact but as a process of which he is the master. Having experienced the effect of the event of the gospel in their lives, the New Testament Christians judged that these were the only adequate terms by which they could express the significance of what had happened. The character of the authority who has the whole of space and history in his hands is known in terms of what happened in a few hours of time and a few square feet of space, the event which we call the Cross of Christ. The crucifixion of Christ provides a set of terms in which it is finally possible to interpret the whole range of things, including myself.

The Bible's statements at this point are not offered as contri-

29

butions to scientific research. Historical, astronomical, geo-
logical, or cosmological theories or discoveries cannot dis-
prove them or prove them. Equally, they are not meant to
be a restrictive factor or a presupposed point of arrival for
science. A truly biblical understanding of creation will assert
the autonomy of scientific study; it will insist on the right,
and the duty, of the scientist to make experiments and judge-
ments which are in accordance with the proper method of
his particular discipline, and to exclude ready-made answers,
from theologians or anyone else, which do not emerge from
the appropriate operations of that discipline. It may be a
proper implementation of the biblical understanding of
creation to exclude the theologically loaded word 'creation'
from the discourse of sciences.

The astronomer, therefore, is theologically at liberty to
devise theories of the origin of the cosmos, and to test their
coherence and their viability by experiment. Christians have
tried their hand at the dangerous game of subjecting cosmological theories to theological assessment, and have found
fault, for instance, with the 'steady state' cosmology on the
grounds that it implies an absence of any beginning or end
and therefore a complete lack of need for God. An evolutionary cosmology, on the other hand, leaves plenty for God to
do, so the argument goes; God gives an initial push to set
10^{55} grams of material in motion, in a manner for which the
laws of physics have no explanation. But a god whose function
is to fill in the gaps left by the physicists and statisticians is
not the God of the Bible; 'god' is not a term which can be
meaningfully incorporated into the arguments and analyses
of physics, and therefore the physicist, *qua* physicist, cannot
rest in an account of the origin of the universe which brings
'god' in as a cipher, standing for a gap in his system; if 'god'
is unnecessary, from the physicist's point of view, for the
maintenance of the cosmological structure, 'god' cannot be
properly held responsible for its *origin*. And the theologian
must agree, in so far as he sees God as Creator only to the
same extent as he sees God as sustainer of all things; the two
roles are virtually indistinguishable. God is not known
primarily in terms of those factors which seem to us to be
inexplicable; what was inexplicable for the last generation

has a way of being explained in the next. 'God' is a new way of comprehending things which already are, to some extent, explicable. His revelation operates primarily through our social and personal *experience*, rather than through our speculation. God is not a device to compensate us for what we do not know. He is a new way of knowing what we already do know. If this is not so, every new thing that we know means one less thing to know about God: but the witness of the Bible and of authentic Christian theology is that the more we experience, and the more we are aware of our social and personal history, and the more we are sensitive to our environment, the more there is to say about God. The way in which we do this talking about God is a language of its own, distinct from the language of science: it deals not with propositions so much as with attitudes, and the user of theological language is inevitably involved in these attitudes. The first chapter of Genesis is not only a series of propositions: it is also a hymn of praise. This is not to say that theological language is just a kind of poetry: it differs from the language of science in that it is far less objective: it differs from poetry in that it gives far greater recognition to the danger of error. What the Genesis writer says about the sun, for instance, is about attitudes towards the sun, not about the scientific 'facts' concerning the sun; his language cannot, therefore, be expected to fit that of an astronomer; but, at the same time, the writer is deeply concerned to expose untruth, and to offer an attitude to the sun which is congenial to belief in the true God and which is appropriate to the dignity and rationality of man.

So theological language cannot be expected to deal with scientific questions, and scientific answers should not be expected to fit neatly with theological convictions. If, for instance, 'steady state' cosmological theories have to be abandoned as a result of the arguments of Professor Ryle and his associates, this is not necessarily a victory for God, any more than would be the case if the verdict had gone the other way. We could say that it is a victory for God in so far as it is a victory for truth; and in that case, at least the credit must be given to the proponents of the 'steady state' theory for devising a cosmological theory which was open to obser-

31

vation and which could be accepted or rejected as a result of the normal application of scientific scepticism. Now attention is being turned to the various types of process which might still be possible under the general heading of evolutionary cosmology. Maybe we shall be able to know by observation that the universe started a certain length of time ago in a primeval 'big bang'; maybe we shall be left with the picture of a universe oscillating in long periods between expansion and contraction with no definable points of beginning or end. In face of this, Dr Mascall can assert: 'the whole question of whether the world had a beginning or not is, in the last resort, profoundly unimportant for theology.'[19] This is because God's activity is the expression of his eternal will; it is an activity which is outside time, but an activity which maintains the whole sequence of things in time. Within the terms of reference of theology, the study of God, there is no essential difference between God's activity at the beginning of things – if, cosmologically speaking, there ever was such a thing – and his activity at any other time that we choose to isolate. The theological statement, perhaps the only purely theological statement anywhere, is that, whatever it is that is, and in whatever manner it may have come to the condition in which we say that it is, the fact that it is is due to a word of God.

Whatever 'beginning' may truly mean, this 'beginning' is under the authority of God and in the presence of his Word. One theory of the origin of matter requires some neutrons to have been available as raw material for the original explosion which, according to this theory, sorted out all the component atoms of the universe into their present proportions. So the explosion was not the real beginning. But the real beginning was not even the first neutron. The real beginning was the absence of the first neutron. And that is the beginning in which the Word was.

WITHOUT FORM AND VOID

St Augustine tells us of his desperate search for some effective meaning to give to the idea of 'formlessness'. 'I used to picture it to myself in countless different forms, which means that I

did not really picture it at all, because my mind simply con-
jured up hideous and horrible shapes. They were perversions
of natural order, but shapes nevertheless. I took "formless"
to mean, not something entirely without form, but some
shape so monstrous and grotesque that if I were to see it, my
sense would recoil and my human frailty quail before it. . . .
Reason told me that if I wished to conceive of something
that was formless in the true sense of the word, I should have
to picture something deprived of any trace of form whatso-
ever, and this I was unable to do.'[20] St Augustine tried to
grasp this 'formlessness' visually, and felt that he had failed.
Haydn made a wonderfully successful attempt to express it
musically, in the Overture to his oratorio *The Creation*. This
overture is entitled 'Representation of Chaos'; but 'chaos',
for Haydn, is not a condition where everything is madly
rushing around in complete disorder; it is simply a condition
where nothing really *is*. The music is full of shifts and vague-
ness; an approaching cadence never arrives, because the
music wanders off towards another destination, which in
turn is discovered to be illusory. The scene is not 'chaotic'
in our usual understanding of the word; it is a profound study
of the instability which, according to Genesis, is the primal
condition into which creation can break.

Formlessness, voidness, darkness are absences; they add
up to 'nothing'. The story of creation is a journey from this
'nothing' to the 'fullness of being, the fullness of God himself'.[21] For those who feel that God is a tyrant, such a process
is the worst threat; non-being has the greatest attraction,
unbirth the greatest seductiveness; they dig for death 'more
than for hid treasure'.[22] If men ever succeed in establishing
themselves on the moon, the greatest advantage may be the
overwhelming presence of 'nothing' there. Scientists have
been ardently pursuing the total vacuum, with great expenditure of energy and skill. On the moon, there will be all
the vacuum that could be desired, just for the asking; there
will be almost unlimited amounts of nothing. This will be
fine for vacuum research, which is no doubt a highly com-
mendable pursuit. But much religion has been offering
'nothing' for generations, and men have been seeking it with
all their powers; if religion does not lead forward to God it

will lead to 'nothing'. Without God, says the Anglican Prayer Book, 'nothing is strong';[23] 'strong enough', comments C. S. Lewis, 'to steal away a man's best years not in sweet sins but in a dreary flickering of the mind over it knows not what and knows not why'.[24]

And Chesterton has a story in which an Indian is asked if he wants anything and he three times answers that he wants nothing: 'When first he said, "I want nothing", it meant only that he was impenetrable, that Asia does not give itself away. Then he said again, "I want nothing", and I knew that he meant that he was sufficient to himself, like the cosmos. And when he said the third time, "I want nothing", he said it with blazing eyes. And I knew that he meant literally what he said; that nothing was his desire and his home; that he was weary for nothing as for wine.'[25]

The earth was without form and void. There was nothing there. Even the first neutron (if there ever was such a thing) was not nothing. The beginning is when something happens to change this situation. But change involves a 'before' and an 'after': it can be measured only in terms of time. The beginning, before the first change, was out of time, *ex tempore*.

And God as the Christians know him is *par excellence* the extemporizer, the improvisor. If this were not so, our failure would have doomed us long ago, and day by day our mistakes would not be providentially overruled. But God is the one who breaks into our setting, who interferes, who justifies us by grace. And this character of God was shown once for all in history. Again, without causation, there was a creation out of a void – in the first instance the void of the womb of the Virgin, which symbolizes a new start, a new creation dependent on God's initiative. More centrally, the void of the new creation is the empty tomb. In the central word of the Passion, 'My God, my God, why hast thou forsaken me?', God himself, his providence and his relationship, are put in the negative; here is the summing-up of man's dissociation from God, resulting in the fragmentation of God himself. This is the darkness, the eclipse, the undoing of the creative act.[26] And yet this is not the end. It is a new nothing from which a new beginning, the new creation, can start. No one saw the Resurrection. Something happened, but no one can say when. The act of new creation is also *ex tempore*; and because of this, it can go on happening. Certainly the first day of the week after the Crucifixion is a day which is potentially locatable in history. But when we talk about the risen power of the Christ, the Son of the living God, we are talking about something which cannot be located only in a specific time and place to the exclusion of all other; we are talking about something contemporary, as the God of the old Genesis is contemporary.

DARKNESS AND CHAOS

Christian teachers have greatly stressed the doctrine that God created the universe out of nothing; this has been partly to oppose the strong arguments, advanced early in the Christian era, that matter was created by a bad god. Luther insisted that there must be a nothing for God to work upon in all situations. 'God created the world out of nothing. As long as you are not yet nothing God cannot make something out of you.'[27]

Now, this is an excellent stress, in so far as it insists that the initiatives are all with God: in the Bible, God's work is not limited, as it is in Plato and many other mythologies, to the reshaping of basic material which is supplied to him from another source: he is truly unconditioned; he supplies his own materials. But the stress on creation out of nothing can be unfortunate, if it implies that the real creative work could take place only at the beginning of things, when there was plenty of nothing to work on. The Bible does not speak much of a creation out of nothing. The nearest that we approach to such an idea in Scripture is in 2 Maccabees.[28] Hebrews refers to God's work of making visible things out of what is invisible,[29] and this is the master specimen of faith; God is the one who calls and chooses things that are not.[30]

But the most clear and certain teaching concerning creation is that it is the bringing of order out of chaos. God sorts out the various factors that compose chaos; he names them and distinguishes them, and, as we shall notice later,

he calls man in to share in this task. The final goal of this is
not a universe stuffed tight with lots of things made out of
nothing but a complex harmony of beings brought into
reconciliation with each other – the image of the body in St
Paul, the image of the city in Revelation. I suggest that if
Luther had given priority to this in his application to the
individual person, he would have produced a better word.
'God created the world out of chaos. As long as you are not
yet chaos God cannot make something out of you.' This is
truer both to personal experience and to the model of
Christ's death and resurrection. I cannot become nothing
except by destroying my real and potential value, which is
something I wish to do in my worst moments, not my best:
and I do not believe that Christ waited to be nothing before
starting his creative activity. What he did do (and in this he
is so different from the less effective revolutionaries) was to
become really part of the chaos and disorder of the existing
state of things. He waited so long in the old order that he
could move from within it. He waited until he was thirty
years old before he made any significant move – and who
knows how many people he might have saved from suffering
if he had moved earlier? 'When our Lord did move, it was
not out of his tradition, but still deeper into it. He did not
start a new movement; on the contrary, he joined the
revival of John the Baptist. He went down into the waters of
John's baptism, down to the lowest place on the earth's
surface and to the barren grimness of the lower Jordan
valley, down to the eerie and symbolic and very filthy and
humdrum waters that flowed down the middle of it.'[31] Here,
as in the first creation, the waters were the material supplied
by the old as the point of departure for the new. In Christ's
baptism, the Spirit moved on the face of the waters, waters
of deep symbolic character. 'Jordan' was the water that had
once been pushed back at the entrance to the Promised
Land; it was the water of healing; it was the water of
national boundary; it was the gulf separating God's people
from those outside. All this chaos of meaning formed the
convention in which Christ immersed himself, from which
he moved forward. His creative action did not start from
'nothing'; on the contrary, his whole life's work is the best

36

possible proof of Jung's great saying that 'creative life is always on the yonder side of convention'.[32] Jesus started from the disorder of convention, from the chaos of what is, and only on the yonder side of it did he start his revolutionary and creative work. He emptied himself, certainly; but this was not becoming nothing so much as submission to chaos, to disorder, to sin, to brokenness; he suffered the effects of disorder on himself to the degree that he was made 'to be sin who knew no sin'.[33] And where a man is prepared to face the chaos in himself, and to be involved in the chaos of society and suffer under it, there most particularly can God do his creative and recreative work.

Chaos is there, but it does not *do* anything; there is no myth of chaos, it is not treated as a person. The same is true of darkness. Nothing is said about where they come from, for they are not reckoned to be positive things; they merely indicate an absence of order, an absence of light. Such an absence does not have to be created, for it speaks of an absence of creation, an area where creativity has not yet moved in. But darkness and chaos *are*; they have names. God's word allows them existence, and, in the case of darkness, God allocates certain rights to the absence of light. But, for the Hebrews, both darkness and chaos took their meaning not from theological speculation but from historical experience. They knew, as a nation, what it was like to be in darkness and chaos, and to be delivered from them. They knew the chaos of being oppressed, and the darkness of being downtrodden. 'At a point in history from which Genesis 1 takes its meaning, Chaos ruled in a land called Egypt, where a people called Israel was forced to make bricks without straw.'[34]

Later, it was Egypt, the oppressing nation itself, which had to bear the experience of darkness, as God prepared for the deliverance of his people.[35] Later still, the light-bearing bodies experienced a denial of their created nature, when there were three hours of darkness ending at 3 p.m. on a certain Friday afternoon. Christ is crucified at the storm-centre of history, and in his victory he overcomes darkness and all its powers. The gospel takes the timeless and generalized insight of Genesis and applies it to a date known in history, when a certain Pontius Pilate happened to have power. And the same person who was revealed as the master of darkness is known as the one who operates in history now, in my history; it is possible for me also to face the oppression of my darkness in the power of this same master. Chaos, and Darkness, and the Deep remain; disobedience is to turn from the light of God, and to be forced to call for rescue from the overwhelming waters.[36] But the terror and threat of these areas is overcome when they are entered by one who moves into them in total obedience, by the Christ who conquers hell by descending into it. And for some of Christ's associates, those who are set where they meet most potently the spiritual or social agonies of our world, the most significant blessing may be: 'Go forth into hell in peace, for your Master has mastered even it.'

Chaos, like creation, is not something over and done with long ago. Chaos is always a possibility; there is the threat of formlessness, facelessness, namelessness, non-being, and these are never very far away. The environment which gives me a life-setting and sustenance is always potentially collapsing, and I am in danger of collapsing with it. Faith in the Creator means faith in his power to hold me in his hand, and this hand is made visible to me in my experience of the whole environment in which I have a place. This environment can reveal itself against me in complete hostility, as it did most characteristically in the experience of Elijah.[37] Elijah characterized himself in terms of his isolation and hatedness; all that could be relied on for security had failed, and his extreme depression was expressed in a death-wish; along with his political isolation and physical exhaustion, he felt that the whole moral basis of his life was discredited as well: 'Take away my life; for I am not better than my fathers.' God's treatment of Elijah was to give him the full-scale experience of the chaos which he had complained about. He faced the wind, which broke up the landscape; all the things on the horizontal plane around him lost their solidarity, nothing was left for him to grasp firmly in his hand. He faced the earthquake, which broke up the earth's structure; all the things vertically beneath him lost their solidarity; nothing was left on which he could firmly place his feet. He faced the fire, which broke up the very basic nature of things, turning reliable solids and liquids into insubstantial gas; the very elements of which he himself was made were shown to be fragile, ephemeral, unreliable. This is the depth of chaos. And the mastery of the Creator is shown in the next event. The Lord has not been in the overwhelming chaos, in all its strength and destructiveness. The Lord is in the word of constructive dialogue, however quiet and ineffective it may seem in comparison with the powers of destruction. However quietly such a word may come, this is God, for this is what 'God' means, the one who provides a perceptible alternative to chaos. He comes deliberately weakly to this weak man, with a simple enabling question. The question and the questioner are there after the events of chaos just as they were before; chaos has not defeated them; the depression in Elijah's soul has not defeated them. For a person in Elijah's situation, the only fact which can give any assurance of a Creator, of any possible goodness, is the persistent quiet presence of such a questioner, for whom chaos is not the end of everything but a beginning of some new direction of activity. We cannot know whether anything of this kind was in Haydn's mind when he wrote the first chorus in *The Creation*; there must have been all sorts of wonderful possibilities for the expression of the first divine words, 'Let there be light'; but in fact he chose to make the voice of God as still and small as possible, the simple voice of a quiet child; and those four undecorated words are the most powerful of the whole oratorio.

A MIGHTY WIND

The picture of chaos is completed, according to the main text of the New English Bible translation, by this 'mighty wind'. 'Wind' and 'spirit' are translations of the same word in Hebrew; the English language can make distinctions at this point which are not possible in Hebrew and Greek (or in Zulu, Sotho and many other languages). The New English Bible margin gives the traditional interpretation, which tells of the Spirit of God hovering over the waters, waiting and

39

preparing for the creative word. The main text follows Professor von Rad's opinion that these words have nothing to do with the creative process; rather, they belong to the description of the disorder in which the creation is to happen. The terrible storm was stirring up the waters.[38] There is, here, no preparatory brooding, no anticipation of the radical reversal which is to come about with the divine command for light. But the storm is God's storm; he is its master, and it will yield to his command; the darkness, therefore, is also God's darkness, and will yield to his command; there is no suggestion of a battle with other gods or any such mythological ideas. But it is in the immediate context of darkness and storm that creation comes; and perhaps this needs no comment beyond Bishop Fison's observation that 'if the cross is the clue to Christian faith and the place where the secret of God the Father is found, then it will not be so much in the stability of an ordered society as in the anarchy of the breakdown of all law and order that we shall rediscover its secret today. . . . For Jesus – and for us – the place of peace is the storm centre, not its circumference.'[39]

Jesus showed himself as the master of the storm, as the one to whom wind and sea were obedient. He discouraged volunteers, but those whom he called found themselves helpless in the storm-centre precisely because Jesus had called them; they recognized him not just as a wonder-worker but as the one who rightly and properly had authority over the created order. Jesus shows himself as the creative person; he pushes back the boundaries of chaos, and so enables his associates to live on the fringe of chaos, in the place where creation is essential as the only alternative to destruction.[40]

So the New English Bible gives us a much more vigorous picture than the traditional version. Creation begins in a head-on confrontation between God and every kind of disorder. God comes into the story as critic, and his first word is a word of doom to the *status quo*. But we probably ought not to abandon the traditional translation completely. There is great value in the notion that the Spirit of God is active in the first creation. The Spirit of God is the mighty wind that comes at Pentecost;[41] he descends on Jesus at the waters of Jordan.[42] Wind is essentially air moving into an empty

situation, and this is the character of the Spirit of God. If
Jesus does not depart, the Spirit cannot come and fill the
vacancy, to enable the apostolic community not merely to
do what Jesus had done but to work on a far wider scale.[43]
So here, at the beginning, the baptizing Spirit is hovering
over the emptiness, ready to make electrons or apostles and
to send them working, whirling, illuminating.

'Wind' or 'Spirit' also means 'Breath'. 'Breath' enables
'word': we breathe to be able to speak, and the breath of
God is hovering, waiting there, immediately before the speech
of God. So now we wait for the first word, the first real event,
God's first move in creation.

GENESIS I: 3–5

*God said, 'Let there be light', and there was light; and God saw that
the light was good, and he separated light from darkness. He called
the light day, and the darkness night. So evening came, and morning
came, the first day.*

GOD SAID

It is God's nature to create. But this familiar truth should
not make us assume that creation is a sort of automatic
result of God's existence; the creation does not naturally
flow out of God; it is not a sort of emanation, an unavoidable
overflow of divinity; it is not even just a good idea, an event
in God's mind. There has to be a specific initiative from God;
we are brought into existence by a deliberate, purposive act
of will, and therefore we *matter*. This is what is represented
by the story of God's *word*, the specific speech by which he
summons us into existence. God calls us into life. He calls
men to be his servants. Most characteristically, he called his
Son into life from the dead. 'God's creative call is identical
with his power to raise the dead.'[44] God's word is the calling
of both creation and re-creation. God's Word was made
flesh, and spoke the calling of God to people to come into
genuine existence, to come into community and accept the
status of being guests at the festival of God; when Jesus told
stories about people being invited to banquets, he was draw-

ing on his own experience of being in his own person the invitation of God.

The character of God is firstly that of a God who speaks. This is true all through the Old Testament: 'The Lord's word made the heavens . . . he spoke, and it was; he commanded, and it stood firm.'[45] 'God *said*' is the first main verb in the Bible; his word is the first event.

So, here comes the word of God, for the first time. God speaks, and it is a commandment. The commandment of God is seen by fallen men only as rules and regulations, a series of fences not to be disregarded: but to man as he is supposed to be, to man as he really sees and shares the nature of the Word, it is a liberation, a blessing. 'I will run the way of thy commandments: when thou hast set my heart at *liberty*.'[46] 'The Commandment of God is permission to live as man before God.'[47]

The Koran expresses this as succinctly as possible. 'God will create what he wills. When he decreeth a thing, he only sayth, Be, and it is.'[48] This is the whole tenor of the Sermon on the Mount; the will of God is the releasing of man from the inhibitions on his blessedness and his community. This is the nature of the Word through whom all things were made. In Christ, this Word became flesh, and then it was even clearer than in Genesis that the Word of God does not just result in effects, it is itself the work of God: in the Word was life, and the life was the light of men.[49]

Although it is true that God's Word of creation is a wonderful and powerful thing, there is not the slightest hint of *how* it operates; the method of creation is entirely hidden. 'He spoke the word and they were created.'[50] This is all that we are told. It is utterly clear that the writer is not at all concerned to give even the most rudimentary answer to what we would call the 'scientific' questions – the questions of cosmological and biological process. The writer of this first chapter is at work several generations later than the writer of the second chapter; but he does not *know* any more than his predecessor in the sense of having before him the results of a larger body of research. Both the writers are concerned to affirm that God is Creator; but this does not mean that we have the means to answer every kind of question that may be raised. What is true, however, is that the writers' faith is in the Creator himself and not in any sacral or supernatural characteristics in the creation; and this faith releases man from the presuppositions which would prevent questions being raised. Man is free to explore and to know, to pursue the 'how' questions; and so it may not be entirely accidental that, in comparison to the earlier version, chapter 1 does show some signs of scientific arrangements, a readiness to see objective classifications of things and to follow some sort of systematic process. Genesis 1 is on the side of science, even if it is not primarily a scientific statement.

God speaks: he utters a meaningful sound indicating that behind the voice there is a mind and a purpose. It is still, apparently, wide open to question whether the study of natural phenomena can yield evidence of purpose. Dr Tournier, for instance, can provide an impressive selection of biologists who discover a significant element of choice in the behaviour of elementary forms of life.[51] Others would question this; and in any case, the purposiveness of individual creatures does not necessarily require a purposive creator. The faith of the Bible does not depend on it being possible to prove the fact of the Creator from the study of creation. But the interesting fact about contemporary investigations, for instance into the DNA molecule, is that man, whatever his theological opinions may be, seems to be unable to avoid language which *implies* purpose and meaning, such as 'code' and 'message' and 'genetic instructions'. Man has committed himself to a search for meaning, and finds it difficult to talk meaningfully about meaninglessness. Even when he tries to argue that the basis of human life and activity is not meaningful and purposeful, in his attempts to argue the matter persuasively, the manner of his argument is extremely likely to contradict the content of it. If the life and activities that happen in the universe are reducible to the analysis of physics, can physics also account for what happens in the minds of the physicists? However this may be, men who do believe in a meaningful and purposeful basis of existence must also acknowledge that this is a matter of faith; the arguments against us are powerful. God, if there is a God, is continually in conflict with chaos and meaninglessness;

and only in pulling chaos forward into clear manifestation of its character, and in suffering its effects to the utmost, is God able to assert the ultimate validity of his purpose.

LIGHT

Light is not only a thing that is seen; it is the means by which all things, including itself, are seen. So, here in Genesis it appears first, before all other things, even before the light-bearing bodies. Light breaks upon the new-born infant's eyes, causing it to have either lifelong fear or lifelong love of light; light floods the senses long before any particular light-source can be identified.

Light stands for the primacy of *seeing*; the disciple of Christ is not, first of all, a man who understands, who listens, who ponders, who decides, or who is wise, good or holy. The disciple of Christ is one who *sees*, even before he hears. For centuries before Christ, God had been trying to get through to his people by means of their hearing apparatus; his agents had for generations made announcements in terms of 'thus says the Lord'. But the incarnation of the Son of God recognizes that, in the purpose of God, man is actually motivated by what he sees rather than by what he hears. Again, in our more recent history, we have had several centuries in which we have been moved and influenced by words; words have been adequate, it may have appeared, for communication and for worship. But this has been a cultural freak of a small minority of mankind, and it is on its way out. People are demanding more visible means of expression. A switch from one theological formula to another no longer works any magic; audible noises are no substitute for visible bread, and impressive statements against racialist ideology carry little weight unless the churches show their commitment in visible action. That which is perceived by means of the light, therefore, has priority. The light is first-made.

Light and darkness are the first basic things, and the distinction between them is the first basic distinction. For the author of this chapter, everything is characterized by the factors which distinguish it from everything else. Creation is

44

the record of the development of an ever subtler and wider distinctiveness. Up to this first event of creation, everything has been a vague, homogeneous mess. Now begins a process of increasing precision and definiteness; the boundaries of chaos are pushed back by the advance of order and pattern. Whatever you choose to represent the most basic distinction of all, whether you call it the distinction between light and darkness, protons and electrons, knowledge and ignorance, here this basic distinction appears, on the first day of creation.

EVENING CAME, AND MORNING CAME, THE FIRST DAY

Light is the positive thing; it represents the Creator's victory and good will. Its appearance is the commencement of the first day, and its reappearance after a period of darkness is the completion of the first day. Our culture tends to make us think of 'morning and evening'; we assume that the day begins and ends in darkness. But this story refers all through to 'evening and morning'; the day begins and ends in light. Night has its name, its permission to be. But darkness can only interrupt light; it cannot master it.[52]

This is the first 'day'. When we think of time, and especially when we recall a period of time, even the most sophisticated of us forget about clocks and watches and scientific measurements; rather, we think of time simply in terms of what it contains. This was the Hebrew manner; the 'day of the Lord' was not a twenty-four-hour period on a calendar but the time of God's activity. 'His activity determined its character, and his activity was always conceived by the Hebrews as swift, sudden, and complete in a moment. It was so in the beginning when he finished each day's work of creation in plenty of time to contemplate the success of each creative experiment before proceeding to the next.'[53]

The 'days' of creation are all 'days' like this, days when God creates and judges. If God is a God of decisive action, what word of time other than 'day' could be used? We cannot picture a being making such an action for x-million years, or for a 'period'. With regard to the scientific questions,

45

it is a good thing that we have this word 'day' which is so clearly not representing an attempt at scientific accuracy. On this argument, it does not matter whether the sum of all the days in the Bible before Christ is 4004 years or 4004 times 365, or any other figure. But a day is a unit of activity, a unit with a start and a finish, evening and morning, a time in which a job can be done and assessed. A day is a unit of movement. Until man could find a means whereby individuals could move faster than the speed permitted by unaided human muscles, people were largely bound to the communities into which they were born, and the unit of distance was a 'day's march'. It is recalling something deep in our consciousness when, in these days, the main significance of a 'day's march' is a communal protest against political wrongs which threaten to dehumanize man.

Many factors combine to weaken the significance of 'day' to us – shift-work, the wider experience of living in polar regions, and the speed of travel; a sophisticated Christian Indian tells us that after a jet journey he has to wait for a day for his soul to catch up; Westerners may be more conscious of having left some of their digestive operations behind. Even so, the 'day' remains the only universally agreed unit of time; and the point is here that God is associating himself with *time*, universally recognizable time.

According to the Bible, our association with God does not depend on our ability to get out of time. We enter eternity not by leaving the time-world but by entering new relationships within it, not by dying but by being born again. Our godly fathers used to inscribe their clocks with the words 'I mark time, dost thou?' Our present age not only teaches many of its youth deliberately to kill their fellow-men but also gives them a military exercise which we call 'marking time'; it is a deliberate killing of time – which unfortunately sums up many men's experience of peace-time armies. Jesus, in whom the Day of the Lord came, who appeared in the fullness of time, was a genuine time-marker, a proper clock-watcher. He was constantly aware of being timed by the purpose of God.[54] He showed that the clock-hand, going vainly round in circles, is not the deepest truth about time. As in the first creation, so in the second, time became the agency through which the eternal God worked, the only agency through which he could work if his works were to speak to us as we are, in our timed condition. And so in the Nicene Creed, after all the high-flown theologizing about the nature of Christ, we proclaim how this same eternal Son of God was crucified under Pontius Pilate. There was a time, and an action. If there had been no such time and action, no such 'day', we should have no salvation; equally, if it had not been the eternal one, the one who was before the 'days' of creation, who was thus involved in time and action, we should have no salvation. And so this present moment too is to be the time of the eternal one for action and judgement.

GENESIS I: 6 8

God said, 'Let there be a vault between the waters, to separate water from water.' So God made the vault, and separated the water under the vault from the water above it, and so it was; and God called the vault heaven. Evening came, and morning came, a second day.

The first distinction is between light and darkness. But light is itself the fact which enables all other distinctions to be perceived. The whole of the rest of the chapter is an account of distinctions which can be made as a result of this basic distinction.

The second distinction speaks to us of the controlled security of our existence under God's providence. The borders of chaos are pushed back, and the threatening waters are given their specific boundaries. The unfirm waters are kept in place by something firmer, the vault or firmament in heaven with waters above and below it. This introduces, therefore, as the second distinction, the difference in solidity between the three states of matter. This is a vital distinction, without which nothing can really happen; it is a flexible distinction which makes change possible. Only because gases, liquids and solids are distinct from each other and yet can be changed into each other, is it possible for useful changes to occur. 'It is the condition of combined permanence and change. In the narrow range between too hot and too cold, too runny and too still, things begin to happen. How dull

47

the sun and moon are compared with the earth! One is too hot for anything to stay put, and the other too cold for anything to alter.'[55]

'What arouses the physicist's interest in this globe . . . is the presence of composite chemical bodies not to be observed anywhere else. At the extreme temperature occurring in the stars, matter can only survive in its most dissociated states. Only simple bodies exist on these incandescent stars. On the earth this simplicity of the elements still obtains at the periphery, in the more or less ionized gases of the atmosphere and the stratosphere and, probably, far below, in the metals of the "barysphere". But between these two extremes comes a long series of complex substances.'[56] It is this complexity, itself made possible only by the simultaneous presence of many permitting factors, which has made possible the development of organic compounds, and of rational minds to observe them.

SEPARATION

God not only distinguishes; he separates; and this is recognized as an essential part of his character and of his justice. We shall, later in this study, consider the work of Christ in overcoming separation and the mission of the Church in opposing various kinds of apartheid. But here it is quite clear that God has a role as separator, and this role remains with God until the Last Judgement. In this instance, God is introducing a new type of substance, characterized by its firmness, and he is putting this block of new material into the middle of the mass of old unfirm material; the firm vault is inserted into the sloppy water, and so gives the water a firmness, a precision, a locatedness, which it did not have previously. The firmament does not come in to keep two different elements apart from each other; the water above and the water below are identical in nature, but the firmament comes in to distinguish them from each other by their relationship to itself. As well as keeping them apart, therefore, the firmament gives to each block of water a character, a security which it did not have before; that which separates also unites, for the firmament becomes the link and bond between the water above and the water below. In a similar manner, Christ comes between this floppy, vague thing called me and the other floppy, vague thing called my neighbour; he comes as separator and therefore as mediator. My neighbour and I no longer have direct access to each other, we no longer have direct power or claim against each other; Christ separates us, and we meet each other only in him. We receive each other, not to dominate or trick each other, but only indirectly, at the hands of Christ; we have contact with each other through him; for he is the firmness which makes the relationship valid. Christ comes between us and each other, and is therefore able to give us to each other in a new, unprecedented and surprising way, just as God came between Abraham and Isaac and then gave Isaac back again.[57] Thus God the separator makes us genuinely independent individuals; thus God the mediator makes us responsibly related to each other through himself.[58]

The other aspect of God as separator concerns the vital separation between sin and righteousness. Compared to this separation, all our tactics of social or racial or ecclesiastical separation are mere games. This, of course, does not excuse or justify these separations of ours; it merely exposes their basic silliness. We play at this kind of separation and ignore our real calling to serious separation; sex across the colour-line, for instance, becomes Immorality with a big 'I', and everything else is relatively moral. Christian disciples are seriously called to distinguish between righteousness and un-righteousness, truth and falsehood, God and devil, and at this point there can be no reconciliation or tolerance; at this point, Christian obedience demands separation.[59] Christians cannot compromise with an idolatry which puts some other value in place of Christ.

Separation here concerns our obedience and discipleship as believers in Christ. It is clear that God truly has a character as separator; it is equally clear that this has nothing whatever to do with separation between people according to the ethnic groups into which they were born; and it is a tortuous and disorderly logic to misappropriate this characteristic of God in support of a political scheme of racial domination.

GENESIS 1: 9-10

God said, 'Let the waters under heaven be gathered into one place, so that dry land may appear'; and so it was. God called the dry land earth, and the gathering of the waters he called seas; and God saw that it was good.

Together with the previous paragraph, these words give us the picture of the basic system of sky and sea and earth as we know them. The earth is the place of our roots, the place on which we can take our stand. It is the point of our departures and the haven of our returnings. It is the source of all our supplies; it is 'mother earth'; it is that *from* which we come, *on* which we live. It is that principle of solidity without which we are not free to learn how to move. It is the form which is characterized by having a definable surface. In contrast to this, there is the vault of heaven which over-arches us and contains us. It speaks to us of our boundaries, not only vertically above but also horizontally; the joining of earth and sky is the horizon, at which we can never arrive however fast we move; our visual boundaries move with us. The vault of the heavens is that *through* which we move. It is that principle of flexibility without which we should be unable to move. These two factors of earth and sky compose the dwelling-place of man; the regular combination of these two factors gives man the feeling of being the 'right way up'. And when their positions are reversed, when, for instance, we stand on the firmness of a cathedral tower or a mountain precipice but see the perspectives receding below us, vertigo tries to tell us that we are the wrong way up, that gravity has got reversed.

Creatures which live on earth have to learn to live and move *on* something as well as *through* something; they have to learn the difference between several kinds of friction, between adhesion and aerodynamic drag; they have to have a grip on earth so as to be able to move through air. Quite apart from physiological considerations, a creature that lives on earth and in air has a greater chance of education than a creature that lives only *in* something, most obviously a creature that lives in water. It may be that only a creature which has learned to be *in* and *on* can effectively exploit the conditions of being only *in*; having been educated by an earth existence, man can contemplate existing in space, without any surfaces, or up or down, or back or front. Nonetheless, for man, weightlessness is a nightmare, whereas for a fish it might be just an excursion.

But the fish has only a poor experience of surfaces. What we call the surface is for the fish the absolute barrier, the ultimate limit. For creatures of earth, life is largely a matter of learning how to recognize, handle, use and penetrate surfaces. We tend to use words like 'superficial' with scorn; but the fact that there is a surface is the first blessing about everything and everybody that we meet. The encounter with the surface is the essential enabling factor which liberates us for everything significant which may follow. We need to take care of the surface if we expect healing or renewal in the roots.

An excessive concentration on the image of 'depth' in theology has its dangers; to find satisfaction only in the God who is the ground of my being may be to run the risk of knowing God only as the interior basis of my being; as an image, it may not have power to break through my preference for finding God in my own mental constructs, and for avoiding encounter with that which comes at me from outside; it may allow me to be satisfied only with those ideas of God which can get through the filter of my imagination or conceptual presuppositions. Nonetheless, this image of 'depth' has great value, for we have a need for rootedness, for knowing the firmness of God in the basic depth of ourselves; St Paul escapes most of the possible misunderstandings by stressing the need to be 'rooted and grounded in *love*', in that aspect of God which is essentially expressed in relatedness.[60] This is the great validity of our life on earth as an image of our life in God; we can send down deep roots into the hidden resources of our creative ground, into the common centre which binds men together in their reliance on their common source of nourishment.

Then God said, 'Let the earth produce fresh growth, let there be on the earth plants bearing seed, fruit-trees bearing fruit each with seed according to its kind.' So it was; the earth yielded fresh growth, plants bearing seed according to their kind and trees bearing fruit each with seed according to its kind; and God saw that it was good. Evening came, and morning came, a third day.

Earth and water and air have been provided; these are the necessities of life; and life is movement. The first creatures to take advantage of these conditions are the herbs and other vegetable forms of existence. The author does not see these things as being really *alive*; living creatures come as a very distinct new departure in verses 20 ff. But he does assert that the characteristic, obvious feature of vegetable life is its sense of movement, of concern for the future; it has a constant cycle of germination, growth and seeding; and this is so, whether we look at the plants which bear almost naked seed, like the various types of corn, or whether we consider the various kinds of fruit-bearing trees. The plants are unable to move themselves across space, which is why they are not thought to have life; but they do move across time; there is in them the whole mystery of hiddenness, and the fact that the plants stay in their orders; the observable difference between seeds may be quite negligible, but they produce widely different plants.

This is the aspect of plant life which most appealed to Jesus; parables from this sector of life evidently were more useful than any which could be drawn from the apparently more exciting sector of life which we call animal. He noted the progress from visibility to invisibility and back to visibility in the progress from seed to plant; he noted the power of growth to overcome hazards and to survive danger; he noted the sheer increase in size which occurred in the life history of a plant; he noted the role of plant life in indicating and responding to the changes in the seasons. And from many such illustrations the disciple community was enabled to have a clearer vision of its own calling and a more specific faith in the creative Christ who was both the seed and the guardian of their existence.[61]

The significance of the power of seed, which was so clearly the supreme feature of vegetable life in the mind of the author of this first chapter of Genesis, comes to its final evolution in the great parable of the resurrection of the body in 1 Corinthians 15, verses 42 onwards. There is a real continuity between what is sown and what is raised; a carrot seed does not end up as a daffodil; the me that now is continues to be identifiable as me, in spite of the changed situation. And yet, there is a radical discontinuity, sufficiently drastic to be recognized as death. The seed is not *used*; it is not, for instance, taken to be ground into meal. It is thrown down at the earth, rejected; and on the far side of the secret process in the ground, which cannot be observed or interfered with, there emerges not another seed but an unrecognizably splendid new thing, the final plant. Resurrection is not collecting together the old worn-out molecules and giving them another chance; it is the entry into a new structure of existence. And it is remarkable that the most helpful image for this final development of human life should be taken from the simplest observation of botanical life which, in our author's programme, is the first sign of movement in the world.

GENESIS I: 14–19
God said, 'Let there be lights in the vault of heaven to separate day from night, and let them serve as signs both for festivals and for seasons and years. Let them also shine in the vault of heaven to give light on earth.' So it was; God made the two great lights, the greater to govern the day and the lesser to govern the night; and with them he made the stars. God put these lights in the vault of heaven to give light on earth, to govern day and night, and to separate light from darkness; and God saw that it was good. Evening came, and morning came, a fourth day.

In the middle of the creation of living things, we hear about the creation of sun and moon and stars. The writer has deliberately separated the creation of light itself from the

53

creation of light-bearing objects, and so has given an obvious instance to Bishop Colenso and others who have been concerned to show that this account of creation is unscientific. But it does not require a modern scientific specialist to observe that light comes from the sun. If, against the most elementary observation, our writer sandwiches the creation of the sun between the creation of carrots and of codfish, there must be some good reason.

Surely the reason is this: to emphasize as vigorously as possible that the sun and moon and stars are lumps of the created order along with carrots and codfish, no less and certainly no more. Yet, in biblical times as in our own day, there has never been a shortage of people who have wanted to claim a special sacral character for the lights of the sky. For the majority of the centuries during which the stars have been studied, this study has been based on the presupposition that the stars govern or reveal the destiny of nations and individuals. The study of the movements of the stars has had a primarily political purpose, and only in the last few hundred years has astronomy become one of the purest and most disinterested intellectual exercises.

For man's mind to grow by his unprejudiced study of natural objects, he has to be freed of the restrictions forced upon him by the religious interpretations which he puts on them; if man is to learn to make responsible political and personal decisions, he has to be free of the influence of enchanted natural objects, of which the sun and moon and stars have been the most widely observed. If man is to explore creation truly, he has to be free of the religious authority which, even today, can force a man to take a special lustral bath to cleanse himself after making a scientific observation of an eclipse. It is this scientific, non-religious interpretation of natural objects that is put before us here; the Babylonian antecedents of Genesis gave heavenly bodies a divine status. For the Hebrews, heavenly bodies were heavenly bodies, to be accepted with thanksgiving to the creator of light, to be studied without fear.

What matters is our relation to God. It is his hand which creates and directs, and he does not yield his authority to any inanimate object; he is not dominated or overruled by any planet or force of nature. My future, my work, my health, are not controlled by mindless things far away or anonymous intermediary agencies called 'fate'.

In Christ, the dark powers by which men felt themselves to be ruled have met their match; at the very opening of his gospel, the evangelist Matthew gives us the story of how men who traded in astrological fates and fears acknowledged that they had met their Master.[62] The sorcerers, magi, so-called 'wise men' (the only other 'magus' in the New Testament was a most disreputable character[63]), were acting on the assumption that the political future was determined by the stars, but they came to yield to Christ the symbols of their claims. The realm of gold is the realm of Herod, from whom they had come, the realm of unchecked political and economic power; those who see the Kingdom of God as just a 'spiritual' matter allow gold to have an unchecked autonomy and restrict 'God's will' to questions of prayer and private morality; and the range of the Kingdom of God is thereby narrowed. The realm of incense is the realm of the Temple authorities from whom the Magi had come, the realm of unchecked religious and ecclesiastical power; those who assume that the Kingdom of God is virtually co-terminous with the Church imply that the Kingdom expands and contracts as the Church does, that it is therefore the Church's true work to put itself on top, to prove that it also can wash whiter than white, and let the rest of the world go by; and again, the range of the Kingdom of God is thereby narrowed. The realm of myrrh is the realm of death, of the fatalism implicit in the methods and reasoning which led the astrologers to Bethlehem; those who see the Kingdom of God as belonging only to 'the next world' elevate death to be a supreme authority, they give death the right to draw the boundaries of God's sovereignty; and again, the range of the Kingdom of God is thereby narrowed. These magi cast before the infant Jesus the powers of wealth and religion and death. They depart for home, not through the realm of Herod, not through the realm of the Temple authorities, not relying on the fatalistic assumptions of astrology. They go home 'another way'. The gospel for which this story is an introduction shows what this other way is, the way of ac-

55

knowledging the total claim of God upon his world, the way of seeing that all things come under his authority and have no autonomy apart from this unitary authority. This is pre-eminently the interpretation of the Epiphany story that is required in this continent, as it was for St Ignatius of Antioch in the second century: 'Everywhere, magic crumbled away before it [the Epiphany star]; the spells of sorcery were all broken, and superstition received its death blow. The age-old empire of evil was overthrown.'[64] This gospel of the over-throw of the powers of darkness was for long the primary meaning of this story, as a comment of St Augustine shows: 'If we must speak of fate, then rather let us say, not that the star was Christ's destiny, but that Christ was the destiny of the star, since he was to it, not it to him, the cause of its rising.'[65]

So the gospel of Christ asserts again the truth so firmly proclaimed in Genesis, that all the objects of nature are parts of one good creation. But let us not underestimate the diffi-culties in this belief. Many people in our world, many people in the Church, feel that they are not really free, that they are controlled by some mindless or impersonal force which makes words like 'freedom', and 'guilt', and 'responsibility' seem to be empty pretences. What they call this force does not matter – fate, or heredity, or luck, or environment, or just 'they'. A person can go through all the drills of piety and still be this kind of slave. Churches which, like most of ours in South Africa, have relied on catechisms for conduct-ing Christian education programmes, must see that success is not to be measured in terms of the number who respond to classroom religion by giving us back the answers which we feed to them; if this is all that we can offer, we have nothing better than totalitarian education which so insists upon a certain interpretation of the present that it breeds minds too inflexible to meet the future. Christian education should produce people who are free to become in response to the unpredictable, who can be described not so much by those features in them which are unalterably determined as by those which are new, individual and undetermined by im-personal forces. It is this kind of outlook which is required in a person who lives according to these verses in Genesis I and according to the Epiphany story.

The heavenly bodies do not govern man; but they are not without authority: they rule the day and the night. Everything else that man deals with is measured by quite arbitrary standards; as we go from place to place, from culture to culture, we have to translate from stadia to kilometres to miles, from ephahs to pounds to grammes, from escudos to dollars to pence. The one form of measurement which is absolutely given is that of time, for it comes not from invention but from experience; it comes from outside. As soon as we talk in terms of past, present and future, we are involved in the governance of the heavenly bodies; the very language of 'days' derives from them in this chapter, even before there are any means of measuring time. This fact confirms the point that I made earlier, that a 'day' in this chapter must mean a period of action rather than an actual period of hours, for how could a period of twenty-four hours be measured or even inferred, if the basic instruments for measuring time had not yet been provided? The fact that there are 'days', 'evenings' and 'mornings' before the creation of the sun is almost more revealing than the fact that there are light and darkness before the creation of the sun. Nonetheless, the terminology of 'days', 'evenings' and 'mornings' is based on our understanding of the regulation of time by the heavenly bodies, and this is understood to go back to the beginning of things and to be universal. This, then, is the function of the sun and moon, a noble and authoritative function, a function which puts all men equally under its discipline, but a function which is nevertheless mindless and mechanical. This is the limit of their authority, and man is surrendering his rights if he allows the heavenly bodies to be more than functional things towards him. However magnificent the star may be, a little child is more truly significant: the child can know something of the star, but the star cannot know anything of the child. 'Sun and moon and stars may all be above your physical body, but they are beneath your soul. . . . There is nothing higher than yourself in the natural order, save God alone.'[66]

GENESIS 1: 20–23

God said, 'Let the waters teem with countless living creatures, and let birds fly above the earth across the vault of heaven.' God then created the great sea-monsters and all living creatures that move and swarm in the waters, according to their kind, and every kind of bird; and God saw that it was good. So he blessed them and said, 'Be fruitful and increase, fill the waters of the seas; and let the birds increase on land.' Evening came, and morning came, a fifth day.

LIFE

Although there is a continuity between the various items of creation, the language of this chapter does indicate some critical points, moments when new and irreversible factors are brought in. These moments are marked by the word 'create'. God 'creates' the heavens and the earth; he 'makes' the firmament and the lights. He 'makes' mineral and vegetable things; but a new start is noted in the 'creating' of birds and fish. Vegetable life was not seen as being significantly alive, for its reproductive system is automatic; animal life is thought of as being receptive to commands, and its reproductive system has some feature of conscious obedience. The questions of what exactly life is, and at what point we can speak of it being present, are less important than the fact that at some time life began. 'The genesis of life on earth belongs to the category of absolutely *unique* events that, once happened, are never repeated.'[67]

The author here does not attempt to define what he means by 'living creatures'; he merely gives examples of what he means. It now seems that as scientific research progresses, it becomes more and more difficult to define what 'life' really is, or whether the concept has meaning: maybe the distinction between 'living' and 'non-living' is just a way of looking at things, which tells us more about the observer than about the thing observed. Maybe these terms are not clear-cut, but represent points on a continuum, like 'hot' and 'cold'. Even if we could locate a point at which life first appeared, there would be no hope of tracing the processes which led up to it, for the processes of production will have been obscured by the actual product. A great deal of energy has been expended, largely by people with religious opinions to defend, on the question of whether life could spontaneously emerge. Pasteur produced incontrovertibly overwhelming evidence that spontaneous generation of life is virtually impossible; it is the most highly improbable of all possible events. But we are dealing with virtually unlimited time; and where time is sufficient, the virtually impossible is sometime virtually bound to happen. By rejecting the cyclical image of nature which is common in other religions, the writers of Genesis offer a picture that is far more appropriate to the discoveries of modern biology: they anticipate the view that evolutionary events are unpredictable and unrepeatable. This is what is meant by religious language which asserts that such events are due to the creative word of God.

Even so, we are still talking about what we do not really know; we do not have a clear definition of life. It is easier to be specific about death, for death is that which ends life and causes the living thing to cease to maintain itself. Death ends the ability of a living thing to restore the *status quo*; death is the sign that the processes of resistance and of self-regulation are no longer able to operate. Possibly, therefore, the best working definition of a living thing is that it is something which can recognizably die. On this understanding, the being in which life is most potent can be identified as the being in which death is most conclusive and significant. And this is precisely the character of Christ; Christ is the one who not only had life for himself, but who came that the rest of us might have life abundantly. And yet, the most conspicuous event in his living was his dying; his dying was summarized in the totality of his death on the cross; this death was not a death only to physical self-maintenance but to social and legal and religious self-maintenance as well. And this was no sudden anti-climax; it was the 'hour' to which all his life had been leading. By his stripes we are healed – by his death a new principle of durable maintenance has been made available for us. And for the associate of Christ, the possession of life is conditional upon a willingness to die; the Christian person is genuinely alive only in so far as he is able to dissociate himself from the elements which are normally reckoned to make up his security – physical and legal and religious security.[68]

Life, therefore, is such a precious and important thing that it is seen as a great new start, a new direction in creation. And yet it can really be had only by those who are prepared not to have it. False offers of security, based on ideologies and corporate selfishness, suggest that we grasp life and security at the expense of other people's life and security. Christ's offer calls its bearers to take up their cross; and any offer of salvation which does not include this element is false. An offer of salvation which guarantees that we shall preserve our life is false. Life is not something which we preserve so much as something which we find anew, and a policy of preservation is offered as an insurance against having to find. Christ does not promise that nothing will ever be lost; he does promise that the really valid possession starts when we find on the far side of losing. Because our life is hidden with Christ, we can risk losing it; because Christ asserts us, we are free to deny ourselves.[69]

LIFE IN WATER

Life first appears in the water; the special word 'create' signifies that here is a vital new start, a novel beginning for which there is no precedent. From the point of view of biological science, the border-line between the non-living and the living may be impossible to draw. But our author is not concerned about the border-lines; he is concerned about the equally true fact that there is a vast difference between non-living things as a whole and living things as a whole. And so, instead of starting off with an account of tiny organisms like bacteria, he introduces first the huge creatures whose ability to move themselves around is absurdly obvious; he stresses the supreme characteristic of life, automobilism, or self-generated movement; and this is first noticeable in creatures which move easily in the media where man finds it unnatural to move, in the media of water and air. Man is the observer on earth; and, quite apart from biological science, he feels that the water-creatures and the air-creatures represent a more primitive stage of things than the earth-creatures who are his closest neighbours.

The sea-monsters are the fun part of creation; this appears slightly in Haydn's treatment of them in *The Creation*, and the Hebrew scripture's closest approach to anything like humour is in the descriptions of the hippopotamus and the crocodile in Job 40 and 41. Man can afford to laugh at the performance of the big sea-creatures, because they live in a different medium to man and therefore man can usually get away from them; it is safer to laugh at a sea-lion than at a land-lion. But, precisely for this reason, they can represent a fear that is less rational, precise and palpable than the fear which dominates us when we are confronted by the great land animals. The sea-monster is that which lives in a medium which is dark and chaotic, in which there are no landmarks, and which is a universal hiding-place. The sea-monster is that great hidden shapeless thing which threatens to jump out at me from the immemorial past; I feel like saying, 'Let me fight against a lion or a bear; give me an enemy which I can identify, which moves and scratches and bites like I do – anything rather than this indefinable great protoplasmic black lump, where there is nothing to get hold of, which is liable at any moment to flop back into hiddenness and remain there as an endless threat.' Monsters like this are not far away from our social and personal imaginations and memories. Genesis is saying to us that even the water-creatures are part of the good creation; they are under God's control, even though they live in the areas of darkness and chaos.

The author of Revelation tells of the demonic power of a sea-monster which comes up on the land and attracts worship and commitment from the people of the world. This is the surrender to the things of darkness, to the hidden threats and pressures in man, which throw the created order out of adjustment. Christ is the master of the sea-monster when it is given such distorted recognition; he is the victor even in that most wayward area of our nature, our imagination.[70]

GENESIS I: 24–25
God said, 'Let the earth bring forth living creatures, according to their kind: cattle, reptiles, and wild animals, all according to their kind.' So it was; God made wild animals, cattle, and all reptiles, each according to its kind: and he saw that it was good.

Now comes the mandate to the dry land. At last we are home. The creatures that the earth brings forth are those that man knows most closely. Cattle come first; they are money, security and prestige for millions of people; man cannot appear on earth until there are cattle to give him some sense of identity. Then come all the ants and bugs and cockroaches: these too must appear before man can appear, because a world without such creatures is inconceivable: they are, for most of us, the first creatures to register in our memory, because of mother's anxiety to keep them away from us. They scurry around taking no notice of us: we crush them underfoot, feeling slightly guilty, because we know that 'they were here first'.

These are made 'according to their kind'. This emphasizes the regularity of nature: but it also affirms nature's freedom to be various. Creatures have to grow, and their distinctive features can develop only in a world where other living creatures are similarly growing. They have to strive to solve the problems of their existence, to live together in these very varied conditions. They have to live with the possibility of alternative answers; they have to adapt themselves to each other's presence. Even when the author is apparently stressing the orderliness of creation, freedom and purposive choice are not very far away: the scene is being prepared for the arrival of mind.

God looks at this part of creation, in all its variety, with all its potential for destructiveness and pain: and he sees that it is 'good'. It is good that creatures have to try to solve the problems of their conditions of life, for these enable them to be what they are. It is good that species can develop, that mutations can occur; and, if this is so, it is also good, not only that a bat can develop from a mouse, but also that a

nasty parasite can develop from a nice free-swimming crus-
tacean; not only that a musical genius can be born of stupid
parents, but that a deaf child can be born of hearing parents;
not only that the law of gravity operates to keep things in
place reliably, but also that it will operate to bring an air-
craft hurtling to earth if its engines fail.

Taking creation as a whole, there may be much to regret.
But when we have to deal with complaints against the
Creator, either from other people, or in our own minds,
when we hear the question 'How can God allow this to
happen?', let us ask conscientiously, 'What other kind of
world would you prefer, what sort of world would it be where
such uncongenial developments were impossible?' It would
have to be a world in which the laws of nature were unreliable, where the rain fell on the just and not on the
unjust, which would, of course, be a kind of bribery and
would deprive man of the possibility of moral freedom; it
would have to be a world in which, in order to avoid the
possibility of uncongenial development or mutation, no
development or mutation at all would be possible; there
would have to be *exact* reproduction from parent to offspring.
A few species seem to have got stuck in something like this,
but we do not envy them. The parent of a handicapped child
(I speak as such a parent myself) has to see that the handicap
is part of the risk of being in such a world of development
and genetic hazards; if we accept the joys and fascination of
such a world we have to accept its risks too, with thanksgiving.

Certainly there is evil; certainly there are afflictions which
are hostile to the character of the Kingdom of God, in the
overcoming of which the Kingdom was demonstrated in
Christ and is still being demonstrated. But this is not the
point here; we come to this later, when we meet the mind of
the author of the other creation story. Our present author
is forcing us to face the demand of belief in a good creator.
If you can believe in God as Father Almighty, you can
believe anything. This chapter forces us to face the question
of accepting life before we go any further, and it is a good
thing that this chapter comes first. It says to us: Which would
you prefer to be – a person as you are, afraid of getting cancer

or begetting an idiot, hoping for the vision of God or for true love with someone different from yourself, alarmed and stimulated by the differences both in character and in situation between yourself and your parents, *or* a unicellular citizen tucked away in a unicellular bed? You can't have it both ways; and the fact remains that this *is* the world you have got, and you are abdicating your place in it altogether if most of your remarks start with 'if only. . . .' It gets you nowhere to say, 'If only fire didn't burn, how nice it would be'; it is no good, because this is what is not. At what is, God looks; and, odd though it may seem, he sees that it is good.

IT WAS GOOD

God knows what he sees, and speaks of what he knows. All through the Scripture, God keeps on saying that it is a *good* creation. It may sound very commonplace to say that God both makes and loves his creation; but these are two different things. Most people do not have the chance to love what they make, to be enthusiastic about it; and even when we do have the opportunity, there are so many checks on our pride that we too easily get discouraged. But, if we are to be good at our own most serious 'creative' work, namely the bearing and upbringing of our children, we probably need more practice, at a less responsible level, in the twin tasks of making and loving. The parent affirms the life of the child by giving him food and warmth; but the child also needs to rest in the affirming gaze of the mother, to practise the contemplation of that which says 'You are loved'; so the mother has to see and know and say that her creation is good. This is just what we see God doing. He takes the first step; he makes. But, as Erich Fromm observes, 'God goes beyond this minimum requirement. On each day after nature – and man – is created, God says: "It is good". Motherly love, in this second step, makes the child feel: it is good to have been born; it instills in the child the *love for life*, and not only the wish to remain alive.'[71] Fromm goes on to compare this with the description of God's country as a land flowing with milk, the essential care, and with honey, the sweetness and happiness of being alive. 'Most mothers', he writes, 'are capable

64

of giving "milk", but only a minority of giving "honey" too. In order to be able to give honey, a mother must not only be a "good mother", but a happy person . . . one can distinguish among children – and adults – those who got only "milk" and those who got "milk and honey".' Mother will love, will be equipped to love, in proportion to her own lovedness. A large amount of her experience, and of everyone else's experience in the world, will have the effect of stressing the power of her unlovedness; if this disease is to be mastered, a new statement of our lovedness is needed, a statement breaking into the succession of other statements with power and conviction. This statement, at its strongest, is Jesus Christ, the Word of God. The Christian gospel states that the supreme, strongest truth about us is that we are invincibly loved by God.[72] And a strong forecast of this is given in the repeated assertion that God saw that what he had made was good.

Christians have an advantage at this point: they have further resources to bring, and they can look at the difficulties more squarely. The supreme moment in the New Testament where the Word of God asserts that all is 'very good' is when Christ himself looks at his work and says 'it is finished'.[73] The new creation is seen to start in the triumph of chaos; its character is shaped by being rooted in darkness. And those who experience now the power of the Creator may find the same principle at work in their situation; those who share in the new creation may come to completeness by the same road.

CHAPTER THREE

Man and Me

GENESIS I: 26–28

Then God said, 'Let us make man in our image and likeness to rule the fish in the sea, the birds of heaven, the cattle, all wild animals on earth, and all reptiles that crawl upon the earth.' So God created man in his own image; in the image of God he created him; male and female he created them. God blessed them and said to them, 'Be fruitful and increase, fill the earth and subdue it, rule over the fish in the sea, the birds of heaven, and every living thing that moves upon the earth.'

LET US MAKE

UP to the creation of man, God's word has always been: 'Let there be . . .' Now there is a pause. God stops and reflects; he soliloquizes. He considers what he has done, the things he has made. He says to himself: 'Let us make . . .' And when he speaks of making man in his own image, part of the meaning must be: 'Let us make a being who can not only do but also reflect on what he has done.' It may sound odd to describe God as the supreme pupil or learner; but it is supremely by reflection on experience that man learns; it is just not true to say that man learns by experience; hundreds of people may have an experience from which only one may draw any learning, because only one may adequately reflect on the experience. If this unique ability of man to reflect is part of his likeness to God, God must be the supremely sensitive being, the one who is being most highly educated. Only so could he respond to the human situation as we believe he has; only so could he be the supreme improviser, able to bring good out of evil at its worst.

Man is simple, one entity. And man is complex, many different forms in one being. This may also be an aspect of man's imaging of God. In spite, therefore, of the strong assertion in the Old Testament that there is only one God,[1] God can still use a plural form of speech when he is expressing

66

the gathering together of his purpose into a great decision:[2] indeed, like other complex entities, such as water, 'God' is expressed in Hebrew by a noun which is grammatically plural in form – Elohim.

Bishop Colenso quotes Paschasius' interpretation of God's word 'Let *us* make . . .' as an indication of the plurality of God the Trinity: 'God said, God made, God blessed'.[3] Of course, as Colenso made clear, the bare text never meant anything like this in the first place. Nonetheless, man himself is in all sorts of ways a multiple being, and if there is any sort of connexion between man as image of God and God himself, man must be showing something of the nature of God through this multiplicity.

God is shown here as experiencing some inner compulsion to share himself and his powers with another being, a different being. This, in one word, is love. Christ, the second person of the Trinity, acts out this love in his own life, firstly by being the perfectly responsible son, and then by sharing this sonship with his disciples by adoption.

So there is a pause, as God reflects; he considers the risk of extending love by extending his image and dominion. Again, the fuller expression of this is seen in the outpouring into man of God himself in the person of the Holy Spirit. This was a risk indeed, for it would mean that man would be understood to be speaking with the voice of God. So St John tells of Jesus' words on Easter night: 'You are receiving the Spirit of God himself; from now on, if you tell someone that he is forgiven, he will know himself to be forgiven: and if you fail to do so, he will be unable to find any other way of coping with his guilt.'[4] An incredible risk. At times, the Church's disciplinary brutality would seem to have removed from persons their one hope of healing, and we can only be thankful that God has the freedom to do his apostolic work outside the apostolic succession. But, without such a risk, there is no real love, only fear. I can be so afraid of the 'eternal triangle' that I refuse to allow myself really to love anyone outside my family; the chances are that I will stop loving my own family too, because I will be denying my family's love the power to include any 'third persons'. If we are in the image of God our love must be committed but not exclusive; it must be able to share itself with an increasing range of 'third persons', and to accept love from them. Otherwise, we betray the essential character of that image and likeness in which we are made, the image and likeness of God who is love. And, as Erich Fromm points out, 'Love is not primarily a relationship to a specific person; it is an *attitude*, an *orientation* of *character* which determines the relatedness of a person to the world as a whole, not towards one "object" of love. If a person loves only one other person and is indifferent to the rest of his fellow-men, his love is not love but a symbiotic attachment, or an enlarged egotism.'[5]

MAN

Up to this verse the word has been about what is other than us. Now it is about us. At this particular moment it is vital that we distinguish between 'how' and 'why'. By and large, the 'how' is the stock-in-trade of the scientists – how did this emerge, and by what mechanisms? In Genesis we have an attempt to put the question 'Why?' against the empirical fact of man, to give a reason for this fact in the light of the presupposition of God. God's creative activity is continuous and eternal: it is not confined to 'origins'. If we remember this, we shall not be unnecessarily harassed by the need to reconcile these verses with the accounts of the origin of man given by students of evolution. For this story is not primarily about the creation of the first man but about the creation of me. This is myth, which, in Berdyaev's words, is 'a reality immeasurably greater than concept. Behind the myth are concealed the greatest realities, the original phenomena of the spiritual life. Myth is the concrete recital of events and original phenomena of the spiritual life symbolized in the natural world. . . . It brings two worlds together symbolically.'[6] This myth refers to man as he was when Genesis was being written and read, not thousands of generations before. Here we have man as the last of the species, capable of consciousness and reflection, with the power to control and direct the evolutionary process of which he is part. According to Sir Julian Huxley, in modern scientific man evolution is becoming conscious of itself.[7] Professor

John Burnaby not unjustly observes, 'Theology is at least not at a disadvantage in respect of intelligibility in preferring to describe the same event as the creature becoming for the first time aware of its Creator.'[8]

At this point, therefore, the idea of 'creation out of nothing' does have something to be said for it, for it stands for the complete uniqueness of this new departure. Life and man do not *only* 'emerge' from a previous condition; something radically new comes in for which there are no parallels. In so far as we understand things by reference to parallel experiences, the vital word 'create' must stand for something which has aspects that are by definition beyond understanding; and this is part of what we mean by 'God'. Man stands too close to his own livingness and humanness to be able to feel complete intelligent mastery over them; there is something about the process of their origin that escapes him, which cannot be wholly related to material which was there before; and the word 'create' is always used without reference to any such material. This is why the notion of 'creation out of nothing', with all its disadvantages, still has value, because of its built-in elusiveness.

The special meaning of 'create' comes out most precisely at this point. The first thing that is said about man is not that he is made in the image of God but that he is made on the same 'day' as the living creatures of the earth. There is no break between man and the creatures made before him. As Teilhard de Chardin puts it, 'man came silently into the world'.[9] Anatomically, the differences between man and the anthropoids are slight, and do not warrant the placing of man in a distinct category. Nonetheless, the coming of man on the earth is an event as significant as the coming of life, not because of the physical newness of man but because when man is born thought and reflection are born; the coming of man is, according to Teilhard de Chardin, a leap from instinct to thought, in spite of the insignificance of the anatomical leap. This is exactly what the writer of Genesis is signifying; on the one hand, he puts the origin of man as almost a tailpiece to an already busy sixth day, the day of the origin of all air-breathing creatures except the birds: on the other hand, he uses for man the special word 'create', used only twice before. Man is made; this means that like most of the rest of the world, he is the result of a modifying or adjusting of material that was already there. But, the really significant thing about man is that he is also 'created'; this means that in him there is something new, something that cannot be entirely explained in terms of what went before. There is in man both continuity and discontinuity with his antecedents; human studies get their character from their judgement about which of these is more important.

THE IMAGE OF GOD

If God be God, if God be the one who is beyond all our words, if he be the one who cannot be understood, but who rather stands over us, then he must have an image if he is to be known about and talked about at all. The image is the visible component of a symbol; it is needed if the symbol is to work. The symbol consists of an invisible reality, and a visible image, and the relationship between the two. Between the image and the reality there must be a connexion, otherwise the image will not work; but also between the image and the reality there must be difference or disconnexion; otherwise the image would *be* the reality itself, and there would be no need of an image to represent the reality. God must have an image. The real question is, what sort of image shall he have. For instance, 'Tutankhamen', the name of the great Egyptian sovereign, means 'the living statue (or image) of the god Amon'; here, the king is the image of God; if you see the king, you see God; what the king does, God does.[10] Genesis makes a statement which is democratic rather than monarchal. The image of God is man himself. And 'man' is not an abstraction; man is specified as male and female. If the king is the image of God, there is no room in the imaging of God for the kind of care which is essentially female; but if man as a whole is made in the image of God, there is room in the concept of God not only for the fatherly attitude which judges and approves a child in accordance with the child's performance, but also for the motherly love which is unconditional, undeserved and unacquired. In spite of all the masculine terminology which expresses it, the

70

doctrine of justification by faith is essentially a stressing of this maternal aspect of the love of God.

Once again, Christians work back to creation from Christ, who is 'the image of the invisible God'.[11] This is truly man in God's image. If we see Jesus, we see the Father. This is man really come of age, man as he was designed to be, in Luther's words, the 'proper Man'.[12] Zoologists and philosophers have struggled to define the essential characteristic that makes man, man – the *humanum*; it may be the opposed thumb, or the shape of the skull, or the developed nervous system, or the moral consciousness, or the ability to reflect. Christian philosophers have suggested sometimes that this *humanum* is equivalent to the image of God. But it is wiser to look at God and see what characteristics of his are visible in man. To look at God, Christians look at Christ, the image of God who is also the proper man; and the most characteristic thing about him was his freedom to be in relationship. He asserted this all along; he drew the line at nobody, and the penalty was the cross. The Resurrection proved that, in spite of all appearances, this is a freedom-loving universe.[13] The Church is commissioned to live according to this freedom, imaging God in the persons of free men. Werner Pelz gives a vivid summary of the implications of this mandate:

'God's freedom is creation. He is free in having chosen his creative work, in continuing it and maintaining it. He is free because he has chosen, and not because from moment to moment he can decide whether or not to continue with the work of his choice. *We* therefore become free when we have been called into God's creative work, when we need not choose any longer. Freedom of choice is not God's gift. It is a curse rather than a blessing. . . . The man who has to choose between two women knows this; so does the general who has to choose between two costly plans of attack. . . . God is free because he is whole, undivided, "simple". God wills what he knows and loves; he loves what he knows and wills; he knows what he wills and loves. That is his freedom. God is not free because he can choose between good and evil, because he can judge. He is free because he *has* chosen – we are not free when we choose between self-assertion and togetherness. We are free when we are pushed, pulled and dragged by the love of Christ into the togetherness we cannot yet bear. We are not free when we think we can choose between freedom and slavery. We are free when we are chosen for freedom. We are not free when we choose, we are free when we are chosen, and we are chosen to proclaim our incredible freedom.'[14]

To look at God, Christians look at Christ, the image of the invisible God; but how can we look at Christ? Christ himself now needs an image through which his reality can be known; and part of the gospel is that he has provided such an image, or (what is in effect the same) body, in the Church. But the Church is not automatically a good image; it can misrepresent the reality of Christ. In so far as it draws people's attention to itself and aims mainly at the preservation of itself or of Christianity or of civilization or some such thing, in so far as it concerns itself mainly with discussing its own authority and structure, it misrepresents Christ, Christ's freedom and Christ's resurrection. At every point, in matters great and small, it must ask itself not 'what is in accordance with our tradition, what will enhance our prestige, what will make people come to us?', but 'what will represent Christ, what will communicate to our fellow-men the freedom, the poverty, the suffering, the victory and, above all, the brotherhood of Christ? How can we express his expression of God's expression of solidarity with the world, especially with the outcast and rejected of the world?' The Church cannot create or destroy the truth about Christ; it can conceal it and it can reveal it. Its concern must be to ensure that if people accept Christ they accept him and not some caricature of him, and that if they reject him they reject him and not some caricature of him; this concern is quite enough for it to be carrying on with.

'God created man in his own image.' This is a statement about both God and man. What we understand about God will affect our interpretation of the statement in respect of man, and what we understand about man will affect our interpretation of the statement in respect of God. Beyond all the features which may be attributed to God, the essential characteristic of God is that he is known only by faith. No man has seen God, no man can prove him. If we say that

man is made in God's image, we are saying that man is an
object of faith too; to see *man*, through all the discourage-
ments and fragmentations of humanity, to reckon the other
person in terms of my association with him rather than in
terms of those features which separate him from me, this is
an act of faith. To see man as a continual surprise, as one
who cannot be adequately described simply in terms of his
heredity or upbringing or status or race or group, as one
who is continually breaking the banks of the language in
which we seek to confine him, to see man as the supreme
example of the situation where, in Sartre's words, 'things
have broken loose from their names',[15] this is faith; this is to
see man as made in the image of that which is known only
by faith. If you are prepared to live by such a faith, in
respect of your wife, your children, your enemies, or those
who are obviously different to yourself, a standard manner
of expressing your outlook is to say that man is made in the
image of God. But if you are not, no lip-service to some ideal
of God can reverse the evidence of your fundamental
apostasy.

In much the same way, we must acknowledge that man
is made in God's image inasmuch as man is truly known,
as God is truly known, only in his self-disclosure. The nature
of God is not available to us in a form which can be sub-
jected to the procedure of externalized analysis; if it were,
God would not be God, because we should be able to claim
the intellectual mastery over God. Those who claim that
man is made in the image of God allow that man, likewise,
is not knowable except in terms of revelation. Much can be
known about man; much can be known about a man –
much, indeed, of which the man himself may be unaware.
But we must say that the facts which can be known about a
man apart from his own self-revelation are not the most
significant things about him, and that we treat him as less
than man if we think of him only in terms of that which can
be objectively known – his ancestry, race, status, or even his
verifiable history. And even those hidden things which a man
may disclose unconsciously, of which he is not aware, cannot
be properly handled except in a situation of corporate self-
awareness, where people are in a situation of loving service

and trust towards each other and are trying to help each other to discover their strengths and weaknesses. Man, therefore, is made in the image and likeness of God inasmuch as, like God, he is known through revelation; his self-disclosure is not self-evident, but is an event.

IMAGE AND LIKENESS

Another application of this kind of reasoning is to be found in considering the phrase 'in our image, after our likeness'. Theologians have academically debated the significance of this double wording, and have tried to discover a difference between the image of God and the likeness of God. The general opinion seems to be that there is really no serious difference, that this is simply a duplicated expression. Nonetheless, in other fields, especially in painting, an effective image is very definitely not a likeness; an observably verifiable likeness, photographically accurate, is unsatisfactory as a method of conveying the truth about the subject which the artist perceives; there is a divergence between the likeness which is seen and the image which is known, which lives in the imagination. The likeness which is seen can perfectly well be seen; it does not need an artist to draw attention to it; his task is to draw attention to that which cannot be seen. So the old Egyptian artists did not draw the likeness of the king, which would have meant making him the same size figure as his subjects; they portrayed his invisible kingship by the visual imagery of drawing him twice the size of his subjects.[16] This principle emerges most clearly in the icons of the Orthodox Churches, where there is clearest opposition between image and likeness. Every icon depends on the doctrine that God can be represented in man. 'St John Damascene observes that while it was impossible for the Jews to depict God at all, it is not so for Christians, for the Incarnation has made it possible for them to depict the second person of the Trinity, the Christ. As Christ became in truth man, and acquired a visible body, and lived upon the earth, and associated with men, it became possible to portray him. To reject Christ's icon is virtually to deny his incarnation.'[17] But the icon does not aim to present a likeness of the outward person of Jesus, son of Mary, as seen by all sorts of people in Palestine twenty centuries ago. The icon is not an imitation of the natural world; it is not concerned to reproduce what we could see if we happened to be on the roadside when Jesus went past. It is concerned to call up an awareness of the inward truth about Christ, which is not seen but is known. In this respect, it is like the Gospels themselves, which record not what most people saw but what most people did not see. Most people saw an eccentric tradesman turned field-preacher, who was always getting into trouble for knocking around with the wrong people; a likeness of this is easy enough to make. Those who had the eye of faith saw a Christ, the image of the invisible God. And this is what the Gospels are about.

But this verse in Genesis identifies the image of God with the likeness of God. If we are to make sense of this, we must do so by stressing the hiddenness, the unlikeness, of this likeness, for this is what we see in Christ. Christ, St Paul says, had the human likeness of a slave, in whom the divine nature was hidden.[18] The truth of this can be accepted only by those who are prepared to have their ideas of God stripped of dignity and splendour; and this in turn means that this whole element of the creation story can be accepted only by those who are prepared to accept their brother man in terms of that which is hidden in him; the pressures on us encourage us to define our fellow-men according to that which can be outwardly verified, of which verifiable likenesses can be made. We must insist that the only likeness of our fellow-men which is valid is that hidden likeness which is characteristic of Christ; for only in this likeness has man a likeness according to the image of God. Only such an acceptance of a man's likeness in terms of faith rather than sight will enable us to break through the easy and rigid discriminations which are made against men, when they are classified in terms of features which are outwardly verifiable.

A SPOILED IMAGE?

The other great argument that has been conducted by theologians about this passage concerns the effect of the Fall upon the 'image of God' in which man is made. This is a matter for the systematic theologians; personally, I find it difficult to be enthusiastic about this question, and I am satisfied with the following answer.

The Priestly writer of this passage (Genesis 1: 1—2: 4) was content simply to let this account of creation stand. The story of the Fall and all its implications comes in the other account, which was written earlier, and was presumably known to the Priestly writer. He knew all about the Fall; he was himself part of fallen humanity; yet for him the important work was to make this straight, uncompromising statement. There is no sign anywhere that the writer is dissociating himself from the man about whom he is writing; he does not say 'This is how man *was*, but look at the mess he's in now'. He is writing about man as he knows him, just as earlier he has written about cattle as he knows them. He is writing about himself. He is writing about me. Therefore, in spite of all the signs to the contrary, we must say that man not only *was* made in the image of God but that he *is* so. This is a fantastic statement of faith, especially when we recall that it was written by people who had recently and deeply experienced man's inhumanity, in exile and enslavement. But this very phrase, 'man's inhumanity', may be the clue, and it appears far more clearly when we look at Christ, the true man. In so far as we are less than Christ, we are less than man, we are inhuman, for Christ is the normal man. In so far as we are satisfied with definitions of our fellow-men in terms of the outward verifiable classifications which are less than human, we are less than human; we are failing to be in the image of God, of which the normative specimen is Christ. In so far as we offer to others a Christ whom we can adequately describe, over whom we have a verbal or intellectual mastery, we are less than human and we are expecting the other people to whom we thus offer him to respond in a manner which is less than human. Man is indeed made in the image of God; but am I man?

Man can, for better or worse, dissociate himself from the nature of his species. It is impossible for an ant to be unlike an ant; it is possible – or at least we ourselves have devised language which says that it is possible – for a human being to be inhuman. Man has the unique ability to fail to be what he is designed to be and still somehow to survive. He can fail to be in the image of God. Konrad Lorenz's objection is surely unanswerable: 'To regard man . . . as the final and unsurpassable achievement of creation, especially at his present-day particularly dangerous and disagreeable state of development, is certainly the most arrogant and dangerous of all untenable doctrines. If I thought of man as the final image of God, I should not know what to think of God.'[19] We dare not assert that we ourselves, as we are, are an adequate image of God; this is not because we are not divine enough but because we are not human enough. But we can say that Christ is human enough. In fact, without Christ, the idea of man as made in the image of God has practically no contact with reality. As Martin Niemöller summarized the matter, 'Jesus Christ is human; we are not'.[20] Christ is what is possible for man. Man is somewhere on the way. Lorenz suggests that man himself is the long-sought missing link between animals and the really humane being. The Christian can accept this observation and this evaluation of man, because he has seen a delineation of the really humane being in the person of Jesus, and he measures his own sin in terms of his deviation from the humaneness of Christ. For the Christian, therefore, this really humane being is not just a future hope.

The phrase 'Image of God' has a meaning much wider than this verse suggests, for it includes discussions of all the verbal and pictorial ways in which we seek to communicate with each other about God. This is a vast subject, and is not strictly relevant at this point. But, by giving priority to *man* as the point where the image of God is to be found, this verse releases us from much anxiety, anxiety which is the commonest cause of idolatry. Words may turn out to be fragile and unreliable; visual images may need adjustment; we may feel insecure in our efforts to communicate what we want to communicate about God; but we need not be ultimately anxious. We can acknowledge that words are our own constructions; their significance depends on the innumerable circumstances of our history; they should be our servants, not our masters; they must be judged rather than act as judges.

We have not been given a series of absolutely fixed words by which to assess the validity of our ideas about God. But we have been given a Word-made-flesh; we have been given a person, with all the inexpressible hiddenness of a person. Beyond all words, the supreme imaging of God is to be found in a man. Belief in God is belief that there is something essential and durable that is beyond knowledge. If man is made in the image of God, the deeper things of man are safeguarded, the things that are perceived not by analysis and classification but in encounter. If I believe this about God, I am believing that, however highly developed they may become, analytical language and dogmatic statements cannot tell the whole truth or even the main truth about me. If I do not believe this about God, I am virtually saying that the whole system of imagery, the whole experience of sensitivity and intuition, and the whole phenomenon of art, are all part of man's immaturity and will in due course atrophy and cease.

MALE AND FEMALE

God created them male and female. God did not start off, according to this account, by making an individual person but by making a marriage unit. Man and woman's association is not a matter of occasional convenience; they start off together; the couple, the community, is the meaning of 'man', and the one half has life and validity in sharing this createdness with the other.

God makes man as male and female. He deliberately invents sexuality. The author, of course, was perfectly well aware of the difference between a cow and a bull; but he does not mention sexual difference in his account of the making of cattle; it is something of very particular significance for man. Man can reject and devalue sexuality in a way in which cattle cannot. He can treat it as something alien and hostile, as an invention of demons. There are many implications and consequences of this; one of the most significant is that to reject sexuality is to reject variety and change. For the importance of sex is not only in the vast difference between male and female; but this whole method of reproduction is the guarantor of biological variety and individual uniqueness. The geneticist Theodosius Dobzhansky has written, in a book which is wonderfully summarized in its provocative title, *The Biological Basis of Human Freedom*: 'Sexual reproduction is the superlatively effective mechanism which creates novel constellations of genes. . . . The potentialities of this mechanism are immense. With 1,000 genes, each capable of mutating in 10 different ways, $10^{1,000}$ genotypes are possible. This number is vastly greater than the number of atoms in the entire universe. Obviously, only an infinitesimal fraction of the possible gene combinations are or ever can be realized anywhere in the world. And any one gene combination is unlikely to arise repeatedly. Every human being is, then, the carrier of a unique genotype. . . . Sexual reproduction is thus a creative process; it originates biological novelty.'[21]

This biological novelty has all sorts of implications for human relationships. Some people are keen to insist that a man is primarily what his group or ancestry has made him, that biological boundaries of race are of absolute importance, that everyone must conform to the 'traditional way of life' of his group, that novel departures from the life-styles of parents or forebears are dangerous – in other words, that human distinctions are rigid classifications which allow of no change. Is it entirely accidental that this kind of attitude seems so often to be accompanied by a devaluation and suspiciousness of sexuality – 'puritanism' in a very narrow and rather unfair sense of the word?

The creation of sexuality is the creation of creativity. Creativity, as we have already seen, continually brings new distinctions. But, in order for creativity to proceed, most of these distinctions must be plastic, flexible, continually shifting. Such distinctions cannot be absolutely important. Certainly, God's character includes his role as the maker of distinctions; specifically, he makes the sexual distinction. But this is the last distinction that he makes. He makes male and female. This is a profoundly significant statement; but it is also a profoundly significant silence. Plants have been made in great diversity; birds, fish, creeping things, and animals have all been made each according to its kind. We might expect that all this emphasis on classification and distinction would come to its climax in man. But the only classification is between male and female. There is nothing about Semitic, Negroid or Caucasian man; there is nothing about Hindu or Israelite or Christian man; there is, oddly enough, nothing about Methodist or Moravian man. The adjectives by which we distinguish various 'kinds' of man are very notably absent at this point. The emphasis in the previous sectors of creation has been on the range of difference within the various types; here the emphasis is on the unity of man, as made in the image of the one God. If we people see ourselves *primarily* as a series of groups, to that extent we are obscuring God's image and disobeying our basic mandates in creation; and the same judgement is to be made, as we shall see in due course, with respect to the 'dominion' which is given to man. It is quite impossible to quote this creation story in support of a doctrine of racial distinctiveness; its witness is entirely in the other direction. The fact that man is classifiable into racial groups is certainly true, but it is not a central feature of God's plan. Still less is it part of God's plan that these groups should be seen as opposed to each other, with a rigid demand to keep separate. The story of the tower of Babel shows very clearly that the consciousness of our dividedness is part of the disorder of man; variety of language is introduced to emphasize this dividedness; it represents the consequences of human sin, not the original mind of the Creator.[22] The curse of this dividedness appears as a result of man's faithless effort to devise and grasp at a status for himself, instead of trusting in the security provided by God. In fact, the sin of the builders of the Babel tower is identical in motivation to the sin of Eve, and dislocation of relationship comes as a result.

According to the Christian gospel, Babel has been overcome, and the created character of man has been reasserted. Babel was a measure of divine precaution. Just as God made it impossible for Adam and Eve to grab immortality by a stupid use of their skill, so he took steps to curb the tower-builders' ambitions. But this was a temporary remedy in an emergency. It does not represent God's final will for man. Man was scattered into nations at Babel, but at Pentecost

men were called together 'out of every nation under heaven'
into a new community.[23] The Church, as a new inclusive
race, was being assembled to be the image of God once more;
a miscellaneous collection of Africans, Asians and Europeans
came together and at once formed something that we ought
to be able to call a 'communism' – a community sharing
property, eucharist, meals, worship and residence. It is true,
of course, that these men were all Jews; but their Judaism
had not enabled them to break through the barriers of
nationality and language in this radically new way. And
very soon the Church found that even the common origin
in Judaism was a thing of the past; it started the social
revolution for which it should always be responsible, the
revolution of demonstrating the one community for which
man was originally designed.

This is really a very simple matter; it does not necessarily
raise highly elaborate political questions, about which men
of faith can surely differ considerably. But the Church,
especially in a country which claims to be Christian, cannot
avoid insisting on the right to live according to the gospel of
Pentecost; it must insist on the right of its members to be in
fellowship with one another in a deep and realistic way
irrespective of their racial origins. If it is refused permission
to do this, it might just as well be refused permission to
preach the gospel, for the gospel is an account of an experience of an act of God in Christ which has happened and has
wrought a significant change in real life. Racialistic policies
are an attempt to outlaw Pentecost, in effect; in South
Africa, for instance, it would be extremely difficult, and in
many places illegal, for a group of Turks, Persians, Italians,
Arabs and North Africans to get together and live together
as a community formed by Pentecost.[24] And if the Church
ceases to bear witness to Pentecost, it really ceases to be the
Church; it is like a dead factory or an extinct mine.

The primary type of group affected by Pentecost is, of
course, the national group, in the sense of a group of people
sharing a common ancestral origin. But this is not the only
way in which mankind is divided; there are generation gaps,
income groups, social classifications, which divide man from
man; they all supply adjectives which can be attached to

'man' to satisfy his desire for someone on whom to fix his hatreds and prejudices. Where the author speaks of every 'nation' he means more than just the ancestral groups – and so does the author of the end of Matthew;[25] 'nation' means any group in which man finds himself. And the Pentecost incident fulfils Joel's prophecy, that the Spirit will break down the barriers not only of race and language, but also of age and class; the working of the Spirit will be most conspicuous in those two most notoriously troublesome sectors of mankind, youth and labour.[26]

So the story of creation demands a continuous social revolution; it requires the exercise of a continuous critique upon the customs and attitudes of society. It comes as bad news for those who feel a strong need to assert differences, whether national or racial or social or moral or cultural. And the gospel of Jesus Christ, as always, asserts and underlines the gospel of creation. The death of Jesus was brought about by people who were afraid of losing their national and moral identity. They could not face the possibility of being 'man' without a whole string of protective qualifying adjectives.[27] They were afraid of losing their clearly identifiable status as children of Abraham, and getting only a vague, elusive humanism in place of it.[28] Jesus was threatening the symbolic centre of their national identity;[29] he was offering genuine life instead of a national tradition, and the authorities felt, rightly, that this was a threat to their status and uniqueness.[30] So they expressed their rejection of Jesus by investigating his ancestry and origins; and in proving that these were unacceptable they proved that he was unacceptable himself.[31] It was this kind of sectional motivation which led directly to the crucifixion of Jesus; by his death and by his resurrection, Jesus proved the validity of the old creation teaching; he proved that man, when he is obedient to his mandate simply to be *man* in the image of God, is stronger than sectional man; he is fulfilling the nature in which he is made.

It is also worth noting that the author of Genesis 1 did not write in casual ignorance of man's racial divisions. It is generally agreed that this chapter was written during or after the period of the Exile, during which the people of Israel had experienced, as never before, a deep corporate suffering caused by their conquest by another nation. In fact, this experience did lead to a great intensification of the Jewish people's group-consciousness; it is therefore all the more significant that such an emphasis is so notably absent from this account of the creation of man.

GOD SAID TO THEM

God makes man, in his own image. And as soon as he has done so, he characterizes man as the first being in creation to whom he can disclose himself. The intention of God is that we should know him as he knows us.[32] For the Genesis writers, God was known as the one who had opened relationships with his people by an act of self-disclosure at the Burning Bush,[33] and therefore they depict him as losing no time in opening conversation with man as soon as man is made.

God speaks; clearly, therefore, he is understood in personal terms. His word is a loving and encouraging command; so it is not surprising that people have felt for a long time that the most suitable personal term for God is 'Father'.

But, as we read of man's creation by God, let us note the discontinuity as well as the continuity in this image of Father. There is no suggestion of physical paternity here, such as one finds in other traditions outside the Hebrew people.[34] God was Israel's Father, and our Father, not as an inevitable natural fact but by an act of grace, taking effect in a covenant, the whole point of which is that it is an agreement linking two parties that are otherwise not linked. To make sense of the image of Father, we have to accept the complexity of St Paul's language of 'adoption'.[35] We cannot address God as Father as by natural right; God is Father of our Lord Jesus Christ. The name 'Barabbas' means 'Son of the Father'; one 'Jesus Barabbas' was released from the punishment for his own crimes in order that another Jesus, a more universal 'Barabbas', who had been formally declared innocent of crime, might be punished for the sins of the whole world.[36] Those who are prepared to be associated with this 'Son of the Father' can share his sonship by being incorporated into the family of God by adoption. This is both the depth and the limit of the Christians' use of the image of Father with reference to our Creator; if we overuse it, and speak as if in the image of 'Father' alone we have unmediated access to divine reality, we have only ourselves to blame if the psychologists accuse us of holding the concept of God simply as a father figure.

BE FRUITFUL

God gives the command to the male and female human 'Be fruitful and multiply'. This is the word which gives divine authority for the procreation of human life. It means that marriages should not aim at being childless where child-bearing is possible. This is taught clearly in our marriage service. But it is possible that the word can be overstrained. The instruction is to responsible adults to multiply, and this command is not adequately fulfilled simply by the production of as many infants as possible. The mandate is directed to the whole of society to enable infants to achieve complete maturity and responsibility to God and man. This is a matter of education, public health, politics, local government; a whole range of civic concerns receive their commendation or condemnation according to this mandate. And certainly it should not be assumed that this commandment automatically excludes all kinds of family planning. On the contrary, it demands the whole range of concerns implied in responsible parenthood.

DOMINION

Man is ordered to be fruitful and multiply. This is the same mandate as that already given to the sea-monsters and other living creatures; man is part of the natural order, and some of his characteristics are derived genetically from his ancestors. But the mandate to 'rule' is of a different order altogether; this concerns a series of cultural attitudes and activities which are inherited not genetically but socially, which are learned from environment by each person, not automatically communicated by heredity. The confusion between biological and cultural inheritance has not only had gruesome effects on the doctrine of original sin; it has also led to a wide variety of interracial prejudices. Such features as technological prowess, humanitarianism towards people and even towards (selected) animals, and democratic ideals, are assumed to be racial (and therefore genetically-based) characteristics of the white groups; laziness, savagery, incompetence and superstition are likewise assumed to be racial characteristics of the darker-skinned groups. ('You feel a Native's skull', I was once instructed by a white man, 'and you will see that there is a dent in the top; that shows he has no soul.') Where people assume that such characteristics are not really *learned* but are genetically inherited, they will ensure the maximum rigidity in preserving the groups intact with their characteristics, and the results will gratifyingly confirm the assumption to all outward appearances; the stereotypes will be reinforced, because the social conditions which produce undesirable behaviour, for instance, will be made more inflexible. The stereotypes are easier to learn than the real truth; so we tend to select evidence which appears to be in their favour, and to manipulate language accordingly. One of the most important tools which man has for his task of 'subduing' is language; yet this tool can in itself reflect man's failure in mastery. Man's biological evolution is of vital significance, of course, even at the points where it has not quite caught up with itself – hernias and prolapses show that we have not completely adjusted to the 'dominant' position of balancing on our hind legs and having our hands free for other occupations: a study of survival patterns in areas where, for instance, diabetes or certain types of anaemia are prevalent is enough to show that man has not ceased to evolve biologically. Nonetheless, at the present stage, it is clear that man depends more than ever on his social inheritance, his learned characteristics. To ascribe to biological factors characteristics which are *learned* is to reduce man's humanity to a minimum. It is to ignore one of the most hopeful characteristics of our social inheritance, as opposed to our genetic inheritance, namely its flexibility. Learned characteristics, even prejudice, are far more adaptable than genetically-inherited characteristics.

To accept this distinction between biological and cultural inheritance does not carry with it any implication of an absolute division between man and the rest of the animal world at this point; it is clear that several other species possess social characteristics; and, according to a research team at the University of Michigan, it would seem that as humble a creature as the flatworm can not only learn things but also in some way pass on this learning. And, on the other hand, there is plenty of evidence suggesting that a disorder such as schizophrenia, with its obviously 'spiritual' features and significance, may have its basic causation in genetic mechanism. Nonetheless, man is distinctive inasmuch as he has come to depend for his self-awareness more and more on those characteristics which are essentially and uniquely human, the characteristics in which there is maximum flexibility, mobility and choice. Christianity has entered our cultural development and has given these aspects of man an immense stimulus, by insisting that the supremely human act is the act of free commitment of faith in Christ, in response to the grace and love of God. And, as a derivative of this theme, Christianity has encouraged us to see our personal distinctiveness not in terms of the insignificant and unalterable racial characteristics which we carry in our skin, but in terms of the various skills and talents which we can acquire and so supply to the community as a whole. Any system which suggests that a man's racial inheritance, for instance as a Zulu, or even his ancestral status as a 'gentleman', is more important than his functional character, for instance as a doctor, is out of conformity with the Christian gospel which this text in Genesis foreshadows, and is undervaluing the most significant aspect of what it means to be human. The biggest cost of racialism is in the end borne by its own advocates; for, if I say that a man's racial identity is the most important thing about him, I must agree that my own racial identity is the most important thing about me. I must insist that it takes priority over my individual characteristics and over the genuinely human features which I share with all human beings. This false gospel of the supreme importance of racial identity requires the sacrifice not only of other people's humanity, but also of my own.

God shares his image and likeness with man by giving him *dominion* – not by giving him procreative power. The man-

86

date to 'be fruitful and multiply' is a completely distinct blessing from the sharing of the image of God; there is no mandate here for sacred prostitution or the deification of sexual activity, both of which reduce the human value of persons by elevating an activity or a principle instead. Just as the creation itself is not an automatic emanation from God, the commonest form of human creation – that of sexual union – is itself not an automatic emanation of the divine method of creation. It is not entirely unrelated to the creativity of God, but it is certainly distinct from it. So, in the first move of the new creation, there is both similarity to and dissimilarity from the normal process by which a person comes into existence. Jesus was a man born of his mother; but the doctrine of the virginal conception of Jesus expresses the truth that in the Incarnation there was something beyond the creation of a new human being; an eternally living divine being was receiving a new nature, and was being made man. Sexual creativity is certainly part of the divine mandate, but is not a direct imaging of God; in fact, according to traditional Christian teaching, it was precisely in the suspension of this type of creativity that Christ, the image of the invisible God, was born into the world, not abhorring the virgin's womb.

FILL AND SUBDUE

Before man is told to 'rule' the things of the earth, he is given the mandate to fill the earth and subdue it. The authority which is given to him is not just to keep an already orderly system in good order. Our author, who has such a strong sense of the power and orderliness of God, still allows a significant area of work for man in bringing creation to completeness of order. Man has to work hard to occupy the earth's territory; his reproductive urge is not just to enable himself to survive but to take responsible possession of the earth, to 'fill' it. We can look around us and see how this mandate is being obeyed. Apart from his most ubiquitous enemy, the rat, man is practically the only creature which has succeeded in becoming established all over the earth; hardly any other creature has remained so unspecialized and therefore so adaptable. For instance, to find a lion in the snow is so rare an occurrence as to be really noteworthy.[37] But man has managed to inhabit the earth from the poles to the equator, and we almost take this for granted. T. H. White caught something of the significance of this fact in his account of how God, at creation, gave all the embryos the chance to select their various specialized equipment, and one of them refused to specialize and insisted on staying as it was. The Creator is mightily pleased with this, and calls up the others. ' "Here all you embryos, come here with your beaks and what-nots to look upon our first man. He is the only one who has guessed Our riddle, out of all of you, and we have great pleasure in conferring upon him the Order of Dominion over the Fowls of the Air, and the Beasts of the Earth, and the Fishes of the Sea. Now the rest of you get along, and love and multiply, for it is time to knock off for the weekend. As for you, Man, you will be a naked tool all your life, though a user of tools: you will look like an embryo till they bury you, but all others will be embryos before your might; eternally undeveloped, you will always remain *potential* in Our image." '[38]

Man, therefore, has this unique freedom, this adaptability and mobility: thus he can fill the earth. So it is characteristic of the true man, Jesus Christ, that, in overcoming death and ascending on high, he should fill all things, and claim them as his dominion.[39]

God blesses the rest of his creation by supplying people, to control and develop it. These are going to be people with *power*, people who will be able to act in a co-operative and purposive manner to control their environment. In a word, man is to be a *political* being, and the author sees the whole power-bearing aspect of man's nature not as evidence of his fallenness but as an expression of a divine mandate. And this chapter was written, not in a time of political success, but in the context of the most profound political disappointment and after the most shattering experience of the disorder of human power-bearing. Man is created with power, and is responsible to God for his use of it. *Man* as a whole is given this mandate both to work and to exercise power; and any system which deprives healthy and adult people of the opportunities to work and to exercise political power is to that extent failing to measure up to the Creator's mandate; it is dividing *man* and restricting some of the characteristics of manhood to a subsection. It may indeed be true that 'power tends to corrupt'; but this is the spoiling of an essentially good thing, and this is no excuse for a godly man to abstain from exercising his responsibilities. Power tends to corrupt because of the dividedness of man, not because of the inherent badness of power. And the history of the Church shows clearly that there is no magic by which a group of people are protected against the dangers of power simply by adopting a religious identity for themselves.

But the word 'subdue' itself implies a struggle between power and power; there will be rival forces in the world, and it will not be enough simply to set up standards. All power is in some sense a threat to justice, yet justice cannot be established without power. This is the reason why many good people feel that power, especially when expressed in 'politics', is not a proper area for the expression of Christian commitment. But, just as man has to rely on qualities other than mere goodwill to subdue sickness in his body, so he has to call in qualities other than mere individual love to overcome defects in society – defects which may not be attributable to the moral wickedness of any one person or group. The subduing of the earth includes, as its highest and most difficult sector, the subduing of the social factors which most profoundly affect man's environment; these factors are accessible to observation in much the same way as are the phenomena of the physical and biological creation mentioned earlier, and their processes are open to the analysis of the social scientist in much the same way as the processes of chemical interaction are open to the analysis of the natural scientist. Both are involved in the subduing of the earth, in the assessing of relative values, and in the extension of order through the appropriate use of power. And when good people refuse to use part of their power because they feel that it is difficult to reconcile such power with the ideal of love, the chances are that they are losing their opportunity to take part in the correction of injustice, and are conniving at oppression; they are usually renouncing power on conscientious grounds, while retaining much more power unconsciously. 'The middle-class Church which disavows violence, even to the degree of frowning on a strike, is usually composed of people who have enough economic and other forms of covert power to be able to dispense with the more overt forms of violence.'[40]

Christians generally agree that it is no part of the Church's vocation to enter directly into political controversy at a party level. This is very likely true, as a general rule. On the other hand, it is definitely part of the Church's work to educate people politically. By this I do not mean that the Church should necessarily teach a particular political attitude; but it should be helping people to develop that whole area of human skill which is properly called 'political'. It should be helping people to discover and use their powers and to dedicate them seriously. It should be helping people to be liberated from the inhibitions which are placed on the range of skills and abilities which they possess. It should be helping people to discover and use the specific leadership-abilities which they possess. But, on the whole, the Church appears to have connived in a conspiracy to keep power in the hands of a minority and to persuade most people that they do not have power and should not try to exercise leadership. This is certainly a widespread impression in the non-white areas of Southern Africa. The Church is virtually seen as an agency for the reduction of available resources, and must take a share of the responsibility for any irrational and unconstructive anti-authoritarianism which may appear. It is evidence of a seriously unholy state of affairs when words like 'dominion', 'authority' and 'leadership' are associated only with unfavourable experiences of suppression and domination. Maybe power corrupts, but deprivation of power can corrupt still more. The Church's educational task is to help members to grow to their full stature in the whole range of their abilities, to help them to overcome the fears and resentments which make the image of authority so bitterly hostile in their imaginations, and so to help them to accept and use their share of 'dominion'. This enables each person to share in leadership, as the situation requires; but it does not make everyone a 'baas'; in fact, it is only when leadership, or 'dominion', is really shared in co-operation that we can see what Jesus meant by washing his disciples' feet; leadership and service are truly one and the same thing.[41]

The Church's educational commitment in this respect is particularly important in view of the preponderance of the element of competition in secular education. Our formal education puts supreme stress on individual performance; it is merely a happy accident if the products of our educational process turn out to be good at working with other people. But the exercise of man's 'dominion' over nature requires people who are not only good at their own speciality but who also have some sympathy with other people's specialities and are able to work with them. This is increasingly the case, whether one thinks of a big project for agricultural development in a tropical country, or if the problem is just getting a ship unloaded. St Paul was suggesting the same principle in his use of the image of the body;[42] and these skills of co-operation are characteristic of the city; they are the essentially 'political' skills, which man must develop to the full if he is to obey this mandate to 'have dominion'.

THE RULE OF LAW

Jesus lived in a time of acute political interest, surrounded by people with conflicting political enthusiasms and ambitions. It is not true that he was uninterested in political questions; in fact, when we recall the short duration for which the first Christians expected the world to survive, it is remarkable how many incidents of political relevance they remembered from the acts and words of Jesus. But, beyond all the details, one great and complex fact stood out; Jesus had exposed the weakness of the power-bearers, the injustice of the guardians of justice; he had stood alone representing the norms of the conventional processes of justice. Faced with the innocence of Jesus, man's enthusiasm for justice quickly disappears; while the law-bearers slip into a panic of lawlessness, Jesus is left alone as the sole representative of God's mandate to subdue the earth. The account in St John's gospel of the trials of Jesus makes this utterly clear;

struck illegally by the authorized representative of the law of God, he answers, 'If I spoke amiss, state it in evidence; if I spoke well, why strike me?'[43] This is the unanswerable response to all bannings and detentions without trial, and to all other methods devised by governments or police to evade the normal processes of law. When the State threatens only with genuine justice, the righteous man can truly say, like Sir Thomas More, 'Then I'm not threatened'.[44]

Jesus asserts the rule of law, and so does Paul after him.[45] They do this, not out of expediency, but because the gospel affirms creation, and part of creation is this 'dominion', and part of this dominion is the rule of law. The rule of law is one of the better things that man has been inspired to devise; Christ asserts it, and therefore the Church is obliged to assert it. In fact, it is the Church in its most *conservative* mood which is obliged to protest against such totalitarian novelties as the by-passing of the rule of law when people are punished without trial or conviction. The Church, at this point, is the guardian of order; it must insist that such abrogations of the rule of law weaken man's dominion, for they undercut the reliability of the whole legal process. If the Church is silent at such a point, its silence implies consent to a policy of undermining creation.

The crucifixion and resurrection of Jesus are the victory of law; they are the vindications of man's power to subdue disorder in spite of all the pressures which make him renounce his mandate. As a result, Jesus is able to claim all authority for himself, as the victor, and as the effective representative of mankind.[46] If Caesar has power, it is because Christ has allowed him to have power; Christ's word is a permissive recognition that Caesar has power, but this can be only in responsibility to Christ.[47] Caesar is not given a 'dominion' in independence of God; his mandate is to express the justice of God and to implement it. And God's justice is not a series of impartial statements concerning who is right and who is wrong; God is not the blindfold figure with the scales. God's justice is active intervention on behalf of the oppressed,[48] and Caesar's mandate is to represent this justice. Caesar's mandate does not give him permission to use law as a means to impose the will of the strong against the weak, for this is contrary to the justice of God who gives Caesar his mandate; further, it is contrary to God's gift of 'dominion' to man, for this 'dominion' is a unifying and not a divisive force, which the agents of human justice are expected to represent. To his own disciple-community, Jesus gives the mandate to go and 'disciple-ize' all groups of people. [49] Here the mandate to 'subdue' reaches its full character; here it means to bring all groups into the range of the justice and love of Christ, the wholly reliable and undistorted authority. The disciple-community is sent to men *in their groups*, in the settings of maximum political strain, in the fields where love cannot operate until expressed primarily in terms of justice.

The effects of this are not, of course, to be seen in the total abolition of the various groups and nations, with their various characteristics. Even after Pentecost, Parthians and Medes did not cease to be Parthians and Medes, but their Parthianism and their Mede-ism ceased to be the supremely significant thing about them. Different languages remained, and new ones developed. But the members of these groups are baptized into the one community of God, Father, Son and Holy Spirit, and therefore their different characteristics cease to be the badges of inter-group hostility. [50] One may say 'Shibboleth' and the other say 'Sibboleth', but this no longer gives them cause to cut each other's throats. [51] We have to insist that it is not our various differences which cause our hostility, for this is to blame our maker; the reason for our hostility is our own sin, and this is overcome in the resurrection of Christ. The Church has to stand for this power of God to reconcile and to overcome our hostilities; it must, in its day-to-day life, provide the evidence that God is changing our enmities into love; it must, therefore, spend itself in bringing people together, and it betrays its calling if it connives in a policy of keeping them apart. There is an enormous responsibility at this point; the reconciliation made by Christ does not affect only the relationship between individuals and groups; it affects and heals every aspect of disorder in the entire universe; [52] but there is no evidence of this unless the Church provides it. The Church has to make this known, to the highest powers of heaven; and the highest powers of heaven cannot know this wisdom of God unless it is acted

93

out in the day-to-day relationship between Gentile and Jew, between people who have been historically and culturally separated from each other but who are now reconciled.[53]

THE CREATION OF COMMUNITY

The world is given to us to rule, to have dominion over on God's behalf. It still remains God's. God shares his likeness by sharing his dominion. The world over which man is given dominion remains God's property, on loan to man. The Psalmist, after reflecting on the superiority of man over the rest of creation, ends by praising the excellence of *God's* name, not man's.[54] But all this does not *seem* to be true. Man, as such, is not lord of the earth. Minorities of men are claiming this dominion, over against the rest of mankind. Power-bearing groups use the earth, not as someone else's property which is reliably on loan, but as their own property which is liable to be snatched out of their hands by other power-bearing groups; the earth is therefore used, misused, worn-out, in competition or hostility. The measure of our deviation is to be seen in the fact that for us the word 'dominion' suggests primarily dominion over other people, not over the non-human creation. We get more satisfaction over being able to shift one wife or one family from area to area than from shifting a whole herd of oxen. For us as *man*, man in human solidarity, earth has ceased to be *our* earth; we have become strangers to it and to each other. We buy ground, and say, 'This is mine, and not yours'. We each accumulate 'dominion' for ourselves, over against each other. We ensure security for ourselves, either as individuals or as groups; and, whether we intend this or not, this nearly always means that we get our security to some extent at the expense of someone else's security; for security is a relative matter, and we feel secure if it is clear that we are more secure than someone else. This is made very clear by Jesus' teaching about 'treasure'.[55] We are anxious about the security of our 'treasure' because we have got it and others haven't.

In a city like Johannesburg, where most big houses have burglar alarms and most smaller houses have burglar bars, one feels the truth of Proudhon's remark that all property is theft. (I should add that I myself have greatly improved the security of my own house since I started writing this book – I say this in case anyone should assume that I am not a hypocrite also.) If it were really certain that we had the right to what we have got, we should not be so concerned about security. But, in a world of injustice, it is impossible to have anything totally justly. Whether we speak of our dominion or our possessions or our securities, we cannot have them without anxiety unless they are properly shared. 'Dominion', therefore, is given to man as a whole, and not to a privileged minority. There is no dominion for those who withhold it from others; there is no security for those who withhold it from others. And, even though prisons may be a social necessity, it remains true that there is no freedom for those who withhold it from others; St Paul, for instance, was free to observe, think, pray, love, write, sleep and wake, when he was a prisoner; his guards were not free to do anything but guard.

Christ comes to affirm man's dominion, by providing a form of security which is for all men. If we accept the gospel of Christ, we no longer need to trust in a security which is only sectional. Christ does not stand for one section of mankind over against another; he does not even stand for 'Christian' man against the rest. He died to gather the whole of humanity together. Those who put their trust in Christ's security need not fear that their security will be taken away by a thief or by a rival group. The whole point of this security is lost if it becomes a sectional possession, if it becomes assimilated to man's habit of subdividing himself. The security of the gospel operates in the same way as the gift of dominion: the refusal of one means the loss of the other. Because of this, St Paul, writing to the Galatians, utters a very severe curse against anyone who offers, as gospel, something inconsistent with the original universal gospel of Christ.[56] These are among the severest words of the whole Scripture; and the form of anti-gospel which was endangering the faith of the Galatian converts was, in point of fact, an offer of security which depended on religious and cultural separation. There are, of course, many forms of deviation from the Christian gospel, in both words and behaviour; but this is a deviation which radically affects the very nature of

95

the gospel itself, and of the Church which preaches the gospel. If the Church allows itself to be infected by our human disease of sectional division, it fails fundamentally to represent the work of Christ; it behaves as just another human association and therefore forsakes its character as Church.[57]

The Church's task, therefore, is to work out and apply the meaning of Christ's reconciliation, so that man may be man once more, so that *man* may claim the dominion which he has been given. The work of the Church, in preaching and sacraments, is not limited to its own self-preservation; its success and failure are not to be measured in terms of its own apparent strength or weakness; it is not its own servant, even for God's sake. In word and symbol and action, it is God's agent for the re-establishing of man's dominion over creation; its task is to call man to recognize the lordship of the one Christ, so that man may receive anew the dominion from the one who alone has power to give it. Its task is to call man to recognize his brother; for unless this dominion is shared with brother man, the gift is withheld. Christ shows that the gift of dominion can really come true. For the most part we act and believe as if the gift of dominion is not true; our actions reflect our belief that we are basically not responsible, that we can blame fate or economic forces or psychological hindrances for our troubles. But the gospel is really spoken, says Harvey Cox, 'when a man knows that he really is free from dependence on the fates and recognizes that his life is now being placed in his own hands. . . . The taming of the powers means that man is invited to make the whole universe a human place.'[58] This means to exercise the dominion which God has given, to believe that the gift is real. It means responsible thinking and exploration. It means an end to the aims of magicians and fortune-tellers who try to find short-cuts and easy answers to questions which need extended and painstaking analysis. The fortune-teller and the fatalist are irresponsible in that they cannot tolerate mystery; ignorance frightens them into a lust for an answer – any answer. The true exercise of God's gift of dominion is seen far better in the scepticism of a scientist who refuses to accept short-cuts, who trusts in the ability of man's mind to handle the matter intelligently and to arrive at a solution in due course. A hasty pursuit of factual answers is usually a form of unbelief. But so often we behave as if all that we want is the facts, and whoever gives us these facts quickly and easily will get our custom. This is what our educational system, including our Christian education system, looks as if it is trying to supply. Our examination system so often appears to be designed to test our ability to memorize facts rather than our competence in handling the discipline. It may be worth observing that some African countries are becoming acutely aware of the inadequate understanding of man which seems to underlie much Western-style education. The Government of Tanzania, for instance, is replacing the ordinary primary-school science course with a course which might be called 'education for discovery' or 'thinking-studies'.

Knowing facts is not the same as being in the image of God; it is not an adequate expression of our dominion over the earth. Education, including science, arts and theology, is more about *how* to do things in our world. It is possible to believe that there may one day be an end to the number of facts to learn: but if we believe, as we must if we accept that we are made in the image of God, that man's creativity cannot reach a point where there is nothing more to do, we will see that our education cannot stop short at giving facts; this would be unscientific, inartistic and untheological. It would be to deny our true responsibility and dominion.

DOMINION OVER THE LAND

In the Old Testament as a whole there were two ways in which God was supremely acknowledged as King, namely in his rights as lawgiver and in his rights as landowner. 'The earth is the Lord's.'[59] 'The earth hath he given to the children of men'[60] – to the children of men as a whole, not to a privileged class or minority. No generation and no individual had the right to call the land his own to do what he liked with, for the land was God's alone.[61] Any kind of monopolizing of land was, therefore, a serious failure in worship, and St Paul is in this tradition when he says that covetousness is the same as idolatry.[62] The families of Israel were all tenants of the God of Israel, and paid him an offering of the firstfruits as a token rental.[63] An attack on the sovereignty of God will automatically involve a weakening of the principle of equal shares in God's land; Samuel saw this when he predicted that if the people chose to have a king against all their best precedents,[64] they would also get a privileged aristocracy, taxation of basic food and property, a landless, servile proletariat, and an expensive standing army to maintain.[65] Failure in relationship to God goes hand in hand with failure in relationship with the land; for the Israelites the landmark represented both the authority of God and the principle of equal right in the land for all citizens; moving the landmark, therefore, was an offence not against a system of 'private property' but against God himself, the rightful owner.[66] Even expropriation with compensation, a method of enforced change of land-occupation which most of us recognize as essential for such schemes as slum-clearance, is something which should be resisted in the Lord's name, according to the story of Naboth's vineyard.[67] Of course, Ahab was not planning anything so benevolent as slum-clearance; but then, the Hebrews' ideas about both land and labour would not permit the growth of slums. Indeed, where compensation is provided for, it is on behalf not of landlords but of those who were permanently landless because of their tribal peculiarity, namely the Levites; the tithe was not a clerical salary; it was their 'inheritance', corresponding to the 'inheritance' of other tribes, their share in the use of God's territory. The tithe was a compensation for loss of land rights.[68]

This may not be so remote from our situation as it seems. Western Christianity has been extremely weak in proclaiming a gospel of creation, and part of the reason may be that we have deviated far from this conviction of the divine ownership of the land, and the equal share of all families in the use of it. Obviously we cannot in these days say that every family should have an equal piece of ground; but we do not even stick to the principle that the value of land, a value created by the community, should be shared by the whole community. In the Site-and-Service schemes in some of our municipal areas in South Africa, we do come fairly close to the biblical concept of land-tenure. The public

authority retains the possession of the land and provides the
plots with essential services; on the plot a householder can
build himself a house more or less to his own plan and
according to his personal needs. As in Leviticus, the land
remains public property. But – such are the marvels of
modern science – the municipality goes one better than the
Bible: it supplies lavatories. It is probably only because we
happen to have a tradition of absolute freehold ownership,
with many rather concealed disadvantages, that this approach to land-tenure appears to be somewhat second-class.
Where the Church has gone into new countries in its mission,
it has sometimes found 'heathen' communities holding land
in a manner far more congenial to the biblical pattern than
the modern European. Maoris have been so conscious of the
land-rights of the unborn that they insisted that the selling-
price of land to settlers had to include an obligation to pay a
further sum whenever a new child should be born in the
tribe.[69] There have been tragic misunderstandings in South
Africa between whites who have assumed that they had
bought land outright and Africans who have assumed that
all that they were selling was the use of the land. Man cannot
be separated from land, and the biblical view therefore places
a divine sanction on the durability of *community*, that most
terribly vulnerable blessing. When this basic reverence for
the land is ignored, it is only too easy for people to be moved
around without their consent, for communities to be broken
up without consultation, for land-tenure to be organized
primarily for the security of the minority of power-bearers,
for boundaries to be manipulated not in expression of man's
dominion over the natural order but in one group's assertion
of its dominion over another. In such a setting it can be very
invidious if the Church, which is supposed to be the guardian
of the biblical witness, finds itself committed to being a
'landlord', with all that this implies.

MAN THE PRIEST OF CREATION

So man does not have direct or automatic relationship to
the land or to its products; man's rule over the earth is a
blessing and responsibility given by God, and is truly valid

only when it is exercised in obedience to God's mind. Jesus came to assert this rule, and thus to be truly obedient. He expressed God's claim on the things of earth, most specifically through the instances of bread and wine: he took these elements into the new creation, so that they represent the purpose of God for all things. The Church has both to continue this demonstration through bread and wine, and to work out the implications in respect of everything else in the physical world. Harry Williams stated very precisely the basic doctrine of the eucharist in these terms: 'The consecrated bread and wine are the physical universe made new in miniature so that it becomes the instrument of Christ's presence and power – that is, his risen and glorified Body. Just as in the new heaven and the new earth Christ will fill *all* things, so now, in anticipation of that divine act of renewal, he fills the consecrated bread and wine. They do not cease to be bread and wine. They do not change into something different to themselves. But when first brought to the altar they belong to the present world in which nature is not yet fully or finally gathered up into Christ. Then, as the service of Holy Communion proceeds, they are *transferred* into the new world where nature, recreated, is in the fullest sense the Body of our Lord Jesus Christ because he fills it wholly and it is fully gathered up to him. The consecrated Bread and Wine, therefore, precisely because they are still bread and wine (though now transferred into the new creation) are a perpetual witness to the ultimate destiny of the physical universe. In them, God's promise is fulfilled, "Behold, I make all things new".'[70] In the eucharist, in microcosm, the things of this world are taken to be made the Body – the effective instrument – of Christ; and this is the purpose of the whole created order. Everything we have is by divine permission. But these things, bread and wine, can be the Body of Christ only through the obedience and co-operation of man. In the eucharist, man asserts that he is the priest of creation, he is articulating the whole creation's Benedicite. But we have often failed to see the significance of the fact that we offer bread and wine, not just wheat and grapes; we offer not just the natural order but our efforts to obey the instruction to subdue it. And these efforts are often less than satisfactory. Nothing, not even money, can stand for man's disunity as universally as bread does. Where people are too unsophisticated to use formal currency, basic food can be the constant cause of discord. And what more universal symbol of man's depravity is there than the bottle? But in producing bread and wine, at their worst, man is acting in accordance with this mandate to subdue the earth. Bread and wine are a microcosm not only of the natural order but also of the manufactured order, and they must not be isolated from the rest of man's efforts in both failure and success. The Church has not neglected to show its concern about the fulfilling of the domestic mandate, 'be fruitful and multiply'; but we have often failed to show any awareness of our industrial mandate to subdue the earth, with the result that in their industrial and commercial and scientific enterprises most people have no sense that they are under any kind of divine mandate or judgement. If the bread and wine speak of the whole created and manufactured order being finally subdued and glorified, if bread can be the Body of Christ, an effective instrument of Christ's mind, then, by extension, time and petrol and flour and printer's ink and emotional energy and intellectual skill can be the Body of Christ too; they too can be effective instruments of Christ's mind (which is what a body is), but only on the same terms as the bread, only through the brotherly obedience and willing co-operation of man. Neither bread nor butter nor bitumen can decide itself. Only man can accept nature and humanize it; he can take nature and convert it into culture, and this is his unique genius; he can share in the summing-up of all things in Christ. This is a function which goes far beyond the mindlessness of biological evolution; this is an essential part of the conversion of chaos into cosmos, when man expresses his dominion over that which has emerged through biological evolution and imposes upon it his own patterns of identification and utilization. Neither man nor animal can significantly choose to reject his biological inheritance; but man faces a unique risk; he has a cultural inheritance which he can choose to reject. He can choose to be inhuman: and the effect of such a choice is that he will be inadequate as a ruler of the earth.

Our relationships are normally both expressed and evaluated by the way in which we handle *things*. Christ came to love people by using things; he came to correct the disorder which was presumably as widespread in his day as in ours – the disorder in which we prefer to love things and use people. Things get out of hand when a man loves them so much that he ceases to have dominion over them; Christ, by restoring the lovableness of people, also restores the usefulness of things; his reconciliation spreads infectively through the whole created order.

In Christ, the two elements of 'image' and 'dominion' converge. He who is truly in the image of God is able to extend his dominion not only over the rest of creation but over himself. And this is the point at which we face our supreme difficulty. For instance, as Denis de Rougemont observed, 'The atom bomb is not in the least dangerous; it is a thing. What is fearfully dangerous is man. . . . Clearly, if the bomb is left alone, it will do nothing. What we need is control of man.'[71] The mandate to have dominion over the rest of creation is a dead-end if we do not see that we are part of that creation over which we are to exercise this dominion. If the control is out of control, that which is supposed to be under the control of the control is bound to be out of control. It is a wonder that the rest of creation has not fallen apart more than it has done; the fact that it has not is due, in terms of this chapter of Genesis, to the providence of God in giving particular mandates to the other sections of creation, so that, in spite of the mandate of man to have dominion over them, they are still directly sustained by the law of God. The Christian gospel states that the deliverance of nature has already begun in the saving work of Christ. The nature-miracles of Jesus are intended to demonstrate the kind of thing which can happen when a totally integrated man, with his obedience to God uncompromised and undiluted, exercises his mandate to subdue the earth. But this exercise of dominion was achieved neither by technical skill nor by a magical short-cut; it was there because Jesus had first of all a genuine dominion over himself. The nature-miracles express one kind of dominion; but a greater kind of dominion is represented by the story of the temptation. Here Jesus asserted his real freedom to have and to exercise true dominion; he showed that he was free from the compulsion to use his abilities to secure his own status and to exercise dominion in a self-regarding way.[72] Jesus, being the most humane being, is also the most dominion-full being – or, to put it more simply, the most powerful being. But his power is not seen primarily in his status; it is seen in his total availability for others. Power is the ability to get things done; and we see Jesus' power, his exercise of dominion, when he is able to point to the blind who are seeing, the deaf who are hearing, the lame who are walking, the lepers who are cleansed, and the poor who are hearing the gospel.[73] This is a more significant exercising of dominion than even the stilling of the storm.

And, as always, we have to ask how Christ's exercise of dominion is to be seen and shared now. The answer which is usually reckoned to be theologically correct would be 'through the Church, the Body of Christ'. The Church has to be powerful in the way that Jesus was powerful, no more and no less. Its power is not to be a matter of status; it has to be judged by the degree to which it is truly available for others. The power of the Church also is an ability to get things done. We saw the power of Jesus in the difference that he made to the world around, and we have to see the power of the Church in the same way. And certainly we can see the power of the Church at work, in healing, in education, in evangelism; blind are seeing and deaf hearing – or at the very least, their handicaps are no longer causing complete isolation; people are going about healthy and active who might otherwise be dead or helpless; and people are hearing a word of truth and justice in a world of lies and prejudice – here is the exercise of the dominion of Christ through his Church; we must recognize that this is so, watch for the signs of God's working, and give thanks. But at the same time, we must also say that the Church's main use of power at present seems to be much more selfish. The main difference that the Church seems to make to the scene is to get hold of bits of land, construct powerful-looking and symbolically reassuring edifices on them, attract people into these edifices for a few hours a week, and organize professional caretakers and publicity agents for them. This *appears* to be the way that the Church uses its power and exercises its dominion. The extent to which this is true is the extent to which we have moved away from Jesus' understanding and use of power. There is much talk about 'stewardship'; but this so often seems to be mainly a matter of getting people to decide how much they should contribute to the institution to pay for the maintenance of its own facilities. The Church, if it is to be the Body of Christ, has also to develop a sensitivity for the use of *all* power, and really its own maintenance should be at the bottom of its budget. Robert Graves, the poet, once described his surprise when 'I met a man in America of my own age, much better dressed and better off than myself, who makes a profession of lecturing about me'.[74] As a professional religious man, educated and employed by the Church, I find this too embarrassing to be very funny. I, and thousands like me, are certainly better dressed and better off than Jesus of Nazareth, and we make a profession of talking about him. The institutional Church channels a great deal of its power into making this possible for us, into providing us with auditoriums and into persuading people to come there and hear us. In all this expenditure of power there is certainly a great deal of devotion, and great desire to be obedient to God's mind. It could be true that without this system there would be fewer blind people seeing, fewer deaf people hearing, fewer people really hearing the gospel. It could also be true that, if the Church were freer from the clamour of its own appetites, the effect of its presence might be more like the effect of the presence of Jesus.

Whatever our practical decision at this point, we must be clear about one thing: the Church is supposed to be an agency of Christ in the world, a community that realizes that it has power, that this power is a responsibility from God, and that this power has to be used to implement the mind of our Creator. The Church, and every Christian, have this calling to be sensitive to the real meaning and purpose of the power that they hold; they have to be a model to the rest of the world in the exercise of the dominion which God has given them.

GENESIS I: 29–31

God also said, 'I give you all plants that bear seed everywhere on earth, and every tree bearing fruit which yields seed: they shall be yours for food. All green plants I give for food to the wild animals, to all the birds of heaven, and to all reptiles on earth, every living creature.' So it was; and God saw all that he had made, and it was very good. Evening came, and morning came, a sixth day.

After distinguishing man from the rest of creation, first of all by the very act of speaking to him, and secondly, by giving him dominion over the rest of creation, God concludes by stressing the indelible fact that unites man to the rest of creation, the fact that he has a body which continually needs nourishment. If we remember our author's exalted understanding of the status of man, it is remarkable how true he is to the biological truth that there is no complete discontinuity between man and animal. For anything creative to happen, there must be continuity and discontinuity, the recognizable and the surprising, just as Jesus was recognizable and yet unrecognizable after the Resurrection,[75] just as there is continuity and discontinuity between the seed and the plant in the image of the resurrected body.[76] Man's nourishment is to be taken alongside the beasts and birds, with substantially the same menu: man is to take the seed and fruit, while the birds and beasts take the leaves. The intention is that there is to be no need for living creatures to deprive each other of life in order to live. This agrees with the author's previous assumption of an absolute boundary between vegetable and animal life – the assumption, indeed, that vegetable life is not really life at all. By the time that this chapter was written the killing of animals for meat was commonplace; but its main significance was that both the killing and the eating of the meat were parts of worship. Meat-eating was mainly centred on the sacrificial system of the temple which, by this time, was no longer a matter of joy and festival; it was, rather, the means of handling a wide variety of types of guilt. Killing had come to be part of a method of dealing with the disorder of the world; and therefore it was possible to imagine that, in the first place, no killing was intended by God or needed by man. At the time when God could look around and see that everything was very good, sacrifices were unnecessary. Only after the Flood, according to this writer, only after the pressure had been felt for a decisive handling of man's moral disorder, was a mandate given to man to feed on animal as well as vegetable diet.[77] But at the beginning, neither killing nor sacrifice was necessary. Except for city-dwellers, these two activities go together; for us who do live in cities, 'sacrifice' has lost most of its meaning; it is a word which means most to people who kill their own meat, and the power of its significance is in inverse proportion to the number of abattoirs.

Christ has made sacrifice of animals unnecessary; and it may well be that our eating of meat is a piece of archaic barbarism which a Christian culture ought to be making obsolete. Certainly the Old Testament picture of the day of the Messiah is one where the hostilities between beast and beast and beast and man are passed away; this is not out of a sentimental love of animals, but because the abolition of such hostility is an indication and a by-product of the victory of God's righteousness.[78] And there is value in the symbolism of the presence of the ox and ass beside the animals' feeding-trough in which the infant Christ was laid. The man in whom the image of God was present in complete purity was born in close familiarity with the rest of the sixth day's creatures. In Jesus Christ, Son of God and Son of Mary, the uncreated comes alongside the creation – the whole of creation, not just the 'top end'; Christ does not come as a despotic authority, stretching out the hierarchies of being; he comes to take his place as a genuine part of creation, asserting the original close relationship between man and the rest of the created order, especially that of the sixth day.

GENESIS 2: 1–4
Thus heaven and earth were completed with all their mighty throng. On the sixth day God completed all the work he had been doing, and on the seventh day he ceased from all his work. God blessed the

seventh day and made it holy, because on that day he ceased from all the work he had set himself to do.

This is the story of the making of heaven and earth when they were created.

REST

We naturally assume that the sixth day must have been the climax of the Creation, because it was the day of the creation of man. But in our story, the impression is inescapable that the real climax is the seventh day – and certainly this was the impression of those who kept the Sabbath. God ceased from his work on the seventh day, not the sixth; his rest is part of the work. Professor von Rad compares shrewdly the Genesis account with the Babylonian creation story on which it is based; in that story, the climax at the end of the creation process is the public glorification of the god Marduk, as all the top gods proclaim his honour and his fifty names. 'How different, how much more profound, is the impressive rest of Israel's God! This rest is in every respect a new thing along with the process of creation, not simply the negative sign of its end; it is anything but an appendix.'[79] Rest is a new thing, and more than any other part of the creation, it has continually to be made new. For the principle of rest is continually threatened, not least by the 'bind' which we call religion. Even Moses, under whose leadership the whole concept of the Sabbath rest was established, did not know how to rest himself, although at least he had the humility to take a few tips from his illiterate heathen father-in-law.[80] Moses was never able really to rest in the household of God, because he never became more than a servant in it; and the one thing that a servant is presumed not to do in the master's house is to rest there. But Christ is related to the household as a son; his security is not in his obedience and activity but in the rights of his relationship to the Father;[81] it is this which enables Christ to be offered to us as the true man, living in the strength of his relationship, abiding in the Father; his work flows out of his resting, whereas, with the servant, if any rest comes at all it is only as a reward for working. Dr Frank Lake, who draws out this comparison in impressive detail,[82] demonstrates that for many religious people this *rest* is the hardest part of the gospel, the acceptance of which requires the most radical repentance. He instances the kind of person who 'cannot rest because the burden of his neurotic guilt and his sin, inextricably mixed, have cut him off from God, as he believes him to be. He cannot rest because his final refuge, his religion, forbids him to do so. Its first and final message to him is to urge him again to the things he must do to be saved.'[83] The message of rest, of deliverance from the works of the law, of unconditional acceptance in Christ, comes as the very core of the gospel; it spells out in detail what the rest on the seventh day of creation already indicated, that there is a strict limit to what can be attained by activism and moral earnestness. This often seems to be a dangerous slackening of the moral imperative; but in fact, by abandoning a mechanical connexion between human obedience and divine acceptance, this gospel opens the way for authentic moral responsibility, based only on a free response to the grace of God. This is why the Sabbath is in principle the great new thing breaking into the moralism of man, which so often seems to be based on a commercial kind of bargain rather than on the love of God; and Christians therefore would claim that in the blessing of the seventh day the old creation has its closest point of reference to the new.

The seventh day, therefore, rather than the sixth, is the climax of the whole account; and this demonstrates conclusively that the writer is supremely interested in the *evaluation* of the created order rather than in the created order itself. The seventh day is the day set aside for the deliberate exercise of evaluation, which we call worship; and rest is essential if effective evaluation is to be made. The fact that the seventh day is the climax underlines the refrain we have already heard so often, that God saw that it was *good*. Haydn caught the spirit of this chapter perfectly. in *The Creation*; he put the narrative in a sober recitative – a recital; but at the end of each 'day's work', instead of merely noting that God saw that what he had made was good, we find a full-scale chorus of orderly, enthusiastic praise; and it is these choruses which make up the most significant and memorable feature of the whole work.

We speak of a 'doctrine' of creation. But the first article of the Creed is no 'objective' statement; it is a celebration, it is something to sing. The first chapter of Genesis, right at the beginning of the Bible, establishes the essential scriptural principle that there is no theology without worship; there is no doctrine without wonder, no logic without surprise. Otherwise, however correct our words may be, they misrepresent the heart of things. The Christian Creed is a psalm of thanksgiving and commitment; and dullness, rather than unorthodoxy, is the supreme betrayal of the Lord of the Creation.

The fact that God values his creation, that he reckons it to be good, is the basic reason why we cannot divide his role of Creator from his role of maintainer. A god who merely sets a cosmic machine in motion at the beginning of things and then sits back to watch it, cannot be the God of the Bible, who continues to care for what he has made. Mother Julian saw the truth with wonderful clarity: 'Also in this he showed me a little thing, the quantity of an hazel-nut, in the palm of my hand; and it was as round as a ball. I looked thereupon with eye of understanding, and thought: what may this be? And it was answered generally thus: it is all that is made. I marvelled how it might last, for methought it might suddenly have fallen to naught for littleness. And I was answered in my understanding: It lasteth, and ever shall last for that God loveth it. And so All-thing hath the Being by the love of God. In this little thing I saw three properties. The first is that God made it, the second is that God loveth it, the third, that God keepeth it.'[84]

So, although God rests, his care continues. Because he cares, he preserves. 'Thou hast made heaven, the highest heaven with all its host, the earth and all that is on it, the seas and all that is in them. Thou preservest all of them.'[85] The great psalms of creation have the same stress. 'Thou makest grass grow for the cattle . . . thou makest darkness and it is night . . . thou makest the sun rise. . . .'[86] God's creation is a continuous work as well as the original initiative in the past, and it is unfortunate that this has been obscured by the stress on the idea of creation 'out of nothing'. If we had retained the biblical idea of God's continuous creativity, ordinary Christians would have probably had much less difficulty in seeing that evolution can be God's creative method. In fact, Christians have a picture of an unfinished, dynamic world, in which hope is a vital element; they look for a completeness which is not yet; in principle, the Christian world-view is much more congenial to an evolutionary interpretation than to one which insists that the universe is a finished product.

SABBATH

But God establishes this rhythm of work and rest. The characteristics he displays in creation are passed on to man – not the secret things, but those that are open and communicable. They are blessings – freedom, relationship, dominion, and now, rest. This last is a blessed provision, and a person is lacking in divine humanity unless he wants it. But it is to be sought only in God – 'you made us for yourself, and our hearts find no peace until they rest in you'.[87] This again is impossible to have properly unless it is had together. The idea of work being communal and rest (leisure) being individual is foreign to this view. The Fourth Commandment lays it down quite clearly that rest is for all on the Sabbath.[88] The South African Prayer Book of the Anglican Church most unwisely requires the reading only of the first part of this verse at the eucharist. If it is to be read, it should be read in full, or else employers may get the impression that they are obeying it if they have one law for themselves and another for their servants. The law makes it quite clear that the employer is breaking it if his manservant or maidservant is required to work, just as much as if he works himself. The commandment puts the responsibility for the rest of humanity clearly on to the shoulders on which it belongs – namely those of people who choose to be employers. The failure of many employers in Southern Africa to take seriously this godly anticipation of trade union conditions brings many headaches for pastors who look after congregations that consist largely of domestic servants. But it is dangerous for such a blessing to be enforced as a restrictive legalism. All that we want is that people should see that it is a blessing, and therefore can be enjoyed only in community.

For the Hebrews the Sabbath stood for several blessings in addition to that of rest. The Sabbath was every seventh year as well as every seventh day. Whereas in our Western educational system it is only the 'top people' in academic life who get a sabbatical leave, in Hebrew law there was a refresher course for every citizen every seventh year in such a range of subjects as civil and criminal law, medicine, theology, courtship and marriage, ritual, sanitation, history, literature, natural science, dietetics, census studies, and so on. All this came under 'The Law'.[89] This system provided against the emergence on the one hand of an arrogant intelligentsia and, on the other, of an irresponsible, irrational plebs.

Our present educational customs in the West appear to be designed to produce a structure of intellectual and social élites; to a considerable extent our churches have encouraged this and assisted in the exporting of these customs to other parts of the world. Some of the most vigorous and constructive criticisms of such education are coming from these 'export markets', which are finding our traditional style of education both undemocratic and unhelpful in a developing agrarian context. It is notable that one of the most thorough and perceptive of these critiques comes not from an academic educationalist but a practising politician and national leader, namely President Nyerere of Tanzania.[90] He suggests a radically different style of education, which would rely on a very close connexion between the school, the community and the land. This is already being tested in practice, and it is from such testing that proper assessment must be taken; but we might observe in passing that the President's ideas do seem to be far more congenial to the biblical understanding of education than are the educational traditions of the West.

The law of the Sabbath year also ensured a year of rest for the land.[91] Not having much of a doctrine of individual immortality, the Hebrews understood that they would have future existence only in the continuation of their race in their descendents; and this concern acted as a check on the greed which would extract every bit of profit from the ground now, with no consideration for the future. This would prevent a process which has turned many more fertile areas into dustbowls.

Further, the weekly Sabbath was not only a rest law but also a labour law. It required of society that idling be eliminated, the idling both of the unemployed and also of the man of so-called 'independent means' – who is in fact the most totally dependent of all humanity apart from the infant and the senile.

But the climax of the whole Sabbath system was in the year of jubilee, occurring every fifty years.[92] This was a festival of the monarchy not of a man but of God, not a celebration of the supremacy of an aristocratic élite but an occasion to straighten out the inequalities of society. Land could not be sold in perpetuity; all that could be sold was the use of it until the next jubilee year; then it returned to the care of the family whose inheritance it was. So the community was protected from the emergence on the one hand of a small aristocracy holding large estates, and on the other of a large landless class. Because land and labour are inseparable, account was taken of improvements made to the land in making the jubilee year adjustments; indeed, where the value of the property was mainly reckoned in terms of improvements (i.e. a house in a walled city), there was no hindrance to outright freehold sale.[93] But the Jubilee law and the Sabbath law both stress a truth which man, especially modern Western man, seeks by all means to avoid, that the differences between people in wealth and ability are of less consequence than their common membership of the human community.

But to implement this in practice demands something stronger than good intentions or even good laws. However carefully the official laws may seek to protect the poor, unofficial custom always favours the rich. The justice of God is expressed in active intervention on behalf of the poor and undeserving. This was demonstrated in action by Jesus, and this habitual attitude of his towards the outcast is both the best-attested aspect of his personal character and the clearest long-term cause of his crucifixion. The Resurrection is the sign that this freedom to be in relationship was not an ineffective ideal but the truest thing about both him and us. So it is no accident that the Christian Sabbath is the first day of the week, the commemoration of the Resurrection; it has become Sunday not because of anyone's laws but because the Christian community has from the first insisted on sharing the cup of brotherhood and the bread of communion on that day, be it holiday or working day. Christians have not always lived under governments which have organized a holiday every Sunday, nor do they everywhere now; but they have always broken bread.

HEAVEN AND EARTH

The heaven and the earth were made. The phrase 'heaven and earth' is, doubtless, a way of saying 'everything'. But it is a very particular way of saying 'everything', for there are things which it is true to say about 'earth' which it is not true to say about 'heaven', just within the context of this story. 'Earth' is that sector of being over which man has, or should have, dominion; it is that sector which he properly knows, of which he can intelligently speak, of which he can feel he is master, the laws of which are open to his discovery, observation and rationalizing; it is the sector within which he can, in principle, make predictions, about things, about persons, about himself. 'Earth' is *here*.

'Heaven' is, truly, the 'other world'. 'The heavens, they are the Lord's; the earth he has given to all mankind.'[94] Here is the distinction. 'Heaven' stands for that sector over which man does *not* have dominion, mechanically, politically, or even intellectually. It is that sector which is essentially unknown, although odd facts here and there may be revealed about it; it is that sector about which man may possibly have some information but no real experience.

Although the inevitable assumption is that 'earth', in fact, refers to this planet, there is no restrictive definition to this effect. Man is entitled to push back the boundaries of 'heaven' in a physical sense, to attempt to extend his life-space. The only reason why there is nothing about space-travel in the Bible is that man had existence only on this planet. But no particular problem is raised for our faith by the fact that this is no longer so, in principle. There are limits placed on man, according to Scripture; but they are limits in terms of ethical responsibility, not in terms of what man may attempt to know.

'Heaven', in spite of any space-travel which man may undertake, will remain as that sector of being of which a man must say: 'I know that this area is governed by laws, made by the maker of heaven and earth; but I feel that however long I could live, however learned I could become, I could never master these laws, for they have mastery over me.' Heaven is that sector within which things are in principle unpredictable, about other persons and about oneself; it is a sector which keeps at a distance from us, yet also approaches us. It is the sector which has come near, and yet it is still the sector *from* which there can be a coming towards us. And so, in the writing which is reckoned to represent his most mature and sophisticated eschatology, St Paul can speak of the future coming of the Saviour *from* heaven, a heaven which exercises its political influence on its citizens who are on earth.[95] The Saviour is the one who characterizes heaven, for he is above all the one who comes to us as a surprise, as the unexpected one, as the unseen one in the midst. The remoteness and the immediacy of heaven are supremely expressed in the remoteness and the immediacy of Christ, which in turn are represented to me by the remoteness and the immediacy of the man next to me.

But there is a further stage beyond this, beyond the beyond. The ultimate distinction is not between heaven and earth but between heaven-and-earth together, on the one hand, and God who made both, on the other hand. Heaven may be a different order of creation from earth, but it is no less under God's authority and limited by him. He is as much beyond heaven as he is beyond earth; and for him the renewing of heaven is as possible and necessary as the renewing of the earth.[96] God is beyond that sector over which we feel we can have knowledge and mastery; he is also beyond that sector over which we feel that we cannot obtain knowledge and mastery. Both are subject to his laws; both may be in revolt; both will need ultimate renewal; both of them present threats to our security; and over the threats from both sectors, Christ has won the mastery, so that nothing in heaven or earth can now separate us from the love of God.[97]

It may be right to speak of heaven as God's dwelling-place.[98] But heaven is not, as it were, God's starting-point; his being antecedes that of heaven; he needs no locality from which to operate. The possibility of such unlocalizedness is what Christians mean when they say that they believe in 'God'. If we say that the Saviour comes to earth *from* heaven, we are still bound to remember that the heaven and the heaven of heavens cannot contain God.[99] God in Christ chooses to move towards us, towards this known world, via the unknown world of 'heaven'; he chooses to move towards my known self via my unknown self; he chooses to make himself known in my neighbour via those aspects of my neighbour which I cannot itemize and measure. All this is part of what we mean when we say that 'he came down to earth from heaven'. But, as it was in the beginning, so now, and world without end, there was and is and shall be that which is beyond the limits of both these sectors in me, in my neighbour, and in the whole range of things; and this is what we assert when we assert 'God'.

At the end of this first account of creation, therefore, we are reminded in the strongest way of the central concern which enables us to look at the rest of the matter with honesty and trust. Man's situation and vantage-point are not of his own devising; they do not depend on his unreliably motivated will or his erratic resources of control. Since the times of the Bible, man has acquired far more evidence of his own smallness in comparison with the immensities of space; he feels more sorely than before that the claim to be master of the universe is just ridiculous, that his glory is only that of Mr Toad. And, in exactly the same degree, and because of the same developments in technology, man has appropriated his 'dominion' as never before; his status as 'little less than God' has become more and more of a visible reality. We become scared of this contradiction; we suspect that the cocksure confidence of technology is only a mask for an anxiety; we fear that our smallness may turn out to be the only truth about us, that the technology we have created may only turn again and rend us. Against all this, the witness of the Bible is that all the initiatives are in the personal hands of the one who alone is reliable, from whom the whole scheme takes its origin and shape. The words of Psalm 8 are the best commentary on our modern anxiety; they reaffirm what Genesis 1 has already stated: that man's situation of insignificance and glory is not self-generated; its origin and its guarantees depend on one who is beyond man, independent of man's motivations and artefacts. Man has not wrested his dominion from a basically hostile universe; he will not have it wrested from him by the revenge of nature. The one who has given man this dominion is also the one who has set the whole universe in order – there is one who is the source and stimulus of both. Man's insignificance is not something about which he can be effectively anxious; his glory is not something in which he can take a pride of achievement. '*Thou* hast made him little less than a god, crowning him with glory and honour. *Thou* makest him master over all thy creatures; *thou* hast put everything under his feet.'[100]

The worship of God means the honouring and accepting of the truth that our situation in the universe has its origin in that which is beyond us, that we can neither create nor destroy it by our own skill or stupidity. This is the theme running through this first chapter; it is reinforced by the setting-aside of the seventh day which in one sense is always present because it has no boundaries, no evening and no morning. And the eighth psalm finally clarifies the matter by actually expressing it in the language of worship; man has been given this status and character, this ability and dominion, *therefore* 'O Lord our sovereign, how glorious is *thy* name in all the earth!'

First Interval

In the last few years there seems to have been an irresistible urge among English people to write and read about the First World War. The fact that dozens of accounts have already been written does not stop the flow. The Hebrews also did not believe in having only one viewpoint and expression of their story. They also did not believe that a later account could simply replace an earlier one. They were happy to have two or more accounts side by side with their different emphases, maybe contradicting each other at times. They felt, very wisely, that it is better to have confusion than to risk throwing out part of the truth.

The truth of God is for all, but some will find it in one emphasis, some in another. The enthusiasm of a whole nation can change in a very few generations. The present power-bearing group in South Africa is so concerned for order that it can approve of such a threat to justice as the Terrorism Act, and many other forms of punishment without trial; the claim can be made that South Africa is the most orderly state in Africa, but at the expense of freedom. Yet, only a few decades ago, the forefathers of this group were passionately concerned about freedom.

As people look at their situation in God's world, some will be more impressed with the orderliness of creation, others with its freedom. For some, experience of the world leads to a sense of harmony, consistency and beauty (we see examples in Raphael, Handel, Bridges); others find a greater value in exploring the conflicts, disharmonies and unpredictableness of their environment (such were Breughel, Schönberg, and Donne). It is always dangerous to try to fit people or traditions into categories like this, but it is clear from the uneasy co-existence of the priestly and prophetic traditions, and from the variety of devotions in the Psalter, that the Hebrews had two such modes of experience of God; consequently, they felt nothing improper in reading back such a duality of God's self-disclosure into their accounts of the beginning of things.

At the time when the book of Genesis was being put into its present shape, several versions or documents were in currency, covering the same main area of concern. Thus there were two current versions of the story of the beginning of things. In the final arrangement the later version, from the Priestly tradition, was placed first; this is the version which we have been considering so far. But evidently the editors felt that the later version did not replace the earlier, primitive tradition, so they simply put the earlier version alongside the later, with all their differences unconcealed. We will reflect on the implications of this later. But perhaps the most obvious and inclusive of all the differences is in their whole idea of story-telling. This reflects a basic difference in understanding of what knowledge is and how it is to be handled; it is impossible to say that one is right and one is wrong; there just are two radically different types of knowing and of knowledge. Although very few people are exclusively identified with only one type, most of us have a tendency to be inclined more to one than to the other; and from this, many of our disagreements take their origin. Perhaps the best way of making the distinction is to speak of cumulative and non-cumulative knowledge. The man who prefers the manner of cumulative knowledge tries to build up a structure, a history, an orderly account of things; one thing will be added to another until a complete picture is available; a foundation of facts is laid, and further facts are assembled on to this foundation. The man who prefers the manner of non-cumulative knowledge is less bothered about orderliness, because he is less bothered about causation and sequence; he is interested in registering reactions to things as they strike him, on the understanding that it is in this manner that significant learning is made and significant decisions take place.

Now that we have had a few centuries of intensive scientific study, we are bound to feel that the most obvious example of cumulative knowledge is in science, where the research of yesterday gives us facts for today on which are based the hypotheses for tomorrow; conversely, we look at such studies

as ethics, aesthetics, or even politics, and we feel that today's
work is not significantly *adding* knowledge to yesterday's, it is
exploring the same ground in new terms. Whatever was
valid in Aristotle's *Physics* has been taken into the accumu-
lated knowledge of physics and therefore need not be studied
on its own; the modern student can safely ignore it. But a
student of literature, however modern, cannot possibly ignore
Aristotle's *Poetics*, and it seems reasonable to say that this
state of affairs is likely to continue indefinitely. This is only
an example; it would be wrong to insist on a firm distinction
between science and the arts at this point, or to classify the
Priestly version of creation as 'science' and the primitive
version as 'literature'. The real distinction seems to have
been in existence long before there was a discipline of
natural science as we now know it, and it is a distinction
which we can observe almost any time we hear ourselves or
anyone else describe something. Recently, I observed a
series of people who were each required to describe a record-
ing of a conversation which had been played to them; about
half the members told a story – 'A said, B said, A said, B
said, etc.' The others presented something more like an
account of two blocks of emotion in contact with each other –
'There was this guy A and he was this kind of guy and felt
this kind of way and seemed to be in this kind of jam, and
there was this girl B and she seemed to be that kind of
character and felt that kind of way and was facing that kind
of problem, etc.' These are two kinds of ways of being a
person; and they are reflected right here at the beginning
of the Bible.

The account of creation in Genesis 1 is orderly, controlled,
complete; there is no sense of tentativeness or experiment.
But we know that, in fact, it was the later of the two accounts
to be written. It was a people who had been through the
disorders of the Exile who framed this great recital of the
orderliness of the cosmos. It was a people that had experienced the social fragmentation of mass removals who so
majestically expressed the supreme authority of a reliable
creator. And their doctrine was not that once upon a time
all was well; rather, they were saying: 'This is what is really
true about us now. In spite of all the appearances, all is well

now, and he who makes us saves us. This is a law-abiding universe.'

The so-called 'primitive' account of creation, from chapter 2, verse 5, onwards, came from an earlier period of history. Here God is not so much the sovereign Lord of the universe as the experimenter, the bringer of novelty: he is free to criticize his work; he is concerned not so much about law as about relationships. His word is not the divine fiat of 'Let there be light', but the word of perceptive concern, 'It is not good for man to be alone'. Professor Ian Barbour has shown how most theologians in the field of creation have chosen to favour one or other of these ways of thinking about God.[1] This general feature of the juxtaposition of alternative attitudes is represented right at the beginning of the Bible; the editors of Genesis allowed each attitude to have its place.

In Christ the tradition of a law-abiding universe and the tradition of a freedom-loving universe both find their doom and their fulfilment. On the cross it would seem that all law and order had come to an end; the one who came to fulfil the law, the one who did fulfil the supreme law of love without reservation, was done to death by the combined efforts of the best religious law and the best secular law in the world. On the cross it would also seem that all freedom had come to an end; under the pressures of an insuperable inner tyranny, a compulsive refusal of freedom, Church and State and common people combined to do away with the truth who had come to set them free. And yet the gospel of the Resurrection proclaims that through this very mechanism both law and freedom were finally vindicated. The various Christian doctrines of the Atonement combine to assert that in the redemptive work of Christ both lawlessness and tyranny met their match. The opening two chapters of Genesis show that it is possible to hold order and freedom together, but the cross shows the cost of doing so. If the Church is fulfilling her calling to be the Body of Christ, the image of Christ, she will be found in the places where this costliness is required; she will discover and assert freedom as the divine therapy for men who are so hypnotized by the love of order that they abrogate law; she will discover and assert law in situations where law is so

misused that it ceases to be the protector of the individual's
freedom. It should be impossible for the Church to live in
such conditions without in some way being crucified. God
did not wait for exceptionally favourable conditions to
vindicate these twin principles of order and freedom. The
Son of God was indeed sent forth in the fullness of time, but
this can mean that he was sent at a time when circumstances
could most effectively conspire to crucify him; if order and
freedom triumph in the gospel history of Jesus, they can
triumph anywhere.

There is a similar kind of duality in the way in which we
talk about God. We have already noted the fact that all our
language about God is inevitably symbolic; and in any use
of symbols, there is always a greater or less degree of connexion and continuity between the image and the reality
which the image is supposed to represent. If we use a very
'sacred' imagery or style in our talk about God, we run the
risk of thinking that this imagery directly represents actual
reality, and that it cannot possibly be doubted or even dis-
cussed. We confuse the image with the reality and worship
it; and this is, in a word, idolatry. So it is possible to idolize
the sacred book, the sacred tradition, the sacred structure,
the sacred ministry, or anything else; it is possible to idolize
a very majestic idea of God, and this is a tendency into
which we might be led by the idea of God which we are
given in the first chapter of Genesis. But there is an opposite
risk, the risk of so emphasizing the lack of connexion, the
discontinuity, between the image and the reality, that
nothing seems to be true or reliable at all; we are left with
nothing better than subjective opinions, and we abandon
the real truth to which the image, however distantly, refers;
and this is, in a word, apostasy. It is a kind of apostasy to
say that the stories in the second and third chapters of
Genesis are '*only* myths', in the shallowest sense of the word.
This is the tendency into which we might be led by the idea
of God which we are given in these two chapters.[2]

In the very first two chapters, therefore, the Scriptures
give us specimens of man's two basic tendencies which appear
when he tries to respond to and to communicate the revelation of God. These two tendencies must always be in the

Church if it is to be true to its calling. There must always be the tension between the conservative and the radical. The conservative will tend to think of the radical as an apostate; the radical will tend to think of the conservative as an idolater. But both are saying, deep down, something vital about the human need to which the gospel of Jesus is a response. So this tension is part of the conditions of existence in which we have to fulfil our discipleship. If one or the other is suppressed, it is not a triumph for truth but a defeat for love, for the Church's failures ultimately are always failures of love. If one emphasis is missing, we misrepresent the range of God's word, we fail in catholicity. The genius of the Church is to keep both in relationship, as do the pages of Genesis. The way of God is not to abolish conflict, which can be done only by killing off one of the parties, but to convert conflict into tension. This is represented in the highest levels of Christian preaching by the doctrine of the Trinity and the doctrine of the two natures in Christ. This is the essence of a covenant; it is the basic discovery of genuine ecumenism. Any church or Christian that refuses to accept this principle has to nourish itself on its own pride in isolation, accepting only the veriest crumbs of the word of God and of the means of grace and of the catholic fellowship.

So, right at the outset of the Scriptures, we find a virtue which is not often attributed to the Jewish or Christian traditions, tolerance. It allows for the validity of two very different accounts of one thing. Erich Fromm reminds us of the story of three men who were asked to describe an elephant in the dark. 'One, touching his trunk, said, "this animal is like a water pipe"; another, touching his ear, said, "this animal is like a fan"; a third, touching his legs, described the animal as a pillar.' Fromm contrasts this attitude to the main stream of Western thought, based on its Jewish and Christian backgrounds, in which the supreme value is placed on correct thinking; this, with its strong underlying attitudes derived from Aristotle, has led to arguments about dogma and to scientific research.[3] The fact is, however, that flexibility of imagination and the ability to hold disparate ideas in tension are essential to scientific progress. In the comparatively 'exact' disciplines, like physics, there are points where it is unscientific to deny that two or more complementary approaches may be necessary to account for one set of phenomena. As man attempts to bring phenomena under his intellectual 'dominion', by means of the language and concepts which he has developed for the purpose, it is found that some aspects of the behaviour of light, for instance, can best be described in terms of a corpuscular theory, while for other aspects a wave theory is more adequate. For the word 'theory' in this remark we could substitute more obviously subjective and fuzzy words, like 'model', 'image', 'interpretation', or even 'myth'. If this last word is at all acceptable, it may stress the validity of alternatives, for it is unlikely that *only one* myth could be true. It is when we start using the word 'only' too freely that we reveal ourselves as being victims of some kind of tyranny which limits our potential as severely as a totalitarian education. Right at the outset, the Bible insists on the validity of experimenting with alternative, or complementary, explanations; the fact of these two versions of creation is God's caution to our tendency to sprinkle our good statements with unnecessary 'onlies', which allow our statements to be true only by the invalidation of other statements. 'Of all forms of mental activity, the most difficult to induce even in the minds of the young, who may be presumed not to have lost their flexibility, is the art of handling the same bundle of data as before, but placing them in a new system of relations with one another by giving them a different framework.'[4] This is precisely what the reader of the Bible finds in its first few pages. This ability to 'put on a different kind of thinking-cap', to break away from the confines of one set of terms, to experiment imaginatively beyond the boundaries of accepted definition, this has enabled much scientific advance, from Galileo's imagining of the behaviour of perfectly spherical balls on perfectly smooth surfaces to Kekulé's dream of carbon atoms holding hands in a dance, which made possible a true understanding of molecular structure.

In spite of the rigidities through which Christians have so often expressed their uncharity, our tradition is designed to breed this tolerance, and it appears with enthusiasm and authority in a writer who is not normally thought of as a specimen of tolerance, namely St Augustine. 'O my God', he writes, 'how can it harm me that it should be possible to interpret these words in several ways, all of which may yet be true? How can it harm me if I understand the writer's meaning in a different sense from that in which another understands it? . . . For this reason, although I hear people say "Moses meant that", I think that it is more truly religious to say "Why should he not have had both meanings in mind, if both are true?" . . . For my part, I declare resolutely and with all my heart that if I were called upon to write a book which was to be invested with the highest authority, I should prefer to write it in such a way that a reader could find re-echoed in my words whatever truths he was able to apprehend. I would rather write in this way than impose a single true meaning so explicitly that it would exclude all others, even though they contained no falsehood that could give me offence. And if this is what I should choose for myself, I will not be so rash, my God, as to suppose that so great a man as Moses deserved a lesser gift from you.'[5] St Augustine elaborates this attitude in great detail; would that all the theological contestants who have claimed him as their authority had meditated on this section of his writings first!

But, as well as tolerance, the mind of the Genesis writers teaches a necessary exclusiveness. There are many other possible interpretations of our situation, but they have been rejected, as the scientist will exclude the idea which in experiment turns out to be unsound. Different as they are from each other, these two accounts of Genesis both assume that God is good, that phenomena are real, that history has a purpose. And such dogmas have to be asserted if people are to be individually valued and if scientific study is to proceed. Archbishop Temple's claim is surely undeniable: 'It may be too much to argue, as some students of the subject have done, that science is a fruit of Christianity, but it may be safely asserted that it can never spontaneously grow up in regions where the ruling principle of the Universe is believed to be either capricious or hostile.'[6] And Teilhard de Chardin notes the strange ineffectiveness of the great wealth and refinement of Indian metaphysics, but asks: 'How indeed could it have been otherwise? Phenomena regarded as an illusion (Maya) and their connexions as a chain (Karma), what was left in these doctrines to animate and direct human evolution? A simple mistake was made – but it was enough – in the definition of the spirit and in the appreciation of the bonds which attach it to the sublimations of matter.'[7]

The editor of Genesis had the wisdom to let the two accounts stand side by side; he did not attempt to harmonize or to conflate them. The dangers of such conflation are perhaps exhibited at their extreme by the following extract from a letter published in a Johannesburg newspaper in 1963:

'White people are all the descendents of Adam and Eve; but when Adam and Eve were created, the world was already populated with people who had been created in the sixth period of the evolution of the universes. The duration of each of these periods, or days as they are called in the first chapter of Genesis, was about 300-million years. It therefore took 300-million years for animal and man in their present form to be created through the slow process of evolution. Man was apparently perfected in his present form about 30-million years ago, but none of these evolved people was White. Typical examples are Africans, Bushmen, Aborigines, Maories, Eskimoes, Chinese and Japanese. The reason God made Adam and Eve was that the people created through evolution had not sufficient intelligence even to "till the soil", let alone invent steam engines, electricity, radio, and atomic power. God needed a much more enlightened and intelligent race of people to do these things and to uplift, educate and civilize the evolved people.'[8]

Not only are there two quite distinct accounts of creation, written in different circumstances and ages, drawn together by one editor who preferred inclusiveness to tidiness; the two accounts themselves, especially the earlier one, each represent a combining of traditions. In Genesis 2 and 3, there are several signs of strain as two or more strands are intertwined, and, for this reason, if for no other, we must beware of thinking that one interpretation will give a complete account of the whole. This is part of the reason for the amazing range of interest in these stories and the scope of human concern which they cover. Right at the beginning of the Bible, it becomes clear that divine inspiration is certainly at work in the office of the editor as much as in the study of the original author.

The most obvious difference between the two accounts of creation is simply in their presentations of the sequence in which things are known. According to the Priestly tradition, man comes as the end and climax of the whole series; according to the more primitive tradition of Genesis 2, man is first-made. There is little purpose in discussing the question 'Which thing actually existed first – man or amoeba?' The real *Genesis* question, the *beginning* issue, is 'Where do we start?' It is interesting to note that two most helpful writers in this field give different answers, which correspond in effect to the two different accounts of creation in Genesis: Professor Coulson says that we should proceed from a study of the things of nature to a study of man and of Christian revelation; this is, in effect, the order of Genesis chapter 1.[9] Professor Birch says that the most directly accessible clue to the nature of the universe is man himself, and that this must be our point of departure; this is the order of Genesis chapter 2.[10] Clearly, this is a case of both-and rather than either-or. The order of Genesis 1 is the order of logical thought; that of Genesis 2 is of intuition; it allows for the fact that I myself am the centre of perception in my world, and that without me there would be no perception for me to be conscious of. This order has at least the advantage that it is impossible to mistake it for a 'scientific' account. Most of the 'Science versus Religion' battles on the question of creation have centred around the first, not the second, chapter. It is more clear from the second chapter than from the first that the main interest is not in what *was* but in what *is*, not in the origin of things at the hand of God but in the dependence of things upon him. The essential question to be asked here is not, 'Is this an accurate account of the way things began?', but 'Does this correspond with the way that I experience myself and my surroundings?' The title

Genesis can be taken as meaning not so much 'the beginning of the universe' but 'the beginning question – the basic issue – the starting-point of our inquiry about ourselves'. And for our writers, the starting-off point is not speculation about origins but the sense of being involved in the operations of a power now, a power that is shaping and renewing, a power which is supremely able to bring us into encounter with each other and to face us with issues of guilt and hope. And if this power does this to us, then by implication it is operating in the rest of the world in the same character, and we can see the rest of the world in the light of what we feel about ourselves.

This is the kind of question which is central to man's problems about himself; and the proper intellectual study of human origins is shackled and overburdened if it has to carry responsibility for questions which are not truly appropriate to it. It can find itself under obligation to 'discover' an origin of human life when in fact it may turn out to be strictly impossible for such a discovery ever to be made. It can find itself burdened with a question about the origin of the universe cast in temporal terms, whereas it may be impossible to talk significantly about a point in time at all, in a large universe. These are dangers to the man who has to try to answer the questions. The danger to the man who asks them may be still greater; if he trusts in a knowledge of human origins to solve his problems, he will almost certainly be adopting the strategy of Linus in the 'Peanuts' strip, who says, 'No problem is so big or so complicated that it can't be run away from'.[11] To 'solve' human questions simply in terms of causation is just a sophisticated way of passing the buck, a game in which, as we shall see, Adam is pretty skilled. On these lines, it is possible to demonstrate that the Great War of 1914 was caused by Charlemagne's coronation as first 'Holy Roman Emperor' on Christmas Day, 800. Teilhard de Chardin sums up the matter thus: 'Fascinating as the problem of our origin is, its solution even in detail would not solve the problem of man. . . . It is not in their germinal state that beings manifest themselves but in their florescence. . . . To grasp the truly cosmic scale of the phenomenon of man, we had to follow its roots through life.

. . . But if we want to understand the specific nature of man and divine his secret, we have no other method than to observe what reflection has already provided and what it announces *ahead*.'[12] The study of origins is inevitably a highly specialized undertaking, the results of which the non-palaeontologist just has to take on trust; but in the central questions about man, every person, every human being capable of reflection, is a scientist and can contribute to the continuing research, because the essential question is about himself.

CHAPTER FIVE

The Experimenters

GENESIS 2: 5–7

When the Lord God made earth and heaven, there was neither shrub nor plant growing wild upon the earth, because the Lord God had sent no rain on the earth; nor was there any man to till the ground. A flood^a used to rise out of the earth and water all the surface of the ground. Then the Lord God formed a man^b from the dust of the ground^c and breathed into his nostrils the breath of life. Thus the man became a living creature.

a) Or *mist.*   b) Heb. *adam.*   c) Heb. *adamah.*

THE LORD GOD

WITH our new author, the first thing that we see is that God himself has a new name. This is much more like a 'proper name', a domestic name. God is identified in the same sort of way as man is identified, by this specific name which is peculiarly his. This apparently naïve attitude to God is in a way more Christian than the loftiness of the first chapter; for God, as Christians know him, has been identified in a person, a person with a specific name. But the names 'the LORD God' and 'Jesus Christ' are more than mere names; in both cases, what appears to be a name is really a statement. When we say 'Jesus Christ' (even in swearing) we are stating that history has a meaning and a purpose, and that the fulfilment of it has appeared in Jesus of Nazareth. If we do not mean this, let us stop using this wording. In the same way, the phrase 'the LORD God' means that the being who revealed his name 'the LORD' at the Burning Bush[1] is the one true object of worship and is the source of life. This is the confession made by the crowd on Mount Carmel.[2] This crowd is not criminal in its state of ignorance;[3] it is not blamed for its silence; it is not expected to have an automatic knowledge of the identity of God. It is simply waiting for a disclosure; and such disclosure comes by the gracious act of God. In almost exactly the same terms, the Christian disciple responds to the supreme disclosure situation – 'My Lord and my God'.[4] This is typical of the biblical method; the words about God are shaped by experience, not by speculation. So, in spite of the remark quoted earlier from the Preface to the Revised Standard Version, the Jehovah's Witnesses are not completely wrong in speaking of 'Jehovah-God'. It is very correct – although rather pedantic and difficult for public reading – of the Jerusalem Bible to use the name 'Yahweh' right through the Old Testament. We do not start with a generalized abstraction called 'God'; we start with an experience of someone – Yahweh or Jesus – who can be described in the end as nothing less than God.

So, if the title used in this part of Genesis, 'the LORD God', or 'Yahweh God', is similar in form to the title 'Jesus Christ', we need not be surprised if the picture given of him is anthropomorphic. Indeed, it is childish. Who except a child models men out of the dust of a garden path? This is an experience of creation which is denied to people who are old enough to be fathers. We have already noticed that there may be a danger of overstressing the father image of God. Christian faith asserts that through the *Son* of God all things were made. Whatever else this may mean in terms of theological analysis, it must at least mean that in the heart of the creative activity there is the character of the child, the character of experiment, of easily flexible activity, of intuition and searching. If we set up a picture of creation which is too adult for the unsophisticated to share, we de-catholicize the biblical witness, we narrow its range. We distort the truth about God, the world, our families, and ourselves, if we picture God the Father as the central or characteristic figure of God, and the Son and the Spirit as ancillary or secondary figures. Tillich has stressed the importance of this for a truly healthy understanding of God and of ourselves. 'God again and again breaks through the images we have made of him; he has shown us in Christ that he is not only father and mother to us, but also child, and that therefore in him the inescapable conflicts of every family are overcome. The Father who is also child is more than a father as he is more than a child. Therefore we can pray to the Father in Heaven without transferring our hostility against the father image to him. Because God has become child, it is possible for us to say the Our Father.'[5]

THE DELAY

In this earlier version of the story of creation, man comes first, I come first. Verse 5 stresses the delaying of plant life until the coming of man. Man, as we shall see later, is brought in to assist in the creation of his environment. At this point, let us notice that the writer feels the need almost to apologize for the non-existence of the plants and herbs; they arrived late; and it is fair to guess that ninety per cent of the apologies given and received in our world are for lateness. But in some ways, the ability to delay, to be un-reliable, is a necessary aspect of God's nature. Jesus was prepared to be delayed where necessary, even when he was hurrying on an emergency call; with Jairus's daughter at death's door, and everyone around him chivvying him along, he was prepared to be interrupted by the woman with the haemorrhage – who, after all, was a chronic case of twelve years' development, fussily anxious to avoid publicity. In the eyes of Jesus her situation was just as critical as that of the dying child; twelve years of being drained to death was as urgent a matter as a twelve-year-old life being cut off; to reach real salvation through faith, the woman had to be relieved of the personal and religious anxieties which had caused her to touch Jesus without speaking to him, and this was just as much a now-or-never situation as that of the girl waiting to be touched, to be raised to new life. Jesus experi-enced the kind of dilemma which the pastoral and evangel-istic Church has always faced, yet without being harassed by it. The love of Jesus is reliable; his actions are, precisely for this reason, unpredictable.[6] Where all is predictable, there is room for neither faith nor love. Faith is not faith unless it includes an ability to live without a visible future; and love is not love unless it is prepared to live by surprise, the surprising you meeting the surprising me. We have not learned to live with God until we have learned to live with his delays. For Hans Castorp, the hero of Thomas Mann's *The Magic Mountain*, the longest and hardest lesson to be learned in the timelessness of his T.B. sanatorium was 'getting used to not getting used'. He who is committed to God has the freedom to be, in a right and good sense, unreliable. There is a political implication here, which Helmut Gollwitzer perceives out of his profound observation of the effects of ideological commitment: 'Because the Christian does not swear blind allegiance to his party, because his party is not his religion, because he adheres to his party conditionally and does not regard it as always and in every way right, because he therefore can never be a fanatic, he will always be regarded by his own side as "unreliable", he will give offence to them and be uncomfortable. H. J. Iwand's statement: "The Confessing Church is always in opposition", contains an essential law for the political action of the Christian.'[7]

In the creative relationship between God and man there is a gap. This is the heart of Michelangelo's picture of the creation of man, the gap between the finger of God and the finger of man. God loves man, and so allows man space to move in, he allows man to surprise him, he creates without touching. In James Thurber's *The Thirteen Clocks* there is a most interesting scene, where the Princess, set the task of restarting thirteen clocks that have been magically stopped, tries first of all to get them going by touching them with her hand, the only warm thing in the castle; when this fails, her adviser suggests: 'If you can touch the clocks and never start them, then you can start the clocks and never touch them.' And so she goes round all the clocks again, not touching them, holding her hand a certain distance away from each clock; and the clocks start; time begins again; a vulture called Then flies away; and suddenly it is Now.[8] At the heart of the motor engine, there are the gaps of plugs and points. At the heart of the art of music, there is the system of intervals. At the heart of a marriage, there is the acceptance of a person as a person and not as a predictable functionary. At the heart of the gospel is the 'leap' of faith. This is expressed in Michel Quoist's prayer:

I recognized you without seeing you.
I felt you without touching you.
I understood you without hearing you.[9]

Because God so gently and firmly gives man this autonomy, he is able to forestall without brutality man's tendency to idolatry; he is able to insist that he, God, also be allowed the freedom to love and to be loved, and not to be locked up in a scheme or system. So the Son of God was able to live with a gap between God and God, asserting the distinction between himself and the Father.[10] By this he earned the right to refuse to be touched and held even by his most loving associates.[11] He must be allowed to ascend, which means that he must be allowed the freedom to 'drop in on' people whoever and wherever they are. When we have finished with the disadvantages of a 'God up there', we may discover again the value of the simple image of a God who is able to 'descend' on places and meet people. As at the Burning Bush, we are met by a God who is unlocalized, unpredictable, unconjurable, a God who is not tied to natural objects, be they mountains or trees or church buildings or wafers, or even special identifiable personages; this God meets us by his own choice; he is free to be known to us in the persons of the brothers of Christ.

MAN AND GROUND

The story starts with God making man out of the ground. There is a direct relationship here between man and the ground – in fact, in the Hebrew the word translated 'ground' is in form the feminine of 'man'. The basic elements of which man is made are not different from the basic elements of the earth itself. Man has continuity, not merely with the living animals, but with the inanimate earth itself. Man's existence starts as a clay doll, of the substance of the earth. The significance of this was seen and felt long before Freud and Darwin came on the scene; it is there in the graveyard scene in *Hamlet*; it is there in the song 'On Ilkley Moor' – 'Then we shall have to bury thee; then worms'll come and eat thee up; then ducks'll come and eat up worms; then we shall come and shoot up ducks; then we shall come and eat up ducks; then we shall have eaten thee.' In short, where did you get your atoms from? Ground and man are inseparable, and the material of which we are made is continually coming from the ground and going into the ground. And very many people instinctively feel that there is a continuing connexion between ourselves and the discarded bits of our bodies; Picasso, for instance, is said to share the belief that is widespread in Africa, that hair-clippings and so on maintain an identity with their late owners and give power to anyone who may get hold of them.[12]

The ground needs water, so as to nourish living things; but man not only needs water; to a considerable extent he *is* water. The face of the ground has to be saturated before God can make man out of the dust of the earth. Man here becomes the prototype of living things, some of which, like cabbages, may be over ninety per cent water even though they be solids. We see the killing effects of dehydration with every summer's crop of gastro-enteritis, when thousands of babies die simply because their bodies have lost an excessive proportion of this water. Man typifies the whole of the world of living things, in this power and need to turn water into life. And so Christ, the typical or normative man, appears as himself the living water, water which one does not only have to receive but which one has to be, and to have available for others.[13]

Man is first-made. In contrast to the animals that we hear of later, man receives the breath or spirit of life. Man is a unity, and it is only a sign of our deviation from the truth about man that a word like 'psychosomatic' has to be devised and seems to be so recondite. There is a without and a within of man, but these are not *things* which he *has*, according to this account. Man does not *have* a body from which he can distinguish himself; he does not *have* a soul from which he can distinguish him*self*; further, the soul does not take the body as a dwelling.

In fact, the whole distinction of 'body' and 'soul' is an impossible one for the author to make, as there is no word in Hebrew corresponding to our word 'body'. Man is seen as a being with life and the power of thought. He is not man if he is only body; nor is he man if he retires into a purely psychic realm. God makes the form of man and breathes life into it. Even if we do use the word 'soul', as in the King James Version, the statement is 'man *became* a living soul', not 'man was given a living soul'. The New English Bible more accurately reads: 'Man became a living creature.'

'It is only a century and a half since a group of doctors attempted the experiment of weighing a dying man, and then of repeating the weighing immediately after his death. They sought thereby to discover how heavy his "soul" weighed that had just departed his body. The Hebrews, on the other hand, would never have made such a mistake. They thought of the personality of man as an indivisible whole.'[14] And, if this group of doctors seems to be somewhat remote from our own day, there is an item in the evening paper of the day on which I am writing this, concerning a gold-prospector whose will has just been read, in which he left 200,000 dollars for soul-research, with the suggestion that a photograph might be taken of a soul leaving a body at death.

The distinction made by the Hebrews is not between 'body' and 'soul', as if 'soul' were another component, with a distinct static identity; the distinction is between a living body and a non-living one; and, in this particular case, as no other type of livingness has yet been introduced with which to compare this example, we must acknowledge the character of all livingness as something due to the breath of God; this is not a peculiarly 'spiritual' factor. Life is a motion, a breathing, from God, which animates what is alive and makes it different to what is not alive.

Creation is not over once and for all. The story here of the making of man is the story of how God is always making man, out of dust, out of the detritus of his predecessors. So, we have exactly the same procedure in the raising up of the house of Israel in Ezekiel;[15] God breathes into the dusty assemblage of bones, and they receive life and stand up.

This again is a parable about Christ, whose body was laid in the earth, who has made a living being out of the earth. Christ is still his body, and is identified with it. 'Just as the body is one . . . so it is with Christ.'[16] This suggests that it is not enough to say that Christ *has* a body. If Christ is still man, he must *be* a body in some way; he is still a body-spirit unit. A body without a spirit is a corpse, and a spirit without a body is a ghost, and neither is any use. The Resurrection accounts stress that Christ was neither of these inadequate things in his risen being.

The Ascension was not a farewell to the body but a stage in deeper involvement through a wider range of human kind, through a more extensive body, the Catholic Church, and through a more immediate relationship with inanimate and inarticulate creation, the eucharistic body. It is right, there-fore, to have a strong doctrine of the real presence in the eucharist; for the body is not just what Christ *has* – it is what Christ *is*. The only proviso is that we should not make such a fuss about the real presence in the eucharistic body that we miss the real presence in the baptismal body, i.e. in the fellowship of the Christian community. If it is right to genuflect to the one, it should be right to do so to the other.

DUST

Man is made of that which is infinitely small. The incredible degree of this smallness is graphically expressed by Professor Dobzhansky: 'The aggregate volume of all the genes in all the sex cells which produced the world's population today would probably not exceed that of a vitamin capsule. This tiny mass contains, then, all the biological heredity of the living representatives of our species, and the material basis of its future evolution.'[17]

Dust is both gathered and scattered. This is what happens to the material of which man is made. Its basic nature is impermanent, and so man has a planned obsolescence or preliminariness built into his original design. If he is to seek durability it will be found in a continuity which is not automatic but new and surprising. From the start, we see that man's hope is not to be in immortality but in resurrec-tion, not in the prolonging of the old but in the death of the old so that the new can be born. This picture of man being made out of the most insecure material symbolizes the fact that it is hopeless to expect to discover the remains of the first man. 'Beginnings have an irritating but essential fragility', says Teilhard de Chardin. 'When anything really new begins to germinate around us, we cannot distinguish it – for the very good reason that it could only be recognized in the light of what it is going to be. Yet if, when it has reached full growth, we look back to find its starting-point, we only find that the starting-point itself is now hidden from our view, destroyed or forgotten.'[18]

Dust is the most servile of substances; the clearing of dust is the most basic and menial task of service in a household. At the same time it is the substance which is most capable of glory when it is packed together, for what are the stones of a palace or cathedral but assemblages of dust? Architecture was reckoned by Schopenhauer to be the most limited, the least divine of arts; and yet it is in architectural imagery – the city – that the blessedness of man's final community is described in Scripture. Christ, who took a body of dust, is also the headstone of the corner of the eternal structure. He is the stone which the builders rejected, because he took the form of a servant. So 'creation and service belong together. God himself served the world when he created it. His creation is not the arbitrary act of a great Lord, but the humble service of Christ.'[19]

GENESIS 2: 8–9
Then the Lord God planted a garden in Eden away to the east, and there he put the man whom he had formed. The Lord God made trees spring from the ground, all trees pleasant to look at and good for food; and in the middle of the garden he set the tree of life and the tree of the knowledge of good and evil.

Immediately after the creation of man, we hear of the creation of vegetable life. Man comes first; but from this point on, the order of appearance of things is much the same as in the previous chapter. But in the previous chapter, things had their own validity; trees existed for their own sake; the emphasis was on the plants' concern for their own survival, and on the system of fruit and seed which provided for the continuance of the species. But here, everything is from the man's point of view. Strangely, the satisfying of the aesthetic sense comes first, and the food-producing function of the tree comes in second place. The eye is the most widely-ranging of the senses, and the sense which most quickly leads to decisions, for good or ill. Our more sophisticated critiques come from what we learn by way of our hearing, particularly from the influence of people. Here, man is alone in a world of *things*, and his eyes are enough. The tragedy of blindness is that it hides from us this world of things; but deafness is in many ways more tragic, in that it cuts us off from people.

We see things from our point of view; we value them according to their value for us rather than according to any intrinsic value. This is the difference between our two versions at this point. And when we credit natural objects with value according to our particular needs, then we come close to giving sacral or magical characteristics to them. It is because this present author is seeing things so much from man's point of view that he can think of such a thing as a 'tree of the knowledge of good and evil', which is an idea that would be difficult to fit into the world-view of the writer of the first chapter.

GENESIS 2: 10–15

There was a river flowing from Eden to water the garden, and when it left the garden it branched into four streams. The name of the first is Pishon; that is the river which encircles all the land of Havilah, where the gold^d is. The gold^d of that land is good; bdellium^e and cornelians are also to be found there. The name of the second river is Gihon; this is the one which encircles all the land of Cush. The name of the third is Tigris; this is the river which runs east of Asshur. The fourth river is the Euphrates.

The Lord God took the man and put him in the garden of Eden to till it and care for it.

d) Or *frankincense.*   e) Or *gum resin.*

WATER

According to this story, the earth was in the first place a barren wasteland, and became able to produce living things only after a special moistening. Here is a very interesting difference of outlook between the second chapter and the first. The writer of this earlier account of creation feels that the Creator's primary blessing is to save us from the desert; everything was terribly dry land before God acted; water is a wonderful gift, therefore; and this must appeal to us in Southern Africa, where the word 'Rain!' is a great word of blessing. On the other hand, the writer of Genesis 1 feels that the Creator's primary work is to save us from the sea; everything was terribly wet water before God acted. And so, water is an enemy, a symbol and a threat of chaos; order and life are made possible by the driving back and the restricting of water, and of its partner, darkness. In the final new creation, the power and creativity of God are linked to both these accounts; in the last two chapters of Revelation, the sea and the night are finally abolished. But the blessing of water is retained; there is a river. There is no sea for it to flow into; but, unlike the Okavango, it does not waste itself in a swamp; its function is like that of the river of Eden, to irrigate, and to nourish the healing life of the trees.[20]

Only in a highly industrialized setting is rain more of a nuisance than a blessing, where people have to make long journeys from their place of work to their place of sleeping, and so require mobile roofs to protect them from the elements. And this is exaggerated where the bulk of the workers do not belong to the power-bearing group and cannot prevent themselves being pushed even farther away from their places of work for political reasons. Urban conditions are supposed to bring people closer together, but the sheer length of time spent in transport in a city like Johannesburg deprives thousands of Africans of any real chance of having much social life or church life or of furthering their studies. And when a bus boycott is one of the few legal forms of protest, rain can be converted to a real curse, especially when, as in January 1957, there is a thunder-storm practically every afternoon at knocking-off time.

The idea of the Garden of Eden would make the grandest appeal to people set in the conditions suggested in verse 5. Here, out of the aridity of the outside landscape, man is set in a park (rather than 'garden'), a place where things grow without a lot of hacking and scraping. It is surrounded by these rivers, naturally bounded. Man is in a place of his own, where he can be free and at large. He can be wholly and happily occupied there; life is not going to be one long rest, neither is it going to be one long grind.

Civilization in the proper sense of the word started in river valleys, for civilization requires that men co-operate in common enterprises, and this in turn requires the possibility of some men being able to produce more food than they themselves need. Until the food-producing revolution took place, manufacturing, trade and community were impossible, for each man was fully occupied with getting such food as he could out of the earth. Compared to this revolution, all subsequent revolutions have been almost insignificant; and it was in a few river valleys in the Middle East that man started his godly work of turning nature into culture. From there, civilization flowed out to all the world. A garden, or any other similar human enterprise, without a river would until recently have been unthinkable. So here we have a river, splitting and carrying its irrigating value to the four corners of the world. Here is stressed a unity in diversity which St Augustine could find incorporated into the name of Adam himself, in that the letters of Adam's name stand for the four points of the compass in Latin, representing the one human community of the children of Adam. If man and ground belong inseparably, man and water are linked almost as closely. Water is the first need where men settle, and still today great wealth can be got by those who claim to be water-diviners. It is said that ninety per cent of the murders in north-west India are due to disputes about water rights, and even that the whole intractable Kashmir dispute is intelligible in terms of anxieties about the control of the sources of the rivers which irrigate the lowlands of India and Pakistan. And the next factor which gives land its value is the presence of minerals; so it is not surprising that the land of Havilah comes first in the list of areas fed by the river from Eden. Johannesburg is only eighty-five years old, and yet it is the first and largest city to be built where there is neither river nor sea; and why? 'Because the gold of that land is good.' The Bible takes very early cognizance of the features which cause people to value certain areas of land more highly than others.

Water, and the movement of water, are seen as the greatest natural blessing, representing most basically the abundant goodness of the Creator. All the good that we perceive is merely the overflow of the goodness in the central heart of God's being. Professor von Rad exclaims: 'What an inexpressible amount of water was in Paradise, if the river, after having watered the garden, could still enclose the entire world with four arms and fructify it! All the water outside of Paradise, which supplies all civilizations, is, so to speak, only a remainder or residue from the waters of Paradise!'[21]

PARADISE

'Eden' was translated into Greek as 'Paradise', and the Jews of our Lord's time thought of it as the forecourt of the resurrection, the place of waiting for the renewing act of God. Jesus knew of this Paradise, and made it the place of his appointment with the penitent thief. Christ, the second Adam, makes this appointment with an insurrectionist, a saboteur, a man who bears in his person the strains and brokenness of the first Adam. The only person on the whole Golgotha scene who can recognize the kingship of Jesus is one who has spent and thrown away his life in opposition to kings and authorities and all that they stand for. He has forced himself to incur guilt and condemnation in expressing his hatred of the whole system imposed by the political power-bearers. And, to crown all, he finds himself even in execution stuck next to someone entitled 'the king of the Jews'. He starts to curse this king. But then he realizes that his curses are misdirected, for here is a king who is also being executed, whose crown is of thorns, whose throne is a cross. Here at last is the kind of king that makes some sense, the kind of kingdom where he can find a home. So he prays that he may have a share in this kingdom, and his prayer is answered; this man enters Paradise before the rest of us.[22] The Church and its members, who are supposed to be crucified with Christ, have sometimes been so self-assured, so unsympathetically confident, so insensitive to the demands of atonement, so unwilling to act on the principles of corporate guilt and corporate loss of liberty, so concerned to pursue individual innocence, that their place at the side of the Crucified has been taken by the unchristian existentialist, the political trouble-maker, the man who feels that he might as well be hanged for a sheep as for a lamb. Critics tell us that our Church and its leaders get too much involved with politics and suchlike sordid things. But when we appear before the judgement, I am sure that I and my Church will be found guilty, not of getting too much involved in the sufferings and brokenness and misery of our society, but of not getting involved enough. We shall be found guilty of not allowing ourselves to love enough. It is better that I should risk doing wrong for the sake of love than insist on doing right because of my lack of it. Our consciences may be clear, but we can still miss the gate of Paradise if we find the character of its first new citizen too uncongenial.

This 'Paradise', the forecourt of the Resurrection, was the scene of our Lord's encounter with the 'spirits in prison'.[23] We believe that Christ descended into 'Hades', but we have not realized the evangelical power of this belief. Some Africans have been deeply distressed and discouraged from accepting Christ, because they have thought that this would mean deserting their ancestors. If Europeans do not feel this, it is because they either do not have any useful sense of community with the past, or because they assume that all their ancestors have been Christians. But if I think of all my ancestors back to the beginning of the human species, it is obvious that practically all of them were heathen, and on this score there is no difference worth noting between me and the newest convert. But by associating with Christ, I do not lose touch with my ancestors or alienate them; on the contrary, I draw closer to them all, Christians and heathens alike. J. V. Taylor stresses the potency of this teaching in Africa; in this field, which is so important to Africa, Christ comes not destroying but fulfilling.[24] Paradise is the inheritance of Adam, of man as man; and Christians come to it not in distinction from but in association with the rest of mankind; the Christian may come to Paradise and find that he has been preceded by one who has been an 'outsider' to the Church on earth. This is not because the 'outsider' has by some trickery stolen a march on the Christian; it is because the Christian always *follows* Christ, including the Christ who is associated with the 'outsider'; the Christ who is master of Paradise is the same Christ who is there before us as we go out in our mission to the 'outsider's' home or country or culture.

Paradise remains the forecourt; Eden is the greatest blessing to man under the old covenant. The Resurrection takes place in a new garden, where the second Adam is in a true sense recognized by Mary Magdalene as the gardener.[25] So it is a good tradition for the forecourt of a church building to be called a 'paradise' or 'parvis', for the Church itself is the 'garden' of the Resurrection, where the risen Christ is known in the breaking of bread.

MAN'S NEEDS

Our story seems to recognize four primary needs which have to be met if man is to be satisfied; these are territory, activity, food and companionship. The order in which these four needs appear is worth consideration. The need for companionship, or society, is the need to which most attention is given and which is most difficult to satisfy. As we shall see, it includes sex, but includes a great deal more than sex. Society is not an exclusively human invention, but it certainly is a fairly sophisticated form of animal behaviour. Food is a self-evident need, and comes third. Activity, or meaningful work, has priority in attention over food. Man does not live by bread alone; he needs to have something to do; he needs, to use the word of the previous chapter, some way of expressing his *dominion*. Unemployment is a social problem, not merely a personal problem. Society as a whole is hurt when some of its members are forced to undergo this very specific and painful form of unwantedness; it destroys its own resources when such unwantedness gradually causes people to become unwantable and unemployable. And one of the most unfortunate effects of our customary methods of punishment is that they cause a man to spend a great deal of time in non-productivity and inactivity. I remember the joy with which a prisoner told me of his 'promotion' from the mailbag department to the bakery, where he would be able to work four hours a day instead of only two.

But the first need of man which is satisfied, in this story, is the need for territory; he is given a place which is his, to work in, to identify himself with, and to defend. Studies of animals, birds and fish in their wild state are showing that the territorial instinct is far more deeply rooted than most people have realized. Only when this instinct has had some satisfaction do we attend to other needs. On the whole, our need for life-space is so deep and so instinctive that we attend to it without realizing that we are doing so. We are much more conscious, for instance, of the sexual instinct; but we are conscious of it precisely because it is, by comparison, a relatively occasional concern. One of the subtlest forms of cruelty, therefore, is to insist on keeping people insecure in respect of territory and home. Obviously, there are many individuals who can tolerate a lot of such insecurity, and may deliberately choose it, just as there are many individuals who can willingly be celibate and others who can tolerate conditions of hunger or inactivity. But it is difficult to imagine anything more calculated to cut at the roots of a man's security than to insist that he has no rights to stay in the area where he was born or where his spouse lives or where his parents stay. In Eden, the man is given the right to stay in the area where he works; if this right is denied, a man ceases to be a man and becomes merely a labour-unit, to be thrown out when his period of profitable usefulness is over. It is virtually impossible to pass a law which makes it illegal for a person to eat; but it is only too possible to devise a system of laws which may leave a person with no place where he can legally be; in which case, there might as well be a law against eating, for there is, in effect, a law against existing. Such a system of laws is forcing more and more people in South Africa to exist illegally. Such laws offend the very first gift of God to man, according to this story of creation.

GENESIS 2: 16–17
*He told the man, 'You may eat from every tree in the garden, but not
from the tree of the knowledge of good and evil; for on the day that
you eat from it, you will certainly die.'*

The trees are in the centre of the garden, representing God
as the source of life and of moral judgement; these are to be
observed, not seized as man's rightful property. The man has
to realize that he is not the centre of the garden. He is
dependent; his life, like all else, is on loan. But there is no
danger that he could be deprived of life: so he has no incentive to seize the fruit of the tree of life, and at this stage no
prohibition is needed in respect of that tree.

But a prohibition is needed in respect of the tree of the
knowledge of good and evil.

This prohibition must seem completely arbitrary. The
words 'good' and 'evil' in Adam's situation can have no
meaning. But here is a limit in the midst, representing man's
lack of autonomy. Adam is free, as a creature. The tree in the
midst is a sign indicating the freedom to be, as God's command to a creature is permission to be that creature, and
not some other creature. The freedom of a competent pianist
is to play whatever he decides to play; it is not freedom to
switch from one sonata to another at the whim of the
moment, or to propel the piano at the audience like a tank.
In the middle of Bethal (a small town in the eastern Trans-
vaal, piously named after 'the House of God' by the Boers)
there is a crossroads, and in the middle of the crossroads there
used to be a traffic-light which faced in all four directions.
When the light shines green, that is permission for the vehicle
to stop being stationary and to be what it is designed to be –
a vehicle; it is permission to move, left, or right, or straight
ahead. The one thing that is not permitted is for a car to act
as a bulldozer and drive straight at the traffic-light itself
and knock it down; this is an offence, however green the light
may be. The law of God is in the midst; this is the moral
message of the Bible, which the Church is in constant danger
of denying if its moral theology appears to make the law a

series of fences at the side. All law, political law, moral law, family law, church discipline, has to face this question – is the law to reduce man's ability, or to enable him to be the best that he can be?

What God gives is always gracious; his word is always a word of grace, which is why we are required to say 'Thanks be to God' after the gospel, however castigating the word of the Lord in the gospel may be. So this prohibition is gracious, like the traffic-light. There is no temptation to sin here. The idea of good and evil, of moral dualism, is not open to the man. He is in the state like Saul – 'Do whatever the occasion demands; God will be with you.' This is not far from St Augustine's 'Love, and do what you will'.[26] The idea of unbroken association with God is there, but not yet any opposite. For example, to judge from what has to be put up on church notice-boards and from what has to be read out at the eucharist, one might suppose that the main indications of God's will concerning marriage are to be found in the prohibitions 'A man may not marry his grandmother' and 'Thou shalt not commit adultery'. But in the state of marriage, if all is well, these commandments are irrelevant. One is not aware of the goodness of the fact that one is not committing adultery. Is therefore the commandment of God irrelevant? No, because it is not in fact summed up in these negative commandments; it is primarily there in the very presence of the Creator at the centre of the marriage, giving it permission to be. This again the Prayer Book marriage service makes clear, in its reference to the wedding at Cana. 'The divine prohibition of adultery is no longer the centre around which all my thought and action in marriage revolves. (As though the meaning and purpose of marriage consisted of nothing but the avoidance of adultery!) But it is the honouring and free acceptance of marriage, the leaving behind of the prohibition of adultery, which is now the precondition of the fulfilment of the divine commission of marriage. The divine commandment has here become the permission to live in marriage in freedom and certainty.'[27]

To go back to the traffic-light; it is as if the Council first put up a plain white street light in the middle of the crossing, in order to permit traffic to flow by shedding light on the road; the traffic is given permission to flow, to be traffic; but it is forbidden to attack the light itself, which is contrary to its nature as traffic. But if two vehicles approach each other at ninety degrees and swerve into the light standard in their attempts to avoid a collision, and thus, contrary to their nature as vehicles, make an attack on the light, then the Council will remove the plain white light and substitute for it a red and green traffic-light at the centre of the crossing; the simple obedience has been replaced by a twofold one. The tree is there, in the midst, as far as Adam is concerned, with only potential significance. In respect of all the other trees, there is no problem; there is a simple permission, for in them there is simple goodness. But in the tree of the knowledge of good and evil, there is a form of goodness which so far can make no sense to Adam, the form of goodness which needs badness to differentiate it and identify it. This polarity between goodness and evil cannot be absolutely permanent and universal. There is goodness before there is badness, and badness is parasitic on goodness, just as forged cheques are parasitic on a system of good cheques, but good cheques are possible without the existence of forged ones. There is a distinction between goodness which is known only in contra-distinction to evil and goodness which can be taken for granted; there is not the same distinction in the case of evil, which has not the same autonomy as good. That is why there is, for us at least, a 'problem' of evil but not a corresponding problem of good. This is represented in Christian picture-language when we say that the Devil is not the opposite number to God; these two figures do not correspond to each other, they are not equally-matched champions from two hostile sides. The opposite number to Satan is Michael the Archangel, the leader of the hosts of heaven. Satan and Michael are on a level, they are of the same rank of creation, but one is corrupted and the other is consecrated. The manner of the corruption is expressed in the idea that Satan is a fallen archangel. Satan, like Babylon,[28] claimed to be able to be on an equality with God and as a punishment was cast down from heaven. This idea was worked out in the Middle Ages by Duns Scotus, and led to Milton's picture of Satan as the one whose lust for power can make him say:

'Better to reign in hell, than serve in heaven.'[29] 'Evil in its most developed form is always a good which imagines itself, or pretends to be, better than it is.'[30] We shall come across evil in this form more than once in the rest of the story; it is there, perhaps, in the serpent's estimate of its own wisdom; it is certainly there in the woman's daydream as she contemplates the fruit; it affects man's estimate of the sacred importance of his own work. Christ, the Son of God who has the primacy over all created things, overcame this fundamental character of evil, not by *pretending* to be less than he was, but by refusing to allow his status to be the overriding fact about himself; he did not treat equality with God as a thing to be prized or grasped, but was careless of his reputation, and so was free to be associated with the powerless. Through this man's total availability to others, the power of evil was broken, not just for himself but for all who are in association with him.[31] Jesus, significantly, did not see the Devil being cast out of heaven as a result of his own work; he saw the overthrow of evil taking place as a result of the mission work of his disciple-community, the group to which he had passed the infection of his own concern for serving and healing in the world.[32] The Church is sent into the world to restore a right understanding of the character of good and evil, to be a community with a right sense of proportion, overcoming the basic dishonesty which characterizes the figure of Satan. This is a mission of healing; and its only responsible method is that of Christ the servant, who found his status only by not claiming it.

So, in general, and most characteristically in Christ, we see that evil is not a force which is eternally equal and opposite to goodness; it is goodness corrupted and thwarted; it can spoil and ruin everything within its range, but first of all there must be things to spoil and ruin. Evil depends on a supply of things to spoil and ruin; it cannot create them.

But, although there is no power of evil that is equal and opposite to God, we have to avoid the other extreme, namely the idea that good and evil come equally from the one source called God. There are a couple of occasions where the prophets seem to come close to this idea,[33] but this is part of their argument that the one God has total responsibility;

and if calamity (rather than moral evil) comes, people must ask whether this is not in truth part of the purpose of the one God, who can use even unconscious agents like Cyrus in his enterprises.

But, as a whole, the Bible does not try to maintain that God is the cause of everything that happens. He is the causing purpose behind the universe and history, but he is not every cause in detail. What he created was not a machine that would run exactly according to a predetermined line; he created a universe in which the events of ultimate significance would have the character of a response to persuasive love, rather than of automatic reaction to a coercive mechanism. Different people are bound to give different accounts of the degree of this freedom, according to the circumstances which have shaped their awareness. Some people have a great sense of being in a law-abiding system – or else their experience has caused them to feel a strong need to assert that, in spite of appearances, they are in a law-abiding system; such people will be inclined to find the idea of predestination congenial, if their cultural language happens to be Christian, or else they may find satisfaction in the ideas of psychological or sociological determinism; and both these sets of ideas stress the general view that all things, congenial and uncongenial alike, come from the same ultimate source or system. At its most rigid, this view allows no room for any factors to break in and modify the present plans, and it therefore is obliged to insist that the whole concept of freedom is an irrational fiction. But this conclusion is possible only when logic is allowed to push on beyond the limits of experience, which, in theology at least, is an extremely dangerous state of affairs. In the form in which we find it in the New Testament, the doctrine of predestination stands for the vital truth that our freedom ultimately lies in the fact that we have been chosen rather than that we can choose.[34] On the other hand, there are many people for whom salvation and hope is needed in terms of a release from bondage, to the extent that God himself must be unbound and free to respond to the unpredictable, free to enable man to be free; in this case, the principle of freedom and choice is built into the created order itself, and then it becomes a matter of faith to insist that there is an element of spontaneity, indeed of surprise, in the working out of God's plan. God is then characterized as the supremely sensitive response to that which meets him; and this is not a bad way of expressing the meaning of 'God is love'.[35]

So there are two extreme ideas: first, that God must be responsible for the minutest detail; second, that God's activity is only in the unpredictable, the otherwise inexplicable. Neither of these views can be reconciled with the total witness of the Bible; the truth lies somewhere between the two, and at different times one or other of these emphases will be more valued. The first chapter of Genesis gives us the more orderly, determined, law-abiding view; the second gives us the more exploratory, responsive view. But in each case, there is a potential which is available to be realized; and therefore there is in both an element of choice. According to the first chapter, there is a potential for order in the first disorder, a potential for development and maturity in the earliest simple things; and as the creation becomes more complex, so God is more and more in conversation with the creation, encouraging it and persuading it to be the best that it can be, but never employing threats or coercion. Although the main emphasis in that chapter is clearly the sheer power of God's creative word, it is still fair to say that God is drawing things into the fullness of existence by the power of love, and that therefore there must be, as the Priestly writer knew only too well, the opportunity for resistance and refusal. The second and third chapters present a different emphasis. Here there is no development from an original chaos; man is made full-grown at the start; and from the start there is a potential for deviation and evil. The emphasis here, therefore, is on the freedom within creation, the freedom of choice which makes God a searcher and questioner; nonetheless, it is still fair to say that God retains the initiative; and the rest of the Bible is about the working-out of God's initiative as he draws the world to himself by the persuasion of love.

To have knowledge of good and evil, to *know* good and evil, is much more than merely to be informed about them. It is to experience good-and-evil as a strain, as a bind, as a choice which inhibits all action until it is faced and decided. For, at this point, this is what the word 'know' is about; it means virtually 'to have competence in' something. The connexion between the eating and the gaining of the knowledge is not arbitrary or magical; the physical act of facing up to and of breaking the prohibition would itself be the 'knowing' of good-and-evil in the most significant sense. The intention of God, therefore, in prohibiting the eating of the fruit of this tree is not to keep man ignorant and immature, which often seems to be the intention behind religion; the intention of God is to protect man from the moral inhibition and dilemma of the good-and-evil ambiguity. There is a sense, of course, in which man does become mature by wrestling with the moral dilemmas in which he finds himself; but it is also true that both his achievement and his freedom are radically limited by the condition of moral ambiguity; and, as we shall observe in the case of Jesus, real maturity is now to be perceived in those who have faced and beaten the inhibiting effects of moral ambiguity, and so are free to act authentically in the specific situation in which they find themselves.

Twice later in the story, it is stated that there is a being who has the knowledge of good and evil, God himself.[36] When we speak of 'God', we mean that there is One in whom this knowledge can exist without being destructive; the pain and anxiety of this experiencing of good-and-evil is not the last word. It can be mastered; and it has been mastered in the Son of God. Jesus had this 'competence' in good-and-evil; he faced the goodness in the evil and the evil in the goodness of the three ideas which came to him in what we call the temptation; he worked through the anxiety of this experience, and from that time on was able to go through his ministry without being harassed by the internal strain.[37] The eventual strain of his passion and death was, therefore, not unprecedented; he had faced the implications long ago; the cross had been his daily bed.

So, at this stage, Adam is conscious of the tree only as something which is present to him but not his to do what he likes with; like the white street lamp, it is there only by the graciousness of the Authority.

Death is promised as the consequence of eating the fruit of the tree of the knowledge of good and evil, death to true freedom, death to man as he was supposed to be. As it turns out, the eating does not bring immediate physical death. But knowledge of the compulsion to choose is the deadly, inhibiting thing, delaying action until the choice is made. To be dead, as St Paul saw, is to see life and opportunities and goodness not as grace but as burdens, as codes; to be dead means to *have* to live, to have life as a burden. Death in the sense of extinction can then be a hope of salvation, it can be a fascination; this makes life a horror and forces attention even more on the hard demand to have life and live life. It is the making of life a commandment or rule that makes people want to commit suicide, *and* makes society classify suicide as a crime. One thing is clear, that this kind of dilemma can be resolved by no bold acts of will or imagination, by no good resolutions. Christians reckon to see a solution in one who, far from behaving as if there is no tension, went deeper into it. He suffered the inhibitions of having to choose (as in the temptation); and he suffered the terrible and familiar experience of being unable to do the entirely good. If you will put on one side the presuppositions of Jesus' perfection, you will find there are many ways of picking holes in his behaviour; look, for instance, at the appalling burden of responsibility which Jesus laid on that frail character, Pilate, so that his name echoes round the world whenever the Creed is recited; can you say that Jesus was utterly and unambiguously fair to Pilate? Pilate gets the blame for a judicial murder which Jesus brought on his own head. We say that Jesus was without sin. He always did the right thing, but, in a world of moral ambiguities, the right thing is hardly ever the ideal thing. Jesus saw more clearly than anyone else the absolute of goodness; it was a real part of his lifelong passion experience that he was unable to do the absolutely ideal thing, that he was involved in the moral contradictions which we are involved in.[38] The point is that Jesus met all this evil, shared the inevitabilities of having to choose between unideal courses, shared the full effects of the brokenness of our world, and came through to the far side.

GENESIS 2: 18
Then the Lord God said, 'It is not good for the man to be alone. I will provide a partner for him.'

In the account so far in this chapter, we have had a permission and a prohibition. Now, for the first time, we have a statement in the mouth of God. We might expect that God's first statement would be something of great consequence, and indeed it is.

'It is not good for the man to be alone.'

God is the critic of his own work; he stands back from it and sees that there is something about what he has made that is *not* 'very good'. God is not only the guarantor of permanence: he is also the initiator of change. He is not only in the beginning of things; he is also in the response to things.

Immediately God, in planning his response, isolates the most significant characteristic of the situation – that loneliness is virtually the same as helplessness, and that the remedy for both is the same, a partner.

The first man Adam was alone. In so far as we are of the first man, we are alone; this aloneness is a curse, and we are called to rescue each other from it. This is one of the great incentives to Christian action, to overcome each other's isolation. It is not good that man should be alone; this is the word of the designer, it is the mind of God, and the Church has to act in accordance with the mind of God. If this statement of God's mind is not articulated in word and action by the Church, it goes by default, and the mind of God is credited with willing our segregation. The Church has to participate in God's participation in the world's troubles.

The whole work of Christ is an expression of this word.

The whole work of Pentecost is an expression of this word.

The continuing work of the Holy Spirit is an expression of this word.

The whole mission of the Church is an expression of this word.

Every work of opposition to apartheid is an expression of this word. It is not good for the man to be alone.

The second man Adam was alone also. In so far as we are of the Christ, we are alone. This aloneness is a blessing, for it is a blessing to suffer with the Christ, to share his isolation. He claimed no one's friendship as of right. He expressed fellowship towards those for whom fellowship was denied, and at the end they were the only relievers of his isolation. St Luke spells this out as plainly as could be, in his story of the penitent thief.[39] St Mark at the same time stresses our Lord's aloneness, his separation even from the Father.[40] How can this be blessedness? Luther knew part of the answer:

'The Kingdom is to be in the midst of your enemies. And he who will not suffer this does not want to be of the Kingdom of Christ; he wants to be among friends, to sit among roses and lilies, not with the bad people but with the devout people. O you blasphemers and betrayers of Christ! If Christ had done what you are doing, who would ever have been spared?'[41]

So one of the most splendid and moving stories in the New Testament (especially for us in this continent) is that of the Ethiopian eunuch, who after his baptism did not turn round and come back to the little community of believers in Jerusalem, but went on southward, in *our* direction, deprived, by the Holy Spirit, of his new friend Philip, but rejoicing; he came alone, baptized, into this territory which they used to call the Dark Continent.[42]

It may well be *good* for man to be alone, if he has the aloneness of Christ.

Christ was *able* to be alone. The threat of isolation was not so fearful to him that it dominated his life. He was not attached to people through an inability to stand on his own. Such attachment may be vital for some people, but it is not love. Erich Fromm goes so far as to insist: 'The ability to be alone is the condition for the ability to love.'[43] On the other hand, he was not attracted to aloneness through a preference for living in his own thoughts. When he was with people, he was in a two-way traffic of giving and receiving, for which the simple word is love. When he was alone, he was renewing his sense of community with the Father, dwelling in the knowledge of the Father's love and sure purpose.[44] Christ enables his disciples to use their aloneness with joy, but only in the service of love. On this pattern, the disciple will find that there is a straight way from aloneness to community; he will share Jesus' own experience of being alone yet not alone,[45] for this kind of aloneness is the basic nurturing of love, which is the basis of genuine community.

GENESIS 2: 19–20
So God formed out of the ground all the wild animals and all the birds of heaven. He brought them to the man to see what he would call them, and whatever the man called each living creature, that was its name. Thus the man gave names to all cattle, to the birds of heaven, and to every wild animal; but for the man himself no partner had yet been found.

MAN AND ANIMAL

But here, in the original condition of man, it is not good for man to be alone. And God experiments, as we do, in finding an answer to this problem. He experiments with animals. A good attempt, but not good enough. Animals are possible companions; they are of the same origin as man, out of the earth. But they have not received the Breath (or Spirit) of God; there can, therefore, be no reciprocity. The relationship between man and animal is a one-way traffic; it depends entirely on the imagination and care of man; the animal cannot properly be accused of desertion or cruelty. But a true relationship is always two-way, whether we are talking of a woman loving a man or a mission converting the heathen. 'On the cross was revealed to believing eyes and at Pentecost was vindicated the supreme secret of the universe: that it is a structure of reciprocal relationship. It is only in that two-way relationship that we can understand the great fundamental Christian affirmations that God is love and that there are three persons in one God. Apart from this reciprocity a trinitarian formula is otiose and meaningless . . . the secret of life is neither giving or taking, neither offering nor receiving, but both together in indissoluble yet unconfused unity.'[46]

Only a reciprocal relationship is a free one, and can be an adequate image of the freedom of God and of Christ, the image of God; anything which falls short of this is less than divine and therefore less than human.

Our story shows the animals in friendly subjection to man. Although there is not this essential reciprocity, the relationship of man to animal is certainly not simple; its elusiveness is reflected in the story. In giving a thing a name, you express a dominion over it. But you are also allowing the other to have an identity over against you; the identity is truly there, but you have taken an initiative over it in acknowledging its identity. This is most obviously true of a domestic animal; a relationship can be established with it, but it remains a relationship in which one party has value because of the value put upon it by the other party.

MAN THE SYMBOL-MAKER

It is not clear what everything is. God waits to see what man is going to make of the things which have been made. He waits to see how man will refer to them, how he will divide them up. Man is assumed to have already the power to make words. This is the equivalent, in our writer's method, to the Priestly author's general doctrine that man has dominion. Objects are given differentiation by the word that names them. The animals exist in their differentiation only when they have been 'isolated', given an identity. An unknown, unnamed 'real' thing is less part of reality than the named thing which is 'fictitious'. For instance, until 1930 the planet Pluto had been predicted but not 'discovered'; we could ask, which Pluto was more truly part of the universe in those days, the planet, the god, or the dog?

Nature itself is a continuum: man imposes a pattern or a scheme of reference where there may be no 'objective' basis for it. The colour spectrum is a continuum of wavelengths; what does man do with it? In some languages he divides it into seven, as in English; in Zulu he divides it into four. English has seven words for body postures. Zulu has fifty-four. John Locke maintained that the various species of animals really had no separate existence at all – 'they were created by the mind of man, reducing nature to order, and were not the work of nature herself'.[47] This naming and categorizing is the basis of any scientific activity – the development of an agreed set of terms; these are essentially tools, not rules; they are servants, not masters. Theological argument would have been much less efficient as a vehicle for human uncharity if this had been remembered. Words and symbols are strung together to make 'laws', and here again the same principle applies. 'A scientific law does not control events; otherwise we could not alter it ourselves when we were dissatisfied with it. It is a means of correlating experiences. . . . There is no force of gravitation except in our own minds as they try to comprehend the falling stone . . .'[48]

Here, in Genesis, we are given a picture of man at work as the giver of names, the maker of symbols, and therefore, in principle, the articulator of laws. Man has been brought in as an associate in God's creative activity. In imposing a pattern of language upon his environment and experience, he is extending the rule of order: he is discovering meaning. In so doing, he is not merely noting 'facts' objectively: he is himself biased by his own concern to find meaning and value for himself. He is looking for a partner, and his acts of naming are influenced by his success and failure in this search. His enthusiasm and his despair influence his response to the things which are brought to his attention. He is not concerned primarily with their origins and causation but with their attitudes and functions in relationship to himself; he is concerned about what he can do with them. From this it follows that man has a mandate not only to try to comprehend nature in 'laws'; his response to his environment can rightly include such enterprises as the making of new elements, the acceleration of the evolutionary process by producing new fertile species of plants, and even the striving towards the 'making' of living material. Man has this power and responsibility within creation, to know and to experiment, to test and to reject. The more he does this, the more he needs to be aware, in some sense, that everything has been brought to him by God. His science will tell him what things are, why they have become, and how they can be used: it will not, in itself, tell him what to do with this knowledge; 'ought' is not a word that properly belongs in scientific discourse: and man must allow scientific discovery to stimulate rather than diminish his role as a decision-maker.

The final model or climax of this work of naming is demanded when Jesus asks: 'Who do you say that I am?', 'What do you think of the Christ?'[49] Here, God waits to see what man will make of God himself; and at the same time, true man waits to see what man will make of true man himself. At this point, man's ability as symbol-maker breaks down, not because he is lacking in intelligence but because he cannot face the political and personal implications of giving a true answer. To do this naming demands not only intellect but commitment. This works the other way round also. To hear and accept the identity that the other party gives as his name, this demands commitment. Moses at the Burning Bush asks for God's name; and the answer which God gives is not a neat, factual answer but a very demanding one. He calls himself: 'I will be there as he whom I there shall be' (Buber's translation).[50] In other words: 'You don't have to worry about what I am or shall be; you will find me there in a situation where events and people really meet you and confront you; you don't have to have a name by which to conjure me, I will be there; I will be present in the way in which I choose to be present.' God is not limited to the mountain, nor to the endless series of repetitions which make up nature. He is to be found in the unprecedented and un-repeatable events which make up history. That is why it is reasonable to speak of the personal character of God; for the unique, the really distinguishing thing, about me is not my ideas (which are all derivative – almost everything that I write should honestly be put in quotation marks) or my attitudes, but my history. This is what makes me me. If I am concerned about that which I face in the unexpected, revolutionary events of history, world history, my neighbour's history, my own history, I am concerned about the one in whose image I am made. Buber maintains that history is missing its true character unless it is written with en-thusiasm; the word which came to be used as the name for God, Yahweh, was originally, he says, simply an explosion of wonder – 'HE!'[51] This is the response of man to that which descends on to his path and meets him and commissions him. On this showing, the most genuine history, the most responsible naming, the most specific theology in the Bible is in the exclamation of Thomas: 'My Lord and my God!'[52]

If this is so, the question of what man makes of God is closely bound up with the question of what he makes of man. A Christian can talk of God if he can see that a human form, any human form, is the form in which God approaches him. In one sense, the Son of God was just another person, and persons are pretty much expendable, as Caiaphas pointed out.[53] Buber says that God is never other than *Thou* because his back is never turned; Christians should see that Christ's back is never turned, for he faces us in every human form. Where law or custom makes this difficult or impossible to realize, where people are primarily defined in terms of their status, or as members of one group or another, where neighbourliness and sharing between different individuals are discouraged, this is not just unfortunate; it is the Antichrist.

It was in terms of status and ancestry that the Pharisees answered Jesus' question, 'What do you think of Christ?' They said that Christ is a son of David. And indeed this is true, and must be true. If Christ is to be a person, he must be in an ancestral line; and for those who were of this same line, this was particularly important; the Christ must be of the right race and family, he must be one of us. This is a way of saying that it is important for me that I too am a son of David (which happens to be true of me personally, with my Welsh patronymic). We can make this the most important question about us, as it is so often in South Africa. A man lies injured at the roadside: the first question is not 'Where is he hurt?' but 'Whose son is he? . . . What race is he? . . . Do we get the white or non-white ambulance?'

In its right place this can still be an important question. My ancestry, my parents, have shaped me more than I realize and more than they realized. I found that certain strategies and tricks worked with my parents, and so they have become part of me; I came to value my ability to fight, or to evade issues, or to argue, or to feel sick, or to laugh, as ways of getting out of trouble, and now these things are part of me whether I like it or not; I am a son of David. My neighbour is also a son of his ancestors; and he has found value in ways of being himself which are different from my ways of being myself. Jesus asks the question 'Who am I?' immediately after discussing the commandment to love God and love your neighbour. Loving your neighbour *as yourself* means accepting the fact that, just as your good and bad points are due to your interaction with parents and background, the same is true of the other person; and, just as you need to be accepted with these features, so does he, whose good and bad points do not necessarily fit in with yours at all conveniently.

But Jesus insists that it is not enough to say that he is son of David, for this is to characterize him in terms of that which he cannot change; he is not merely the product of his parents, his background, his race, these so immutable, so easily identifiable, so simply classifiable factors. Howard Thurman's observation is immensely important for people who live in the context of a racialist ideology. 'To place Jesus against the background of his time is by no means sufficient to explain him . . . Any explanation of Jesus in terms of psychology, politics, economics, religion, or the like, must inevitably explain his contemporaries as well. It may tell why Jesus was a particular kind of Jew, but not why some other Jews were not Jesus. And that is, after all, the most important question, since the thing which makes him most significant is not the way in which he resembled his fellows but the way in which he differed from all the rest of them. Jesus inherited the same traits as countless other Jews of his time; he grew up in the same society; and yet he was always Jesus, and the others were not.'[54]

Jesus, therefore, is son of David, but not only son of David. He is also son of God. This means that he is the result of the working of that power which breaks into history and fills it with the unpredictable. He is a new creation; there was a new start when he was born; that is why we say that he was born of a virgin. And we Christians, who reckon that we belong to the family of God, we also are born of God, we are given our names at baptism, which is our virgin birth. The really significant birth, for a Christian, is not his first but his second birth, not his birth of the flesh but his birth of water and of the Spirit. It is this birth which gives access to the durable community; it is this birth which enables us to enter the Kingdom.[55] Those who receive Christ and believe in him become the children of God, and the birth that is primarily important for them is not the birth by which they enter their ancestral group but the birth which comes from the free action and choice of God.[56] Therefore, for us to love *God* means that we have to love and value and respect and allow for and fight for this truth, that we are not primarily characterized in terms of our ancestry but in terms of that which breaks into the determinism of our heredity and makes us new and surprising. This is to live by grace, to live in terms of that which breaks in, the new creation. And where we allow the community of race, the grouping of man in terms of what is biologically unalterable, to take priority over the community of grace, this again is the Antichrist; it is a rejection of that which is supremely good about ourselves. It is, therefore, more than a political or ethical mistake; it is a form of blasphemy against the Holy Spirit.[57]

THE SEARCH

As a solution to the original problem, the animal will not do – still no partner for man had been found.

And it is not enough to look in the other direction, to God 'above' instead of an animal 'below'. What man is needing is a helper, a one who can be alongside, pulling the ropes with man. Despite so many prayers, ancient and modern, God is not man's helper. If God be God it is not *help* that we seek from him, or a friendly push to complete the nice plans that we aren't quite strong enough to effect to our satisfaction on our own. The whole point about God's work in the Bible, especially when he does truly come alongside us in the person of the man Christ Jesus, is that God takes the initiative, his is the grace and the power, his is the mind and the will, that get things done. He is fighting the war; it is his battle, and his people are judged by whether they take their place at his side. This goes right back to the very earliest parts of the Scriptures.[58] What we should expect from the Most High is not help and guidance but equipment and instructions.

So neither from the Creator nor from the rest of creation can man find his 'opposite number'. The solution is to produce a being that is the same. Only with a being of equal value can this reciprocal relationship be established in a real two-way traffic. And yet just another Adam will not suffice either, for man cannot establish a true relationship with his own reflection. The other being must be radically different if there is to be a true discourse. This may be very obvious to us; but the story suggests that it was not obvious always – it is something which has to be discovered. As we discover its truth in personal experience, we seem to be making God's own discoveries after him.

But the unsatisfactoriness of the search so far has one immensely important value; it establishes right at the heart of man's experience the need for doubt and for testing experiment. It establishes a necessary scepticism without which there can be neither scientific research nor a rational attitude towards authority. Man does not simply accept what is set before him as the answer to his need; he tests and rejects. If an authority sets itself up in any manner other than this, it is being ungodlike in its relationships, and is likely to twist the idea of God into the form of a tyrant. The nearer such an authority is to the accepted concomitants of God, the greater is this danger; more damage is done by fathers than by managers, by priests than by generals. There is fanaticism in almost every area of human activity, including science, but religious fanaticism is probably the most dangerous, because it is purporting to speak about things which are central to the whole of humanity. But 'all fanaticism is a strategy to prevent doubt from becoming conscious'.[59] And the scientific method has developed on the conscious and deliberate basis of responsible doubt. This becomes repeatedly clear in the history of science, as expounded, for instance, in Professor Butterfield's *The Origins of Modern Science*. Here we see how much of modern development came about through the doubting of assumptions derived from Aristotle, and how, to a considerable extent, this doubting was undergirded by biblical and Christian attitudes. Bacon, for instance, maintained that it was heathen arrogance, not the Scriptures, which endowed the skies with the prerogative of being incorruptible. 'The warfare was against the so-called naturalism of the Renaissance – the belief in pan-psychism and animism, which gave everything a soul and saw miracles everywhere in nature. It was partly in the name of religion itself that Renaissance naturalism was attacked, and the Christians helped the cause of modern rationalism by their jealous determination to sweep out of the world all miracles and magic except their own. In the circle around Mersenne in the 1630s the idea of a complete mechanistic interpretation of the universe came out into the open, and its exponents were the most religious men in the group that we are discussing. They were anxious to prove the adequacy and the perfection of Creation – anxious to vindicate God's rationality.'[60] 'This disenchantment of the natural world', says Harvey Cox, 'provides an absolute precondition for the development of natural science.'[61] This is the world view of Genesis; the typical man, Adam, is cast in the role of the experimenter who is under no pressure to accord a sacral value to any one item among the things which are brought before him to name; and only by persistently rejecting unsatisfactory answers does he come to a satisfactory one in the end. Once again, we find in chapter 2 an alternative way of expressing the basic doctrine of chapter 1: in chapter 1, this same non-enchantment of the natural world is conveyed in the teaching that the lights of the sky were made on the fourth day.

The arrival of man in the world is the arrival of thought; and the arrival of thought is inevitably the arrival of doubt; this is seen in such widely-separated writers as François Sanchez (who in 1581 stated: 'Hence the thesis which is the starting-point of my reflections: the more I think, the more I doubt')[62] and Teilhard de Chardin, with his observation: 'When the first spark of thought appeared on the earth, life found it had brought into the world a power capable of criticizing it and judging it.'[63] This is one of the criteria of any educational undertaking; if a student tells us, with a reasonable amount of evidence, that his school was bad, the chances are that it was relatively good, because it at least gave him the tools with which to criticize it. This is one reason why church schools are so often, quite properly, criticized; it is even more true about the Church itself. The only way for the Church to avoid criticism, at least until all its members are perfect, is for it to stop telling the truth; otherwise, people are bound to compare the Church with the truth which it preaches and find it wanting; the South African Church, more than most others, is most shrewdly beaten with the whips which it has itself distributed.

To doubt means to exercise a critique upon one's experience and learning. In spite of all its dangers and pains, this is the value of doubt. Adam's experience at this stage is an experience of discouragement; the most reasonable deduction from this experience would be that his search will never be rewarded, that no partner will ever be found. It is his doubt in the validity of this deduction that keeps him going. Where there is doubt there is hope. For people who have grown up in a situation of cultural or political certainty and dominance, doubt may be felt as an enemy. But, for people whose daily experience is rejection, suffering, and death, any worthwhile faith must be a stimulus to doubt, a demand to question the inevitability of their bondage. Even in the case of the most privileged man, the only absolutely certain thing that can be said about him is that he will die; faith makes a person doubt that this fact is truly the most important and significant thing about him. In so far as the man of God is set in a world of death and disorder, he will need training in the discipline of responsible doubting. For the privileged, such as those who have the freedom to be interested in theological writings and arguings, doubt may seem to be primarily a threat to faith; but to the great majority of mankind, characterized here in the person of Adam, doubt is the essential bulwark against despair.

Adam, therefore, comes as a responsible critic into his environment. He is able to say 'No', and to tolerate dissatisfaction. Adam is a man of faith, at this point, precisely because he is able to live in uncertainty; he is not under an overwhelming pressure to say 'Yes' when he should say 'No'.

Many of our traditional Christian attitudes suggest that faith is the supreme possession, the most important thing to *have* and to keep. But, more truly, faith is a not-having; it is a trust in the future; it is an attitude not of having but of seeking.[64] Christianity has often appeared as an almost entirely past-directed scheme, to make men secure in the possession of what they have already got; there is some truth in this, of course; but it brings a real danger that we shall value what we have got, not because it liberates us for further seeking but because it gives us an excuse for giving up the search. If theology has any right to be taken seriously as a form of knowledge, it will be for this reason, that it is based on the deliberate exercise of doubt. A theological statement has authenticity if we can reasonably say of it: 'This appears to us at present to be the least unsatisfactory method of accounting for these phenomena.' In this sort of way men worked out the great dogmatic statements of the Church in the first few generations of the Christian movement. Having arrived at such a statement, they were, of course, not afraid to assert it with conviction and joy, and to shout alleluia; this also is part of faith. But faith does include not-knowing; and this is the aspect of faith which Adam is learning to practise at this point. He is able to keep his critical faculty operative, in spite of the widening range of things on which a judgement has to be passed. But the care and patience of his 'no' is eventually balanced by the rapture of his 'yes'. He is following both halves of Whitehead's motto: 'Seek simplicity; and distrust it.'[65]

GENESIS 2: 21–22
And so the Lord God put the man into a trance, and while he slept, he took one of his ribs and closed the flesh over the place. The Lord God then built up the rib, which he had taken out of the man, into a woman. He brought her to the man,

It looks, at this point, as if the writer is really trying quite hard to answer a 'how' question, about the origin of woman, and to give an account of an observable process. Which may be so – with the considerable disadvantage that the story

explicitly states that there was no one to do the observing;
the only rational creature in existence was heavily anaes-
thetized. He was in a state of not-knowing, in darkness; and
it was at this level, a level deeper than the conscious and
more potent than perception, that God's work took place.
God's activity is revealed only in its results; we cannot, at
the time, point to something and say with certainty 'Lo,
here' or 'Lo, there is God definitely doing things'.[66] And, if
we want to know God himself, as opposed to just his manifestations or his products, we have to develop that area of
the person which is willing not to know, which can rest in
darkness and unclarity. A theology of precision and systematic concept may well be a way of bringing into the service
of God some of man's greatest skills; but it will lead to
spiritual malnutrition unless it is balanced with a more
negative, passive theology. It will lead to a justification by
neither faith nor works, but by gnosis, by skill in making
intellectual constructs. But, 'though we through grace of God
can know fully about all other matters, and think about
them – yes, even the very works of God himself – yet of God
himself can no man think. Therefore I will leave on one side
everything I can think, and choose for my love that thing
which I cannot think!'[67]

The new being is not made separately out of the ground.
It is part of man, and man recognizes it as such. The story is
expressing something of empirical observation, not just the
attraction of the sexes but the sense of involvement of the
one in the other, to the effect that this is not an accidental
or subhuman or occasional fact but part of the deepest truth
about man under the authority of God. Man is not merely
seeking union; he seeks union in a very particular way,
namely through merging in a common life with the other
sex; he pursues a oneness which is seen not just as a far-off
hope but as an original source of unity which draws man
back to itself. The story of Adam's rib derives its power
from the same feeling which inspired another old interpretation of man's male-female nature, the story that the human
being was originally one, but was cut in half; and that, ever
since, the two halves have been searching for each other in
order to join up again. This is, of course, most clearly seen

in the search of male and female *persons* for each other. But it is also to be seen in the search for wholeness that goes on within a single personality, the striving for adjustment between the male and the female components of each person. Despite the scorn poured by some respectable citizens on the Beatles and the hippies, it is surely a good thing that the male human is beginning to stop feeling that he is under a compulsion to pretend to be one hundred per cent male. It is a sign of weakness, not of strength, if a man has to exclude from his life the knowledge that part of him – the 'rib' – is female; if he is afraid of the weakness of his masculinity, he may try to compensate for this by allowing himself to play only what he thinks is the exclusively male role in sex relations. But the womanizer and the sadist escape the implications of this story of Adam's rib; and they therefore miss the wonder of the other person's power to answer to a deeper need.

GENESIS 2: 23

> *and the man said:*
> *'Now this, at last –*
> *bone from my bones,*
> *flesh from my flesh! –*
> *this shall be called woman,*[a]
> *for from man*[b] *was this taken.'*

a) Heb. *ishshah.*   b) Heb. *ish.*

The man, up to this point, has been thinking about himself and his own needs. There is a story that he acted as the perfect English gentleman, and politely introduced himself (in English, of course) with the neat palindrome, 'Madam, I'm Adam'. Indeed, the traditional English translations do suggest that Adam responded to the appearance of woman in grave and measured tones, as would be fitting in a respectable academic setting. The way in which we choose to express the first recorded words of man may reflect quite a lot about ourselves. The original Hebrew is far less inhibited; the New English Bible conveys not only the meaning but the feeling of it. It is not a solemn statement but an ecstatic cry of joy which breaks the bounds of grammar. The man's despair and self-interest are forgotten in the wonder of encountering the other person. His first utterance is an exclamation which is the prototype of every passionate lyric that has ever been written or sung; the one who meets him has captured his interest entirely, replacing the self-regarding concern which has been generated by his own inner sense of need. The shorthand word for this is 'love'.

The man has been looking for a helper, someone to fulfil a certain function. He has been shopping around among various creatures and found no satisfaction. One reason for this is that he has been looking for the wrong thing. It would not be much use to give him a lesson on this; it is not a fact that can be taught from a book. Nonetheless, he is not so bound up with the particular expectation that he has in mind, that he cannot see the true answer when it appears. As soon as he really encounters the other person, he forgets his search for a functionary. He does not say, 'Ah, at last, a suitable helper – a suitable assistant, bedmate, housekeeper, nurse.' He says, 'At last, this is really part of me; with her I am not going to be able to tell the difference between loving and being loved.' This is the strongest reason for putting 'until death do us part' in the marriage service. I accept this person not for so long as she fulfils a function but until she ceases to be. However much planning may go into it, a marriage is an encounter, a surprise. So we maintain that marriage is a work of God, for God is the name we give to the one who has the supreme character of encounter, who is pre-eminently the one who meets us; and we say that God gives us to each other. We express this symbolically in our marriage rite. We do not say to each other: 'I give myself to you (and you had better be as generous to me in return)', but we say: 'I take you . . .' I accept you as part of myself. This is not by some magic that has been on us both from birth; but now that it has happened we bear each other's mark. We are bone of each other's bone now, and from now on. This is because I need no longer be afraid of that which is so bound up with my own tissue. 'Bone of my bone' means that I really accept involvement with the other person – a radically different person. A fear of this involvement keeps a whole range of people in business. This fear provides a market for methods to identify woman only as a functionary, a plaything; many who pride themselves on fearlessness, on escaping from Victorian restraints and so on, succeed only in showing their fear of being really personally involved with the other sex, because their fearlessness consists only in a brave placarding of the other sex as a plaything. To be able to say 'bone of my bone' means also being able to say 'boredom of my boredom, lovelessness of my lovelessness'. 'The other person, whom God has joined to me, is never what he is apart from me.'[68] *This* is real fearlessness, real acceptance; to nurture people so that they can love and be loved to this degree is the real work of Christian education.

'Bone of my bone' means, also, that I have what she has and what she is. Jealousy is my fear that what she has cannot be mine; and, in return, it is my disbelief that she will be able to accept what is mine. But if she is bone of my bone, my interests and relationships and experiences will become hers as well and cannot be used to divide us.

'Bone of *my* bone' is also a liberating and creative discovery of myself. This is yet another way of expressing what it means to say that we are made in the image of God. The other person is the presence of myself, my bone, in that other person. 'I cannot know myself except through the intermediary of another person', says Sartre;[69] the security of being known enables me to see myself. It is this relationship which enables genuine secrecy. Whether it be done by some sort of 'Christian' group, or by a communist cell, the forcing of self-revelation is nothing less than totalitarian. It reduces people to the level of scalps to be counted, of objects to be manipulated. Our story recognizes that in a situation of free choice between man and woman, there is a degree of self-revelation which is beyond that between parent and child. Not to have secrets is to be less than a person, and as children grow to maturity this becomes increasingly important. If they are not allowed to have honest secrets they will fight back by devising dishonest ones. In the old-fashioned, unreformed eucharistic service, which keeps on going as if neither Reformation nor Liturgical Movement had happened, there are a number of 'secret' prayers for the priest to say in silence. Granted that the liturgy is the corporate act, granted that the priest is not doing a special private rite of his own, there may still be something to be said for having a moment during the liturgy where the priest can, in effect, say: 'All right, for the rest of the service I am publicly exposed, and all that I do is shared with the others who are here. But at this point I am going to be a person, I am going to have my secret prayer which is mine and mine only.' This may be a necessary corrective to an over-conscious communism. The keeping of secrets, which may almost look like shame, is a necessary preparation for a one-flesh relationship. Unless self-disclosure is something precious, even costly, unless it has not been prematurely forced, it cannot have the spontaneity which belongs between two people who deeply choose each other. The ability to trust that secrets, once shared, will not be shared further, makes confidence between the two possible. This is part of faithfulness. Sunday-school lesson books nearly always interpret the seventh commandment to pre-adolescents in terms of not giving way to bodily appetites too much. They would do far better to prepare for faithful marriage relationships by helping children to be really faithful in their promises and their secrets; for it is in failures of this kind that the roots of adulteries lie, not in eating too many buns.

'Bone of my bone' means that I am known from the inside, from the areas deeper and more concealed than skin and tissue. Mature marriage is love without illusions; in the earlier stages, we keep up our masks to conceal ourselves from ourselves, but the love of the other person leads us into all truth – it enables us to live with more and more of ourselves and reconciles the area which we do know to the area which we do not know or dare not know. This is disillusionment – the fact that 'disillusionment' is usually a dirty word is the measure of our disorder! Love does not ruthlessly expose truth, it rejoices in the truth,[70] and causes truth to be a blessing and a joy. To say that God is love is to say that he is the entirely disillusioned one.

Man gives woman a name, and so he expresses in a certain sense a degree of superiority, as he did when he named the animals. But there is a great difference here; here he is announcing not that he has found the object of his search but that he has been found by her. And she is different to the animals; she is the equal, the complementary, to himself.

He has been looking for a 'help'; but this is not the term which he uses in order to identify her. She *is* a help, but only in the sense that she helps him to *be*, simply by being an enabler of his own existence. The man and woman together are necessary to make up the new complex unit called 'man'.[71] Previously, man has been giving the creatures names which stress the difference between the namer and the named; but, faced with woman, he invents a name which is different to his own but is also as much like his own as possible. (This is the case in Hebrew even more than it is in English.) He names her, not as a lord exercising a dominion, but as one who rejoices in a discovery of a being who is like himself. The naming is not like a master's naming of his dog, or even a father's naming of his son; it is more like the new name, the private name, which a lover gives to his beloved however many names she may have already. Such a name is a guarantee of the secret character of the new identity which each has for the other; it is not just a superficial or sentimental trick, for it has its counterpart in the ultimate relationship of blessedness between Christ and his true friend. Christ also gives a new, private name, which is written on something which sounds remarkably like the diamond of an engagement ring.[72]

The man who gives woman her name is not the same as the man who gave the animals their names. The languages of the Bible (and many African languages) can make a distinction here which English unfortunately cannot make without a lot of verbiage. But man who named the animals was man in general, man-as-mankind, man-as-opposed-to-animal. But a lesser man now appears, man-as-opposed-to-woman, man from whom woman has been divided off. Man-as-mankind has been split; he has been divided into male and female elements, and the major part of the female element (plus a minor part of the male) has been isolated to form a separate being; the mainly male element has been also isolated to make a separate being. And so man (man-

mankind rather than male-man) becomes conscious of the male-female polarity in his/her self; man is a dual being, capable of bearing the distinction from God and the distinction from animal. Without this duality, the aloneness, or uniqueness (which is the same thing), of man becomes unbearable. Without this, man is alone in his limitedness as opposed to God, and in his consciousness of his limitedness as opposed to animal. Man may try to deny his nature by trying to escape into one or other of the realms which are not his; but at precisely this point man and woman help each other, just by existing as man and woman, not as either god or animal. *But*, where people fail to acknowledge God and put their hopes and adoration on to the spouse as a God-substitute, and on to the marriage and home as a heaven-substitute, something gives way. Father Victor White, commenting on the common assertion that marriage breakdowns are due to a loss of the sense of the sanctity of marriage, says that 'these catastrophes are more often to be attributed to the fact that unconsciously marriage has been regarded as *too* sacred rather than otherwise, and hence required to bear a weight too heavy for it, and which in other days carried *it*. Sex is expected to provide a mystical union, the partner a divinity, the home a heaven – each, in short, is required to provide a substitute for religion and to be saddled with a task to which each is of its nature unequal.'[73]

On the other hand, woman is, like male-man, formed ultimately from earth and has the form of animal. Yet to think only in animal terms makes the physical activity shared with animals impossible through mental or spiritual inhibition. Sex without love does not work, as sex; it becomes, as Dhlamini in Peter Abrahams' *Return to Goli* discovered, like nothing more than passing water.[74]

Often people are oppressed by the inadequacy of a symbol to convey a wide and complex meaning – poets and artists and lovers are always feeling hampered by this; but it is far worse the other way round, where a deep and complex symbol is used to express something which is trivial and undemanding; this is the overwhelmingly grievous thing. When the massive symbol of sex is exercised in all its power for a frivolous and shallow feeling, there is, and should be, one hell of a hangover.[75] Fromm warns: 'Sexual attraction creates, for the moment, the illusion of union, yet without love this "union" leaves strangers as far apart as they were before – sometimes it makes them ashamed of each other, or even makes them hate each other, because when the illusion has gone they feel their estrangement even more markedly than before.'[76] Another well-known authority reminds us of the inadequacy of thinking of sex primarily in animal or biological terms: 'It is customary to illustrate sexology chapters with a cross-section of the human body. The authors have chosen to substitute in its place a map of the North Atlantic, showing aeroplane routes. The authors realise that this will be of no help to the sex novice, but neither is a cross-section of the human body.'[77] In other words, the task of teaching people what sex is really about, which can never be much more than a series of hints at the best of times, should probably not start with the biological aspect, which man shares with other mammals, but with the uniquely human aspect. A meditation on the Song of Songs may be a better introduction than a discourse on Fallopian tubes.

GENESIS 2: 24
That is why a man leaves his father and mother and is united to his wife, and the two become one flesh.

This verse brings us abruptly into the present tense. It shows us that the story which we are reading is not told just as an anecdote from the distant past. It is told because it has an immediate practical relevance. It shows that the story is about *us*, not merely about the inhabitants of a 'paradise' that long ago was 'lost'. In fact, this verse asserts the power of marriage, as a present reality, to modify and judge all systems which are based on the power of the past. A man leaves his past and moves into his present. Nowadays, many people who would claim to be deeply committed to the cause of justice and a new order, condemn marriage as one of many institutions which are decaying and obsolete. But, in its true nature, marriage is one of man's most precious bulwarks against tyranny. The following quotation is not from a recognized Christian theologian, but is nonetheless deeply true:

'The marriage-tie is the fundamental connecting link in Christian society. Break it, and you will have to go back to the overwhelming dominance of the state, which existed before the Christian era. Christianity brought marriage into the world – marriage as we know it. Christianity has established the little autonomy of the family within the greater rule of the state. It is marriage, perhaps, which has given man the best of his freedom, given him his little kingdom of his own within the big kingdom of the state, given him his foothold of independence on which to stand and resist an unjust state.... If we do break marriage, it means we all fall to a greater extent under the direct sway of the state.'[78]

This is the primary relationship, before all others. A tyrannous state will deny this, either in word or practice. A tyrannous state will treat the marriages of its subjects as something to protect only when it is convenient to do so, and as something to disregard if ideology has prior claims. So, a tyrannous state will say that a man may cleave to his wife – *unless* she happens to be of a different race group, or *unless* she happens to have been born in the wrong part of the country, or *unless* there happens to be something wrong with her documents. In South Africa, thousands of families are disrupted every year by a state system which gives to its ideology a higher regard than it gives to the biblical understanding of marriage.

Those who want to control man most effectively conspire against the autonomy of marriage, and find themselves trying to put asunder what God has joined.

Man and woman are to be one flesh. Part of the meaning of this is, of course, that they are to be one unit of activity in sexual intercourse. But sexual intercourse is not itself the oneness; it symbolizes and expresses a oneness which has a much deeper and wider range of meaning.

For God does not say 'It is not good that man should have no sexual outlet' but 'It is not good for the man to be alone'. The chaste unmarried person is conscious of a lack of sexual expression; but the biggest thing he gets with marriage is not really sex but community, with sex as a symbol of it and as a power within it.

When the apostolic brotherhood was trying to find some metaphor that could do justice to the work of Christ, it searched around in its experience and lighted upon this 'one flesh' relationship between man and woman in marriage.[79] For Christians this is the greatest thing that can be said about marriage, that in it we have our best picture of the relationship which is at the heart of our salvation. 'This is a great mystery' indeed, as the writer to the Ephesians says, and he does get splendidly confused. Our marriage service boldly gives us this confusion to expound. It is the most worthwhile word to expound at the marriage service. When, in practice, we can get similarly confused between the character of Christ's work and the character of our marriages, then for us too the symbol will be fulfilling its purpose.

The statement about a man leaving his parents and cleaving to his wife is almost the only generalization in this chapter. As a specific statement in the mouth of Adam, it would be singularly unconvincing, Adam being the one man who had no parents to leave, according to the story! But it is a remarkable doctrine to emerge from the patriarchal setting of the Hebrews; it is, in fact, a statement which is far more congenial to the modern nuclear family than to the tribal society of the author.

There is a lot of talk about differences of culture these days, sometimes from people who have come to feel that naked racialism is a bit indecent but who want some other pretext for maintaining separations and group supremacy. It is said that we must not ride rough-shod over people's cultures, that we must allow them to develop within their cultural inheritance; and, specifically, it is said that we must not force norms of marriage and family life on to people who are not culturally ready for them, and that while the biblical ideal of the family may be good for the whites, with their many generations of Christian civilization, it is unfair to expect 'the Natives' to accept it.

This kind of argument is often pretty nauseating, as it is so often expressed with judgemental condescension and superiority. It shows the same sort of attitude as that expressed in a South African newspaper editorial some months ago, to the effect that we (whites) must do something about the problems of the Coloureds because 'the Coloureds are the product of the white man's lust'. A Coloured man said to me the next day: 'So, it's nice to know for sure that I'm the product of lust; and you, of course, are the product of love, aren't you?' The fact remains that there has, indeed, been a lot of misunderstanding about culture, and a lot of confusion between Christianity and white cultural factors. What ought to be clear is that Christ demands as big a revolution among whites as among everyone else. Christianity is indeed unsuited to Africans, as Africans are by nature; equally, it is unsuited to Europeans, as Europeans are by nature. Quite apart from cultural differences, all men, in all groups, have sinned and fallen short of the glory of God, and all need a radical repentance if they are to find Christ as Lord. Christ is certainly non-European, and non-African. And this little verse about marriage shows this very sharply. The society to which this word was addressed and in which this word was written, was as tribal and patriarchal as any tribal society could be. The natural, cultural character of that society was past-looking, parent-centred, ancestor-dominated, and polygamous, a society which allowed little personal identity for a wife.[80] It would be difficult to exaggerate the revolutionary demand represented by this verse. Its justification is not that it *suits* us but that it is the truth. And its demand is not necessarily reduced in a less tribal society. Many modern, detribalized people find it very difficult indeed to *leave* father and mother, to cease to be dominated by the demands of their parents' images, and to treat the spouse as a genuinely contemporary person. A woman, for instance, may want a man, and get him, and may assume that she has got a husband; but *he* may be really wanting a substitute mother to attend to the anxious baby that is crying deep inside him. The resulting misunderstandings and disappointment may be considerable.

This verse is, therefore, a serious critique of all of us, whatever our culture. The author must have had a very strong sense that, in spite of all the outward relationships of

his contemporary society, in spite of the institutional dominance of parent and the relative insignificance of wife, a
man's main movement is away from relationships with the
past and into relationships of the present, away from areas
where he has had no choice and into areas of his own
responsibility. And he must also have had a strong sense that,
in spite of the fact that man is born of woman and is taken
out of her, in spite of the fact that woman may feel un-
completed without child, nonetheless the primary feeling is
man's sense of incompleteness without woman, that she has
been taken from him and that he is deprived of part of
himself without her, and that he must somehow find her for
himself and not depend only on relationship with mother.
This is a mandate to man to be his own contemporary, to
evaluate things in terms of his own situation and not only
by reference to the past. There is a mandate here both to
parents to give liberation to their children and to children
to receive liberation from their parents; neither of these is
easy or congenial. There can be no history at all if children
are primarily bound to conformity with parents, and there
can be no progress if the children's primary motivation is
hostile revolt against parents, for its own sake. Counter-
dependence can be just as much a bondage as excessive
dependence; they both force the present into an inappropriate subjection to the past. Christianity has often appeared
to be an influence to prevent revolt, to encourage acceptance
of an unacceptable present. This is betrayal of the Lord of
history, by encouraging a detachment from history on the
part of the Lord's conscious agents. However great may be
the problems presented by our young people in revolt, the
conformity of young people is a more serious problem in the
long run.

The most painful form of this strain, which pastors are
often privileged to watch, is when a good child, because of
his goodness, is obliged to revolt against the goodness of his
parents. It can be difficult and costly on both sides; both
sides can feel that the normal inter-personal armaments
cannot justly be used; and human language is probably inadequate at this point, in so far as it has been developed to
express resentment and fear better than experimental trust.

Once again, there is a normative experience of this in the figure of Jesus; Luke's account of the family visit to the temple shows the process starting when he was at the very beginning of adolescence.[81] The effect of his witness was to abolish the boundaries between the family of his past and the associations of his present.[82] And Mary's presence at the cross confirmed Simeon's word, that it is through the ideal mother of the best of sons that the sword penetrates most thoroughly.[83]

GENESIS 2: 25

Now they were both naked, the man and his wife, but they had no feeling of shame towards one another.

Commentators often seem to assume that this verse means that man and woman were not conscious of their sexuality. This consciousness, they say, came with the Fall, and it was because of their lack of such consciousness that they could be naked. It will be more convenient to deal with this matter later in the story, when we have to consider the meaning of 'shame'; but we can observe now that the interpretation referred to seems to be exactly the opposite of the truth. A man cannot say of a woman, 'This is it – bone of my bone and flesh of my flesh', without being aware of sexuality down to the roots of his being. The discovery that another person can be such a complete physical and psychological counterpart makes a difference to the whole tone of life around. Such a discovery may be frustrating, because man has developed his ability to experience much better than he has his ability to communicate. But, frustrating though it may be, this awareness of sexuality is a blessedness; and the more naked the man and woman are, the less they should be ashamed, if they are committed to each other by this 'bone of my bone' mutuality. Shame is not the consciousness of sexuality but a concern to hide it: but this is anticipating a later stage of the story.

CHAPTER SIX

Second Interval

Now begins a real living story. And because of its imaginative detail, we have to take care that we think of it in the proper way. As a story, it is nearer to the form of Christ's parables than to anything in a history book. The proper question to ask of it, as of the parable of the Prodigal Son, is not 'Did this happen?' but 'Does this happen?' This is not an account of the predicament of the first existing man so much as an account of the predicament of me. It is an account of man in revolt. Is it true to at least something of what we observe in ourselves?

This is the purpose of myth; it is one way, a very good way, of communicating truth. For all communication there must be some sort of code; the most bare literal facts are communicated in one sort of code. Myth is another kind of code; it is to be judged good myth in so far as it communicates something useful to me about me. It may be that in some cases the biblical myths do not speak as efficiently as they might do, because of the differences of background between the communicators of those days and the readers now. In that case, it may well be necessary to demythologize. But the best comment on this that I have heard was by a very fundamentalist Pentecostal preacher, who said of Jesus' healing miracles: 'I would agree entirely that we must demythologize these stories. And how? By stopping thinking of them as past history and seeing that they are happening now. Then they cease to be *only* myths and become saving truth about us now.'

We spoil the real significance of this story if we insist on arguing primarily about its historical accuracy.

And yet . . . The educated white man says this sort of thing to his equally educated African friend, and it all seems so obvious to the white man with his confidence in the difference between literal truth and symbolic truth. There remains a pitying doubt in the black man's eyes, and he insists on

some such question as 'But what sort of tree was it, in fact?'
Is this just the persistence of the pious literalism forced into
Africans by the mission schools (which get the blame for
everything), or is it something more?

Two different people may believe apparently similar
things but for different reasons. African literalism seems to
spring from motivations different to those of English-speaking
fundamentalism. For instance, among English-speaking
Christians, biblical conservatism is often allied to political
conservatism; amongst many Africans, biblical conservatism
more often seems to stimulate people to political critique
and activism. History is important in Africa, not because of
what did or did not happen in the past but because it is 'a
remembrance of that which was in the Beginning'.[1] The
people of the past are *our* people, and they must have had a
beginning. For something to belong to *us*, it must be related
to our beginning, and therefore the details of the Beginning
are important for the African, as they were for the Hebrew.
In their traditional ideas about marriage and land-tenure,
and in their myths, Africans are closer to the Hebrews than
either ancient Greeks or modern Anglo-Saxons. They have
not always had an awareness of history; their most ancient
interpretations of the world and of nature have been in
terms of repetitive cycles of events. But the Christian mission
came to them, and at the same time they experienced unprecedented strains in the encounter with better-armed
people from a different continent, with all the ensuing
problems of changes in land-tenure, of enslavement, of
oppression. An interpretation of events in terms of history
was necessary to enable people to live with such problems,
and such an interpretation was there to hand in the teaching
of the missionaries. Hebrew history was the first history they
had heard, and so Africans came to identify themselves with
the Hebrews, and with the hopes and situation of the
Hebrews; they could feel that 'this is *our* history' in a way
that few Anglo-Saxons can. Enoch Mgijima went so far as
to found a new Church which he called 'Israelites', in which
both Sabbath and Passover were celebrated, and which
formed a militant army to fight God's holy war against the
unbelievers (i.e. the whites).[2] This sort of love for and

identification with the people of the Old Testament continually appears in the prophetic movements in Africa, where people feel themselves to be an oppressed and downtrodden people like the Hebrews. English people, who have not known an invasion for 900 years, may find it difficult to sympathize with this; but they have only to cross into the areas of Welsh nonconformity to find signs of a similar outlook – a passion for the great apocalyptic symbols, a wealth of meaning attached to a word like 'Jordan', an enthusiasm for the corporate singing of very individualized hymns. Critics accuse such people of idolizing symbols, and of indulging in escapism with their 'heavenly-bosom' God. This may be valid; but such critics are usually from one of the boss-nations and speak from a situation of cultural security; and they should always beware lest their critique be merely disguised boasting, which is just another kind of imperialism.

Europeans find it easy to forget that 'Christ' means 'Messiah'. Africans really cannot, because their situation so urgently demands a deliverer. 'A Christ is expected wherever history is regarded as potentially meaningful but is still awaiting full disclosure and fulfilment of its meaning.' So says Reinhold Niebuhr, as he distinguishes between peoples who expect a Messiah and value the concept and those who do not.[3] This is the same as the distinction between people who value 'good news' and those who do not. Anglo-Saxons have the saying that no news is good news; it is better, for them, that there should not be news, and therefore the only good news is that there is no news. For those with power and security, news is most probably going to be news of a threat, and an absence of news is blessedness. Therefore, if Christ is good, he is not news; and English-style Christianity often appears to be a conspiracy to prevent Christ from being news. On the whole, the boss-nations do not feel a need for a Christ, a figure who can be a critic and intervener in history; on the whole, oppressed people do feel such a need. This may be one of the many points at which there is a rapport between African and Afrikaner which is quite impenetrable to the English mind. The latter just does not have the same awareness of a need for a deliverer; the only gospel, or good news, of Christ is that he is not Christ at all, but just a religious figure in a holy niche, with no significance for history. For many Africans, the idea of a deliverer and the idea of Zion are inseparable. Here again, the Bible has come to them at the same time as political disturbance, and has enabled them to interpret it. As with the Hebrews, the concept of Messiah came in and took hold in a situation of colonialism and oppression. Previously, in both nations, the concept was unknown and would have been intolerable to their democratic ideals. But now, the demand is for a Messiah, for a Zion, for a charismatic leader and a heavenly brotherhood of followers; and if this is not to be found in the 'established' Churches, the demand will be met elsewhere.

Some Messiah they must have, and if Jesus of Nazareth seems too much of a white tribal god, they will make a Messiah out of Isaiah Shembe or another hero. For them, as for the Hebrews, Zionism and Messianism are inseparable. It is no accident that the greater number of our separatist religious bodies are known as Zionists, and that every one of these many bodies brings the name 'Zion' somehow into its title. There is something here which is reminiscent of the Russian mind, as described by Bishop Fison: 'The futurism of the apocalyptic sects combined with eastern orthodox mysticism to produce a climate of opinion in which it would not have been in the least surprising if Christ really had appeared.' 'To the Western mind', he continues, quoting Christopher Hollis, 'the most childish part of communism is its belief that a political and economic revolution can effect a radical transformation of human nature. It is only as we read the history of nineteenth-century Russia and Russian literature that we understand that the Russians were expecting such a transformation anyway, long before they had heard of Lenin or of Karl Marx.'[4]

Having this instinctive Messianism in common with Africa, together with a much more appropriate tradition of liturgical singing, Russian Christianity might have been a far better evangelizing agency than our 'Western' Churches for this part of the world. It is not entirely irrelevant that at a crucial point in her people's relations with the British, the Xhosa prophetess Nongqause proclaimed: 'The Russians are *Kaffirs* like ourselves. They have defeated the British and will come here to defeat them once more.'[5] (This, we might observe, was sixty years before the Revolution and nearly ninety years before the passing of the Suppression of Communism Act!) For many Africans, Adam is characterized as a *suffering* Adam, and the Russian liturgy repeatedly speaks of 'the suffering people of Russia'. This stress on suffering may be especially apt for the present generations, but suffering is the outstanding historical feature of the Russian people, so disturbed by invasion and warfare similar to that which stimulated Nongqause to her prophecy. How much of their religious character is due just to this openness and vulnerability to invaders – the simple fact that in the whole of European Russia and western Siberia there is only one area which rises above 1,500 feet?

Be that as it may, it does seem that for boss-nations, for communities old enough and dominant enough to be able to despise nationalism, timeless generalizations about religious truth will suffice; but let them beware of scorning the downtrodden peoples who instinctively feel a need for corporate self-consciousness, and express it by taking to themselves the stories of the Beginning. The chances are that such people will be grasped by the gospel in these stories more deeply than the confident extroverts of Anglo-Saxon dominance.

For instance, Sundkler describes at length a magnificent sermon of the Revd Michael Mzobe:[6] in it, the story of man's disorder is given in detail through the eyes of Adam, who has a grandstand view of the world from Paradise: all through, Adam is the one who suffers, seeing the results of his first sin: but the whole point of the sermon is to describe his joy when he sees Christ giving to the Father the good news of the victory won on Easter Day. For this African preacher, it was impossible to preach Easter without going back to the Beginning: the Beginning must be part of the gospel.

Those who have a deep need for the word of God to speak to them of their origins and of their history may well be offended by the use of the word 'myth' as a description of these stories in Genesis. And they will have strong support

183

from no less an authority than Professor von Rad, who says quite uncompromisingly: 'What we ought not to say about these stories is that they are mythical. In respect of inner character, nothing is more opposed to the world of genuine myth than the enlightened and sober lucidity of this account of creation [in Genesis 2], which is so far removed from abstruse mythology.'[7] Of course, it all depends on what you mean by myth. In the profound and significant understanding of myth previously quoted from Berdyaev,[8] the word 'myth' is still appropriate. But we do not have to look far to see how the mythical or mythological element in a story can be so stressed that the story loses its power to speak universally and convincingly; if we compare the simple picture of Adam in Eden, in Genesis 2, with the fancy elaboration of Ezekiel,[9] we see how easily myth can degenerate into something which can no longer be about 'me'. And presumably this is really what most people usually mean by 'myth'. We have a problem of language here; things, as we have seen, are not really known until they are named; and we do not have a word which exactly fits the kind of writing which is before us in these chapters, just as Aristotle did not have a word for 'literature' and Newton did not have a word for 'science'. This material is not quite history, not quite myth, not quite theology, or law, or science, or metaphysics, or drama, or parables, or legend. Possibly the best term is von Rad's phrase, 'inner history'.

But this story of Adam remains an intuitive rather than an analytical method of communicating truth; it is poetry – it is not merely a fancy way of saying what could be expressed more simply in plain language: it is an attempt to express something *more* complex than itself, not less complex. As with a proper poem, there is no simple 'prose translation', there is no satisfactory rendering of its meaning into ideas or abstractions. This is not a *theory* of evil; it is not consistent or organized enough to be a theory. It is fascinating to see how the writer spoils the argument, deprives himself of neat coherence, in order to avoid saying something which would be against his basic beliefs. Neither is it an account of the *origin* of evil; it is a witness to the present character of evil in its extraordinarily paradoxical way of working through good things – the tree, the woman, the serpent, the good creatures of God. The writer will not allow evil to be attributed to God; nor will he allow it to be an equal and opposite force to good. He gives no account of its source; it emerges in the creation with no observed mechanism. There is no one to blame for evil outside itself; it is just there. It is not as if a devil comes in from outside to carry the blame; that would lead us away from experience into an alien world of theological speculation. Even the concept of evil itself is not there. Evil things simply happen, and bring a curse.

There is something very modern about the Genesis story here; it is like a play by Beckett, or Pinter, or Osborne; here is this situation; there is no arguing, no organizing, no rationalizing; there is no 'little solution rattling away down there in the centre of the play like a motto in a Christmas cracker'.[10] The guilt is on man; it is inconceivable; and it is there.

We have considered that there may be difficulties with the idea that the creation emerged *ex nihilo*, out of nothing. It may be much more appropriate to say that *evil* emerged *ex nihilo*; we cannot master the mechanics of its development or isolate its origin. It is just *there*; and we know it.

CHAPTER SEVEN

Tragedy

GENESIS 3: 1

The serpent was more crafty than any wild creature that the Lord God had made. He said to the woman, 'Is it true that God has forbidden you to eat from any tree in the garden?'

THE SERPENT

ENTER the serpent. May we be very naïve and ask, 'Why a serpent?' The characters we have had so far, the man, the woman, the tree, have been universal and central to human experience. But even in Africa, most people do not meet snakes every day. Concerning verses 14 to 19 of this chapter, many commentators say this sort of thing: 'This story is recorded to explain the origin of certain familiar facts of our experience.'[1] This explanation works all right with regard to the pain of childbirth, the hardness of agricultural work, and the certainty of death; but in terms of this theory, man feels a need for an explanation of the snake's method of locomotion as much as he feels a need for an explanation of the pains of childbirth, which is really rather odd; there are so many other features of our life, far more central than snakes, which could be explained. If it is so necessary to have all this about snakes, why not something about rainfall, cow's milk, houses, colour, temperature or disease – things which are of far more importance to man, on the face of it, than snakes?

And yet we cannot get away from the extraordinary fascination that snakes have for the human mind, whether in fact snakes are common in a particular area or not. Snakes are embodiments of the dead (a Zulu may see a snake on his son's grave and say, 'Look, there is my son'). They are symbols of immortality; they appear sometimes as female symbols, sometimes as phallic symbols (St Paul may have accepted the belief that Eve was sexually seduced by the serpent[2]). In one of the most popular children's games, the significance of the 'ladders' for ascending is obvious, but why 'snakes' for the descent? There can be no animal which has attracted more legends around it. In Southern Africa, Zionist faith-healers often diagnose sickness as being due to the presence of a snake in the stomach; on the other hand, it is not very long since, in a more 'civilized' country, snake dung was believed to be a cure for cancer. There is something about snakes which gives them highly optimistic speedometers – most snake stories seem to exaggerate the size and speed of these creatures, the fastest of which moves only at the speed of a man's normal walk; and the belief dies hard that they are slimy. In Scripture they are poisonous dangers to God's people.[3] But they are also holy and healing; to look at the image of a snake cures the snake-bite,[4] and around the throne of God fly the seraphim, the angelic winged serpents that form the highest of the nine orders of heavenly beings.[5] The image of the serpent was a centre of idolatrous worship,[6] and was a forecast of the crucified Christ lifted up for the healing of the world.[7] It would seem that our Genesis storyteller has chosen the snake as a symbol of subtlety because of the unique subtlety which man has exercised in his thought about snakes.

If this is so, then there is a very good reason for giving the snake problem its odd prominence in the story; for it is clear that there is nothing else in the whole of man's symbol-making which is so ambivalent as the snake, there is nothing in his mind which so drastically pulls together opposite characteristics into one thing, there is nothing in his imagination which so continuously expresses a co-existence of incompatibles in one set of terms. The snake can stand for the strain of good-and-evil found together in one entity, the mixed nature of good-and-evil which we know to be such an inhibition in our decision-making, the bi-polarity which makes the cross at once the best and the worst event in history. At the end of things, by the victory of grace, the serpent is defeated, and man is released for the freedom for which he is designed.[8] In the meantime, man's way to the good state of maturity is mainly through the difficult and often wrecking road of compromise and doubt. Man's extreme indecision about the snake reflects his indecision about himself.

THE QUESTION

The serpent in Genesis 3 is not the Devil. Its characteristic is not wickedness, but wiliness or subtlety. Its purpose is to follow arguments where they lead, disinterestedly, but not to corrupt. But those who do this are often accused, like Socrates, of corrupting. And often those who are so influenced may be corrupted; but this again is something bad emerging inexplicably from something good. So the serpent starts a discussion; 'Did God say "You shall not eat of any tree of the garden"?' An innocent question; it wants to establish the exact words spoken. The answer quite clearly is 'No'; God did not say this; the words are an extensive exaggeration of what God did say. But this is the beginning of a religious discussion, which cannot proceed unless there is doubt for it to work on. Religious discussion is an evidence of the fallen world, and doubts about God are an inevitable part of the fallen condition. The task of theology is to raise questions about God, to ensure that people do not fail to give the best of their gifts of thought and awareness to the ultimate questions. The snake is the first theologian. His duty is to ensure that the question is faced, for an unbelief which is repressed is a far more dangerous enemy of faith than any conscious doubt. And the question is not a matter of remote speculation: it deals very directly with my own need and nature. The question, 'Did God say . . . ?' means to me, 'Is this the authentic way for me to be a person – to see a prohibition on every tree?'

The theologian will often find that he is far behind the poets and artists in facing such questions. Breughel, for instance, in his *Adoration of the Kings*, insists that we face the near-impossibility of Christian belief. Most of us are used to pictures of this subject in which the whole scene is obviously divine, with pretty angels as normal features of the landscape. But Breughel's version shows a baby wrapped in a shroud, an environment full of instruments of war, a crowd where everyone from king to peasant is grotesque and uncomprehending; this world is one which crucifies its Messiah. The same kind of ambivalence is expressed most potently in Britten's *War Requiem*; in the Catholic, corporate words of the Requiem Mass, the Church expresses her faith in the care and love of God, which are stronger than death and its horrors; against this is thrown the poetry of Wilfred Owen, expressing the wasteful tragedy of death, the faith-destroying experience of man's refusal to accept his brother man. The brilliant ecstasy of the Sanctus cannot stand without the complete despair of 'After the blast of lightning from the East'; and the Agnus Dei gives us the most potent experience of the discontinuity between the will and peace of God, on the one hand, and the betrayal of that will and peace by the apostasy of God's servants on the other. Anything less wrenching than this cannot do true justice to a world situation which demands a gospel of salvation. If there is no validity in doubt, if the question of God is obvious except to the deliberately dishonest, there would be no need for any incarnation, and the cross would be an impossibility. We may make arguments and theories about the reasons for the death of Jesus, we may try to psychologize or rationalize about it. But the Gospels do not; they tell the tale in a way very much like the writer of our Genesis story; they do not try to explain it, or draw a moral. If we could produce a complete and adequate analysis of the mechanisms that led to the death of Christ, the very fact that we could do so would indicate that we did not really need such salvation after all – but then, in that case there would have been no crucifixion. No atheist polemic can be so hostile to the Christian faith as the play or picture which implies that the birth of Jesus was a pretty nice event in a pretty nice world, that the cross was quite cute too, or at the worst an un-fortunate and uncharacteristic oversight. If the Incarnation was a dire necessity and the Crucifixion its inevitable result, the existence and will of God must be a matter of faith rather than sight, against which argument after argument can be brought. Much of our 'religious' art and drama fails to present the case against God strongly enough to represent the agonies which are at the heart of Scripture.

The snake tries to analyse the nature of God, and asks

whether a certain word is or is not the kind of thing which God says. This may be nothing more serious than a question of imagination; some people make the mistake of thinking that they cannot believe in God because they cannot imagine him, for instance, answering everybody's prayers at once. But difficulty of imagination is quite tolerable in other fields, and is no real worry. I cannot *imagine* what is happening to the molecules of oil in the differential of a car going round a corner at 50 m.p.h., but I can *know* what is happening. As far as imagination goes, I find it far easier to think that the car is propelled by a petrol-loving genie than to picture all the furious activity of roller-bearings and auto-advance and valve-springs at 3000 r.p.m. (But I suppose that the hard-boiled unbeliever would say that this just goes to show how much I have been conditioned to believe in any old nonsense.)

But more seriously, we ask whether this word of God fits in to what we think we know about him. This is the stock-in-trade of theology, and its danger; we make God a subject of study, we try to understand him who stands over us; we try to explain him, to make him clear. It is impossible enough to understand a person; Stephen Potter makes his Lawrence-man say, 'I think a man can make his words clear, and even his thoughts. But himself . . . ?'[9] So one human creature can bandy words about God with another; one person gets a first in theology and another fails; the knowledge of God becomes a subject of competition like botany or bowls, and God becomes a commodity which we can corner.

But it is dangerous for the theologian to think of his subject as the queen of sciences. Isaiah puts the theologian's question back where it belongs: 'To whom, then, will you liken me, whom set up as my equal? asks the Holy One.'[10] How can you know the *sort* of thing God says? It was right of Roger Tennant to say, in the publication called *Theology*: 'Theology is a purely Christian phenomenon; a sin that only Christians commit.'[11] The man of God is not necessarily the theologian but the person who has heard the word of God and holds firm to it. It is *doing* the Sermon on the Mount, not the interpreting of it, that is required.[12] We are not required to put ourselves in the position of judge on his word. If the word is just one among many words, then we can weigh it up – we can decide whether it is good to have a rule about not bearing false witness, whether it makes sense to turn the other cheek. But these imperatives are given as indications of the will of him who says them; they are not just epigrams or valuable bits of advice. If we accept them, it is not because they will make people good or help in the struggle against communism: it is because they speak of the mind of God, and because we believe in God and are committed to him.

In the history of Christian doctrine, there have been many occasions when the biblical understanding has been bent to fit the presuppositions of the day, which have been derived from alien sources. We come to the Bible assuming that we know what words like 'God', 'heaven' and 'faith' are about. We do not let the Scripture judge our assumptions; without realizing what we are doing, we make our assumptions judge Scripture. So we find ourselves insisting that people of other cultures accept not only the Scripture but the distortions which we have worked into Scripture from our culture. This has obvious dangers across the culture-gaps of geography – the linguistic and ethnic differences of mankind. It is equally disastrous across the culture-gaps of history – the differences of attitude between the generations. Inevitably, the young take their learning from the old; but it is easy for the old to systematize and generalize their understanding in such a way as to bind the young to the old people's particular bias and interpretation. The Scripture itself should be a warning to us to beware of the danger of tying down words to limited meanings; it is a continual reminder that a word's primary value is not the generalized meaning which is found in the dictionary, but the actual difference which it makes in the context in which it is used. For instance, it can be very valuable to forget all that we think that we know about the meaning of a word like 'faith', and examine anew all the references in the Gospels to faith and lack of faith and try to see precisely what it is, in each instance, that is present or absent. If we do this, we shall probably find something far less generalized, far less magical, something far more immediate and practical, than the meaning which our particular culture has attached to the word 'faith'. If once we start allowing God's word to judge our assumptions in this way, there's no knowing where it can take us; we will, maybe, find that it will exercise a far more potent critique upon our social and political order, on our church habits and institutions. Without such a readiness to be judged, we will use our Bible-study merely to confirm our existing understandings and misunderstandings; and we will find ourselves perpetuating that extraordinarily successful enterprise, the Devil's ancient conspiracy of making God's word dull.

GENESIS 3: 2–3

The woman answered the serpent, 'We may eat the fruit of any tree in the garden, except for the tree in the middle of the garden; God has forbidden us either to eat or to touch the fruit of that; if we do, we shall die.'

The crafty serpent offers an idea of God which is false and can easily be knocked down. So the woman puts herself, consciously, on God's side, and knocks it down. She makes the effort of judging, and judges rightly. God's command was not as severe as the serpent's question had suggested. But there is a definite attraction in making it more severe than it actually is; part of the value of having an authority-figure is that he is clearly identified as the person against whom we can direct our resentment. We like to have an authority against whom we can feel we have legitimate grounds for complaint. The demands of an ogre-god can be preferred to the less sensational will of the true God. Woe indeed to the church or pastor who seeks to subdue people with rules and pressures derived from this kind of motivation.[13] An ogre-god begins to appear in the woman's answer. She elaborates God's prohibition – she claims that not only eating but even touching is forbidden. All sorts of resentment are emerging in her. She cannot say why there is this prohibition; she cannot even identify the tree properly, because she does not have the proper terminology: the term 'the knowledge of good and evil' has not come into her language – it would make no more sense to her than a term like 'Ptaeroxylon obliquum'. So she just calls it 'the tree in the middle of the garden'; and so the discussion begins.

GENESIS 3: 4–5

The serpent said, 'Of course you will not die. God knows that as soon as you eat it, your eyes will be opened and you will be like gods^c knowing both good and evil.'

c) Or *God*.

The woman has been unwilling to answer the serpent's question with a straight 'No'. 'No' has been the only proper answer, but she has felt that this is too simple, too unsophisticated a reply to give to the sophisticated serpent. So she has allowed untruth to obtain a small foothold in her. By her apparently insignificant exaggeration she has lost part of her integrity. She has exposed an area of vulnerability; and the serpent immediately takes advantage of this, in a direct attack.

The serpent states baldly that what God has said is not true. In one sense, as the subsequent story indicates, the serpent is correct. How is the woman to deal with this contradiction? Further, the serpent promises that she will be like God. How can this be? God has the liberty to make man in his own image, but how can man make himself to be like his maker? Only if 'God' can mean something other than the one who makes us and has dominion over us – only if 'God' can be something that we design. There can be both the God who makes us in his own image and a god in our minds which we can aspire to be like by our own exertions.

We are made in God's image. The new man, Jesus Christ, was the image of God. Christ was the new Adam, the Son of God, the means by which God showed himself; and he did not reckon equality with God as something to be striven for or grasped. The word of the serpent to the woman was not an effective temptation to him; he was content to be apparently unlike God, made in the likeness of men, in the form of a slave.[14] There is a real danger in schemes of piety which give us the ambition of becoming like God. The gospel of both the Old and New Testaments is that God has acted to make and remake us like himself, and that this is the deepest truth about us. Sin is to act as if this is not so, to behave as if we were less than we truly are, to refuse to trust in the existence of the larger part of our being, of which we may be unaware. 'Hence the belief arises that a man is no more than the self he knows. And it is from this identification of the known self with the total self that sin arises . . . this non-faith is denial of God's creativity. It is an attempt to find security in the limited me of which I am aware instead of the unlimited me which issues continuously from the fount of being, and of which I must be very largely unaware. Non-faith is total reliance on what can be grasped and held by conscious reflection and implemented by conscious acts of the will. This is the bogus sovereignty claimed for the smaller part of himself by fallen Adam.'[15]

The woman is in this state of non-faith. Her attention has been drawn to prohibitions and possibilities which make her aware of herself as something less than she really is. She does not see her likeness to God – she sees her unlikeness, and acts as if this is the only truth about her. This is the fault of all sinners, and of the sinful society, the Church, also. Its failure is often that of trying to prove something to itself instead of being satisfied with the greatness of what it really is; because it is insensitive to the range of success implied in being the Body of Christ – a success of sacrifice, identification, atonement – it finds itself having to bolster itself up by competing with the advertising of the world in its clamour, in drawing attention to itself: 'This place is the temple of the Lord, the temple of the Lord, the temple of the Lord!'[16] This is not quite pride and not quite greed. It is feeling that one is smaller than one really is, then believing that this feeling is true, and then wanting to be more than one feels one is. In the corporate history of the People of God, it is significant that the compensation for this feeling is provided in the highest and holiest place. The Israelites in the desert cannot live all the time on manna, the indefinable grace of God, whose very name means only 'What is it?' They pray for daily bread and jam. They clamour for the fleshpots and yearn for the lovely garlic of the unblessed past. They can just put up with living on grace only, for as long as the agent of God is visibly with them. But when Moses has been out of sight for days on end, their sense of inadequacy becomes overpowering. They demand a god whom they can organize, one who will visibly establish them in their insecure identity, one who can be seen and not heard. And, as we have already observed, it is the high priest of the true God who gives them a golden calf; it is Moses' own brother who says, 'These are your gods, O Israel . . .'[17]

The most serious failure of Church or Christian is the failure to live by grace; we fail to realize that the security and the status which we need are already ours, as unearned gifts: and because of this failure, we take some unnecessary step to get or to preserve a security or a status for ourselves. We *get* a particular place in society; we *preserve* our racial identity; we *claim* the rewards of moral goodness. But in all this we are failing to live according to the one thing that matters, the grace of God; we are refusing his gift of createdness and redemption. By acting as if it were not there, we make our security a prize instead of a gift. Then, indeed, all our righteousness is as filthy rags, because it is being earned as a ticket of admission to the favour of God. The real enemy of sin is not the moral striving after virtue, which tends to classify men on a scale of deserving, but the accepting attitude of faith, which sees that even the most discouraging person is loved by the Creator.

It was a whole community's failure in this respect that put Christ on the cross. Israel was Israel; it could not have been more Israel; and yet, faced by the witness of the true Israelite, it felt that it had to preserve its Israel-ness, and so killed him. The law was good law, and Jesus came asserting it and obeying it in unprecedented depth; and yet, in order to preserve the values for which they thought the law stood, the law-bearers of the day crucified him.

This is the pattern of all inadequate behaviour. In the area of personal morality, for instance, the rapist violently grasps at a value for himself which he truly has; but he undervalues himself because this is a value which can properly be expressed to him only as a gift, by someone else's glad and loving assertion of his value. The same process can be seen at a very different level in the definition of

South African citizenship; the power-bearers of the country behave as if the nation were far smaller than it really is; the limitation of the 'nation' to one race-group means that there is no such thing as genuine South African citizenship; that which falsely calls itself South African citizenship is really only white citizenship.

The same kind of disorder affects our church life. In ecumenical relationships, the further we advance in exploration of technical problems, the more undisguised is our unwillingness to be made whole. Indeed, our experience often suggests that the small thing which we know we are works better and stirs more enthusiasm than the greater thing which we truly are.

As individuals and groups, again and again we fall into sin through trying to strain for and grasp an identity narrower than that which we already have; we act as though we can get security only at the expense of someone else's security. We often call this security and identity 'God' – my group's defence against the blacks or the communists, my personal defence against the godless man whose freedom or jolliness makes me ashamed. And so we find the true God to be our rival rather than our friend.

The answer to all this is the central Christian word of justification by grace through faith. We are what we really are because of what God has done in us, not because of any sectional characteristics of our own devising.[18] We have security in our access to God through Christ; we are expected to be bold in claiming and using it.[19] The emphasis which our Western liturgies teach us – both Catholic and Protestant – on 'Lord, I am not worthy' and 'We do not presume' needs to be balanced by the more truly evangelical theme which characterizes the liturgies of the Eastern Churches, 'We thank thee, O Lord, for that thou hast counted us worthy . . .'[20]

GENESIS 3: 6
When the woman saw that the fruit of the tree was good to eat, and that it was pleasing to the eye and tempting to contemplate, she took some and ate it. She also gave her husband some and he ate it.

196

The serpent's responsibility for the tragedy is made as small as possible; it has nothing more to say or do. The woman is not utterly carried away by its suggestions. She ponders, exercising both imagination and intellect; she cannot claim to have been swept off her feet by the serpent. She allows herself to become aware of a large number of considerations which make the fruit attractive to her; they all converge to assert to her a feeling of lack and inadequacy. Harry Williams summarizes her condition: 'The mark of the un-redeemed man is the craving for things to compensate him for not being fully what he is.'[21] Although there is plenty of food for her, she will feel deprived unless she has *this* food. The tree is beautiful to look at, but just to look at beauty is not enough; it makes her feel a lack of beauty in herself unless she can take it into herself; she cannot tolerate it being just outside her, only a thing of beauty. And she feels a need to absorb it intellectually, to contemplate it, to have a mastery over it which can save her from reliance on that which is outside herself, so as to make commitment to God unnecessary. She is attracted by the possibility of getting from a *thing* what can properly be got only from a person, that thing being at the same time a source of sensual and aesthetic satisfaction. Again, it is clear that *sin* is to act in accordance with a *felt* insecurity instead of in accordance with a *known* security; it is the act of non-faith; it is the reliance on a safe state organized by one's own initiatives instead of a trust in what is provided by that which is beyond oneself. And this is seen in its most concentrated form, which might almost be called idolatry, when a single thing is taken as the object of such a wide variety of lusts, when a single thing is given such high value by physical, aesthetic and intellectual assessments.

It is difficult to lock up the woman's offence in a single abstract noun, or in terms of a broken law. The story is not offered to us as an example of pride or greed, or any other generalization; nor is it an example on which a right attitude to law, as such, can be based. There is no universal law which can be based on the imperative which the man and the woman disregarded, and the whole episode is singularly un-rewarding as a moral anecdote. Sin, here, is not a breaking of a law, nor is it a particularization of an evil abstraction. Their action is a peculiar sin, which would not be sin in any other circumstances. The sinfulness is not in anything implicit in the action, but in the fact that in order to commit it, they change their priorities and act as if their relationship to God is not the primary concern of their beings. Sin is a denial or refusal of true relatedness; and so it is shown to us, not as an exemplification of general evil, nor as a breach of a universal moral code (how much easier it would be if they had done something *obviously* wrong, like dropping a bomb!), but as an act of rebellion, of dissociation with that which gives man meaning and a place in history; and this is basically what sin is about, all through the Bible.

The serpent has been talking and thinking; it has been exercising uniquely human abilities. In order to get the story going, it has been credited with the status of honorary, temporary human being. Now, we might excuse both the serpent and the woman by saying that their behaviour is 'only human nature'. The Fall, like so many other 'accidents', was brought about by 'the human element'. The tools used by the woman are her uniquely human equipment. She speaks and imagines; she handles memory, comparison and conceptualization. These are good things; they are not the cause of the trouble. The trouble comes because the woman lets these abilities govern her, instead of giving first place to her relatedness to God. And so she eats. Konrad Lorenz suggests that the apple was thoroughly unripe![22] Man hastily seized the fruit of knowledge and all the wealth that is derived from conceptual thought, but this has not yet been able to give him sufficient security to compensate him for his loss of basic relatedness. The faculties of conceptual thought and verbal speech have given man his most·distinctive mastery over other creatures: yet precisely these faculties give rise to the most serious dangers which threaten man with extinction, because he is unwilling to give priority to learning how to live in terms of his basic relatedness.

The woman accepts the statement of the serpent, and is persuaded by it. She allows herself to be motivated by the sense of insecurity which has been suggested to her. She acts on the assumption that her status is not a thing to receive

but to grasp for, to work for, to devise. A status which is pure
gift is not sufficiently reliable, and suggests the fear that one
may lose one's identity and be lost in the amorphous mass
of those who have no status at all. Christ, as we have noted,
had such a strong hold on the truth about himself that he
could be reckless concerning his security and his status. The
woman could have been so, but instead chose to grasp, in an
attempt to guarantee her status and security by her own
intervention. The same motivation is at work whenever we
find ourselves taking special steps to guarantee our identity.
We fear that we may get lost in the general mass of mankind,
and so we elevate to great importance the ineradicable
physical features which distinguish our group from others.
We make it essential to have the right features in order to
qualify for membership of society. We ensure that everybody
accepts the vital nature of racial identity by giving it
maximum importance in all areas of decision. And so we
learn to put the question of racial identity first, because,
until it is settled, we cannot decide where we can live, whom
we can marry, where our children can be educated, where
we can get medical attention, what work we can do, where
we can be buried. We demand and insist on and grasp our
identity like this because we feel insecure in our relationship
with God. God as Christians know him, God as Trinity, is
the guarantee of the distinctiveness of our identity; God is
eternally three distinct persons. Distinctiveness of identity is
a feature of the very heart of reality, of God himself; and if
we are adequately related to God, we know that our genuine
individuality is not going to be absorbed into an amorphous
mass, but is going to grow ever more personally unique. We
do not have to yield to the compulsion to grasp and organize
a phoney uniqueness, especially where it asserts the claims
of a minority by denying a place to the majority. We do not
have to devise and legalize a sectional status in order to
guarantee our survival. We receive our status as a gift from
God, on the same terms as everyone else. The Church is
supposed to be a model of society in this respect; it is a
community in which this acceptance of status at God's hands
is worked out in specimen form. Baptism and the eucharist
stand alike for the truth that the grace of God is the supremely

identifying fact about all of us; and to allow any other factor to take precedence over this is to forsake not only the brother who is given to us but also God who gives us that gift.

And so both the woman and the man are persuaded; and they eat. There is no explanation of this. Any adequate explanation would be an attack on the Creator; in fact, this is what we shall see beginning in the next section. But once done, the act cannot be undone; if the situation is to be cured, the cure must come from outside; and this is what the gospel of Jesus Christ is about. For this is no less than an attempt by the creature to create himself, and that means a revolt against having been created. The whole idea of createdness is shaken. It has to be rebuilt: and this is what Christ, the second Adam, does – from within the situation. When Christ appeared, resisting the infection of evil so that it could find no anchorage on him, frustrating evil's automatic reaction, religious men said no one could do this but God only, and they were right. They did not want this revolutionary principle of forgiveness to disturb the cause-and-effect of unforgiven habit; and so they crucified him who was the agent of this forgiveness.[23] Forgiveness is the activity of the Creator bringing relationship into existence where it was not. Those who find their createdness intolerable find forgiveness intolerable too.

Almost immediately, the man and the woman face each other in a hostility which can be healed only by mutual forgiveness; but this is not forthcoming.

Inevitably, we concentrate on the element of failure in all this story. We must bear in mind that only where failure is possible is success significant; this applies in every area of activity and endeavour. If man is to be in any sense a willing and responsible partner with God, he must be able to fail. The Fall is a guarantee that we are certainly dealing with man. The inhumanity of that which is pre-human presents no problem. Man is man in so far as he is not forced into being human. His goodness is not inevitable; his goodness does not necessarily bring rewards – God does not bribe man by sending his rain on the just only.

The failure of the man and the woman is a failure such as is common to people. It is not a failure which depends on a high degree of either intellectual or moral sophistication; such sophistication makes remarkably little difference to this kind of disorder. The story of the Fall has nothing particular to tell us about man's intellectual history; it may be worth noting this, because many people still seem to think that the Genesis story implies that the first man had a fantastic intellectual capacity, beyond the capacity of any subsequent wise man. Such a teaching would, of course, make the whole story much more difficult to accept and to relate to our own awareness. But, although Milton clearly believed in it, such a view is no more justified by Scripture than it is by anthropology.

GENESIS 3: 7

Then the eyes of both of them were opened and they discovered that they were naked; so they stitched fig-leaves together and made themselves loincloths.

SHAME

As the serpent had promised, the man and woman do not die; their eyes are opened. But the knowledge which results is certainly not that which was expected. Nakedness had been a blessing, but now it becomes a curse. The Hebrews were particularly sensitive about the shame of nakedness, which was, for them, one of the most horrible features of crucifixion – the universal loincloths on our dead crucifixes show that we can't face the full fact either. Shame comes in, as a means of protecting us from the full knowledge of the other, as a way of obscuring the differentness of the other. The Genesis story does not give us a worked-out argument; it simply states that the unhindered consciousness of sexual difference is part of the blessedness of creation, and that man and woman who are in revolt against this created blessedness discover by themselves, without any divine imperatives, that they cannot cope with this consciousness. The coverings which the man and woman devise have to be removed for the sex act, which the Hebrews called 'knowing' the other. Because of the insecurity now stirred into him by his act of insecurity, man cannot tolerate the continued assertion of the difference of the other, and has to disguise it; thus he dissociates himself from his createdness and from the reason for the existence of the other. The aprons are similar, so that the two may be one in a new unconstructive way, not in the coming together of two complementaries, but one in the combined ganging-up against God in insecurity.

It is therefore sexuality that gets hidden; sex is therefore in danger of losing the significance of its widest, original purpose. The trouble with us is not that sex means too much but too little, and that that little itself gets out of proportion. The trouble with the so-called 'commercialization of sex' is not that it makes us too conscious of our sexuality but that it indicates that our awareness of it is too feeble to exist without artificial stimulus; there would be something wrong with our hunger system if people could make huge sums of money by decorating the landscape and the newspapers with colossal pictures of potatoes.

There is, therefore, no *necessary* connexion between nakedness and shame. When there is such a connexion, it depends not on the nakedness itself but on the fact that the nakedness is due to some kind of unmasking; and this sense of having been unmasked depends in turn on a relationship being out of adjustment. There is nothing in the story here about original righteousness or even original sin. Shame is one of the very few abstractions which are mentioned; and therefore, if we are to draw any generalization from the story it should not be in terms of a sinless situation developing into a sinful one; the story is about the progression from shamelessness into shame by way of 'sin', and the hope of divine salvation in a situation of shame. The linkage is quite clear between: 'They were naked and not ashamed', 'They knew that they were naked', 'I knew that I was naked and I was afraid'; and 'The Lord God made garments of skins and clothed them'. This is not a theory about the so-called 'Fall', or the origin of sin; it is not even a parable about the origin of sin. It depends on the sense that one of the primary puzzles of life is the linkage between the performance of an apparently justifiable action and the sense of misery which follows when we discover that this action has cut us off from the person we are most related to. It is necessary to note again that the action of eating the fruit had nothing at all against it except the knowledge that God did not wish it to be done; in every other way it was entirely reasonable. It is this kind of snarl-up which causes more disappointment and inexpressible resentment than almost anything else – inexpressible because even now we do not have language in which to be clear about anything so confused.

The hope of salvation is that the one who is thus disregarded and rejected takes the initiative to cover the effects of shame and provide clothing. Let us summarize the process. Man has treated the relationship with God as being of secondary importance to the satisfying of his immediate lusts and hunger for self-made security; God is despised and rejected; man suddenly feels exposed and unmasked when this despised God appears; there is nothing that man can do to rectify the situation, except the most ineffective action to indicate that he feels helplessly exposed; and finally God acts as the only one who is still free to act, by making it possible for man to appear before him. This is not a theological proposition; the story could not have been shaped in this way unless it had been based on human experience; apart from its roots in human experience, the story has no points of reference. In the above compressed version, for the terms 'God' and 'man' substitute 'my wife' and 'me', or 'John' and 'Mary'; and the story's background appears. The significant thing is that the writer felt that this kind of experience is so central to the human situation that a normative expression of it ought to come in at the very start of his account of the relationship between God and man; this complex feeling of failure in relationship is the primal factor in man's self-awareness. And this hope of what, in our theological shorthand, we call 'forgiveness' is the primal factor in man's faith in the validity of love.

We might notice that a very similar concern lies at the core of the most developed of the parables of Jesus. The parable of the Prodigal Son (so-called) is often interpreted as meaning 'If you repent, God will forgive you'. In fact, almost all the initiatives are with the father; the son asks for a subhuman existence out of the sight of the father in the servants' quarters; he wants to be deprived of his status as a person; he carefully rehearses a speech to express this desire; he delivers his speech with promptitude and precision. *But* (and this 'but' is the climax of the story) the father takes not a scrap of notice of this carefully prepared 'confession'; he immediately takes steps to *clothe* the son in the appropriate garments and to express in every possible way his son's status as a son. *This* is forgiveness, and it cannot be wangled by good works, not even good works of contrition and confession. Jesus took the basic human experience which lies behind Genesis 3 and filled it out with his own symbols. The introduction at the beginning of Luke 15 shows that this understanding of God was reckoned to be highly offensive, blurring as it did our convenient moral demarcations;[24] and the Church, in preserving and using the story, showed that it too needed a dramatic account of this sort, to answer similar accusations against itself. And one may ask whether the Church of today is so vigorously expressive of God's inclusive forgiveness that it can really make authentic use of the parable.

'ORIGINAL SIN'

If the opposing principle of forgiveness does not break into the situation, the problem remains unsolved; the will to take on a slave-state, however convenient it may be to authority, is no answer; where religion has nothing to offer for the condition of over-dependency except another system of over-dependency, it is bankrupt; it is open to the accusation of replacing one neurosis by another. A son-state is a state of authentic dependency, for sonship does not mean perpetual immaturity; a slave-state is a sub-personal, unauthentic dependency. It has its attractions, and these are infectious, and this whole infectious bundle is what is traditionally called 'original sin'; it is 'sin' because it is the natural enemy of forgiveness; it is 'original' because it is derived from the past and is inherited.

But a great deal of misunderstanding has arisen about this 'inheritance' of 'original sin'. This 'inheritance' operates by cultural, not by genetic, propagation. Its manifestations and its cure are at the uniquely human level of mind and spirit rather than the biological level of genetic apparatus; we cannot expect salvation from the work of the Russian priest who claimed to be able to isolate the gene which carries original sin, and who hoped to breed a human stock with no concupiscence or original guilt.[25]

As we saw before, this is the mistake of confusing biological characteristics with learned characteristics. Natural selection has not propagated genes for what we would call good or bad behaviour, or for such an entity as original sin. As Professor Dobzhansky has stated, 'such genes simply do not exist'.[26] And 'although biological evolution has made cultural evolution possible, it has not determined what this cultural evolution should be'.[27]

It is at this point that we may have to deal with the most embarrassing of all the difficulties which we feel about the idea of the Fall in these days, namely the sense that, biologically speaking, man just has not fallen; he has risen to where he is now. But this is yet another point at which we can validly exploit the difference between our two accounts of the Creation. Chapter 1 does support the biological fact that man represents the ascent of the evolutionary process to its highest point. Chapters 2 and 3 stress the cultural, or existential, fact of man's sense of something being wrong. And man could not have this sense of wrongness if he had not developed to the point where intellectual and moral consciousness became a real possibility. The height of man's development can be measured in the fact that it is possible to accuse a man of being inhuman. There are several other species capable of complex behaviour, such as recalcitrance or boredom; but it still does not make sense to accuse a cat of being uncatty. Therefore, in Professor Burnaby's summary, 'this [biological] Rise of Man is the necessary pre-condition of what theology calls the Fall'.[28] And this in itself is sufficient reason for the Hebrew editor's decision to put the chapter 1 narrative before that of chapter 2.

It is not fair to say that man's fallenness has nothing to do with his biological status, for it is his biological evolution which has made his cultural evolution possible; and his fallenness is a cultural matter. On the other hand, now that he has biologically evolved to the point where cultural factors operate, these factors can be evaluated in their own terms and not merely in terms of what is congenial to biological evolution. There is, or at least can be, an autonomy of the moral order which makes it independent of the demands of biological survival. So, the statement that man is fallen need have nothing to do with man's biological advantage. We may assert that a particular act is evidence of this 'fallenness' even if it may appear to be favourable to man's survival as a species, and it is invalid to argue against the validity of the Adam and Eve story simply on the grounds that the action concerned is not hostile to the evolutionary process. We are, therefore, free to assert that righteousness remains righteousness even if it does not triumph; we are free to assert that the virtue of forgiveness is of supreme value even if it completely opposes the instinct of survival. In fact, so great a pioneer of the study of evolutionary biology as Thomas Huxley was able to state: 'The ethical progress of society depends not on imitating the cosmic process, still less on running away from it, but on combating it.'[29]

DISSOCIATION

The eating is an eye-opener, but an eye-opener to the possibilities of dissociation and suspicion; the eyes of the couple are opened to the need to sink their differences in the face of the common enemy, the Creator. The second Adam comes also as an eye-opener; but he comes fulfilling the prophecy that in the day of the Messiah the eyes of the blind shall be opened; he comes opening minds to the fullness of community. At the eucharistic act at Emmaus on the first Easter day, another pair of humans, Cleopas and his friend, took food, and their eyes were opened and they knew – not that they were naked, but that one who had been unclothed had by the creating act of God been clothed again, that mortality could be swallowed up by life.[30] And this eating for the eyes to open to permanent community is what the eucharist is all about.

When people or groups sink their differences as the woman and her husband do in the story, it is more than likely to be because they are finding a common enemy in God. It needs an overwhelming threat to cause people to engage in such impersonal and unholy wholeness. According to Luke, the common problem of judging Jesus made friends of Pilate and Herod.[31] Mark tells us of the ganging-up of Pharisees and Herodians, to trap Jesus.[32] And John gives us an even more impressive display of religious and secular unity, with his story of a disciple of Jesus gathering around himself soldiers and agents of the religious conservatives and representatives of the self-conscious enthusiasts for revival, in a joint enterprise for the arresting of the truth.[33] Ecumenical enthusiasts may be convinced that isolationism is wrong; but we do have to beware of thinking that any old unity is the highest goal; we too may find ourselves ganging up against the truth. We may find ourselves choosing and volunteering for a shallow unity instead of more quietly following some harder vocation which we prefer to ignore. We may find ourselves united by a common distaste for our diversity, and so act in a combined revolt against our Creator. We may find ourselves united by a common fear of the world, and so act in combined revolt against *its* Creator; we could unite in order to be a better enemy of the world instead of a better servant of it. It *could* be that denominational apartheid is the only way to keep grace available, for the mere abolition of differences between half a dozen conformist and unrepentant Churches would be an ecumenical disaster. Unity, as the gift of God to his beloved, will tarry until the Christian brotherhood has such concern for God's world that it can use the gift rightly.

There are times when we feel that the worst thing that could happen to us would be to be left entirely alone, without anyone to be related to. At such a time, we feel that our differences from people around are a luxury which we cannot afford; we conceal our individuality in order to avoid the threat of isolation. We bind ourselves to a narrow conformity, and we make the strongest possible appeals to others to conform also. We threaten people with ostracism or heresy trials; we idolize our national way of life, so that it becomes obviously unpatriotic to criticize the *status quo*; we put maximum value on impersonal factors of ancestral or tribal community, and so we imply that any deviation from 'the will of the people' is a betrayal of our forefathers. The story of Adam and Eve shows us that this is all due to our broken relationship with God; if our relationship with God is secure, we can tolerate and rejoice in our differences. God as Trinity, God as Christians know him, guarantees that isolation will never be the ultimate truth about us; for God is eternally three distinct persons, held together in an eternal relationship. The principle of community is assured to us; there is relatedness in the heart of God, and so we need not be afraid of being left alone ourselves.

The first Adam acts to suppress the difference within himself, the difference between himself and the woman; the male-female unit makes itself less than it truly is. The horrifying thing about sin is its dullness; we may do our best to dress up our sins in clever language and so appear to have discovered some novel iniquity to confess: but most of the time confession is the dreary old treadmill, and it requires courage rather than verbal subtlety to put our failures into words. A few plain words, in any language, normally suffice to cover the standard sins. In contrast, the character of Jesus as we receive it in the Gospels is extraordinarily diverse; his goodness cannot be classified. Fortunately, the writers felt no urge to make a 'character study' of him; they do not attempt to give an ordered analysis of his personality and so we have a series of stories which unintentionally bear witness to the range of characteristics which he carried in one person – meekness and self-assertion, energy and self-effacement, confidence and despair, uncompromising demand and sympathetic gentleness. It is no accident that his sayings at times seem to contradict each other. The second Adam shows a completeness which the first disguised and refused; in hiding from God the first Adam was hiding from himself. The story of the first Adam does make some sense on its own, coming as it does from a community that was aware of a problem of estrangement from God; but its fullest significance emerges only when it is put alongside the witness concerning the second Adam. As Paul van Buren says, 'the various traditional forms of the doctrine of "original sin" are not empirical observations about man; they are *comparative* statements of man's condition, measured by the historical standard of

Jesus of Nazareth'.[34] This is not to say that some form of a
doctrine of 'original sin' may not come from an observation
of the world from a non-Christian point of view; it is there
in Genesis; it is there in modern writers like T. E. Hulme,
who suspect Christianity because of its association with the
inadequate humanism of the Renaissance artistic tradition,
but who find that the phrase 'original sin' makes some sense.[35]
But Christians put the phrase in a new context; as Dr van
Buren goes on to say, sin is not 'natural' to man; 'such a
teaching would indicate that one had taken one's definition
of man from man in bondage ("Adam"), and not from the
free man Jesus of Nazareth'.[36]

We must again extend this argument to the character of
the Christian community, which has the mandate to be the
'Body' or image of Christ – the means by which the character
of Jesus is to be seen and shared in the present. Granted that
the Church, in this overlap of the ends of the ages, has a very
mixed character; it is the Body of Christ and a body of
disorder; it both receives and communicates God's judgement and salvation. But which in practice does it take as its
norm, the first Adam or the second? Of which Adam does it
most effectively know itself to be the Body? If we say that
it is the second Adam that should be normative of the
Church, this is not a plea that the Church should be more
'divine' or 'spiritual' or 'otherworldly'; on the contrary, it is
a plea that the Church should demonstrate the fullness of
humanity that was asserted by the second Adam and evaded
by the first; it is a plea that the Church should be more free
to meet the world and be its servant, and that it should assert
in its corporate life that diversity and inclusiveness of
character that was asserted by the second Adam and evaded
by the first. The most potent demand for ecumenism comes
when we see how we appear to be emphasizing the isolation
of the first Adam instead of asserting the fellowship brought
by the second. A simple illiterate couple want to marry; they
are of the same tribe, the same language, from the same area,
with almost everything in common – except that one comes
from a kraal where the Lutherans have members and the
other from an Anglican group. The pastor has to explain to
them that one will have to join the Church of the other if they

are to have a united family; he has to try to explain why there are two Churches which do not accept each other's communicants or acknowledge each other's confirmation; he has to help one of the parties to accept a new set of customs of worship, a new lot of rules of discipline, a new system of paying church dues. Can we wonder if the African comes to doubt whether there is any healing or salvation in this fragmented white man's god who seems to exist solely to create difficulties? Can we wonder if pastors prefer to say and do nothing, if they develop a paralysing sense of guilt when they are thus binding simple people with burdens too grievous to be borne?

Part of the trouble may be that we find it too easy to talk about the nature of the Church as if it were an abstract object of discussion on its own. The real scandal of our apartheids and disunities is not simply that they offend our teaching about the nature of the visible Church – about which there has been plenty of traditional disagreement; the deepest offence is that we are throwing the whole reconciling work of Christ back in his face; we are telling him that we would prefer not to be redeemed, that we do not want the gifts of the second Adam but would prefer to keep the first Adam as our model.

GENESIS 3: 8

The man and his wife heard the sound of the Lord God walking in the garden at the time of the evening breeze and hid from the Lord God among the trees of the garden.

All through, this is God's world; he is master of it and it is his home. He does not descend on it for an occasional visit; he walks in the garden as his normal right. The world is not only the place where he *works*; it is the place of his leisure also; he is not a commuting God who goes back to heaven at knocking-off time; he shares the evening breeze with us, as well as the midday heat.

But for people who are guilty, this is a fearful fact; so we pick on the undeniable truth that God does specially reveal himself at certain places, and that he does promise to communicate himself to us by certain covenanted methods – and we take this to mean that otherwise he is virtually absent. The special methods of his presence can be used as evasions of his presence in the whole world. Sacraments and church buildings, as well as educational status and patriotic duty and health, can all serve as 'trees' by which we hide from God. They can all be used as pretexts for evading the demands of obedience in God's world; they can all be used as techniques for keeping ourselves immature and encouraging others in the same way. They can be ways of evading our right to be human. This is the way of evil, capitalizing on the existence of what is good. Against all the pressure to keep God in church, to keep him out of social life and political life and domestic life, it can be a word of most significant and profound conversion when a man can say, 'I feel now that my home is part of God's world'.[37]

The man and the woman flee because they cannot stand before God; they use these good things of creation, the trees, as a means of concealment. The things of this world are supposed to be a means of community between man and God; but they cannot argue the point, they have not the will to disobey. But man can use these things for good or evil; and the surest sign that evil is operative is when man uses things to keep his distance from God.

The man and the woman seek to be secret; they want to be unseen, unknown. Their action has been self-centred; they have broken their relationship with God, and they do not want him to see them. We do not want our ungenerosity to be perceived by the person towards whom our generosity should be directed; when we hide from a beggar we hide from God. It is for this kind of reason that we take steps to avoid being known; and it is this issue which brings to a climax the account of the nature of God's Kingdom called the Sermon on the Mount. Christ warns us that there will be all sorts of divisions within the community of disciples; there will be false prophets who say all the right things; there will be false miracle-workers who do all the right things. The fault with them will not be found in the details of their words and actions; the fault will be that their words and actions have been for themselves; these people will have been known only to themselves; their primary loyalty will have been to their own activity and identity, and not to Jesus. And so he says to them, in effect: 'Get away from me; I never knew you, for there was nothing in you for me to know.'[38]

What, in fact, is the basis of our commitment, of our Church's commitment? Is it to some sort of ideal, a group's tradition, a sectional ideology, a political system, a scheme for self-preservation? Or is it to Christ, who is beyond the sectional schemings of man? The best of these things can be nothing more than a tree behind which we hide, in the knowledge that our religion is basically a method for ensuring a supply of fruit for our own maintenance. It is quite possible that the most impressive Church will be the most attractive tree.

God is the name for the one who by his presence stimulates guilt. Jesus did not accept the conventional distinction between the innocent and the guilty. A large part of the Sermon on the Mount is devoted to teaching that the mere absence of a guilty act does not mean that a person is not guilty; on the contrary, the 'innocent' are accused of exactly the same offence as the 'guilty';[39] the man who has done no killing is convicted of murder, the man who has not had the opportunity or the nerve to commit adultery is convicted of committing adultery. This is the opposite of a moral code; it is virtually an assertion of the uselessness of moral codes.

The story of the woman taken in adultery makes this even clearer.[40] The point is not that the guilty woman is said to be guiltless, but that the 'guiltless' accusers have a sense of their guilt stimulated. As accusers, they are united; in their character of prosecuting counsel, they repress any sense of guilt in themselves, and assert the guilt of the accused. Jesus brings their guilt into consciousness, and divides them, so that they go out one by one. This is the work of grace. Just as the enemy of faith is not doubt but the repression of doubt, so the enemy of grace is not guilt but the repression of guilt. And, whatever defeats this repression is an agency of grace, or of God. The grace which saves the woman taken in adultery is relatively straightforward; it is a more costly and complex grace which saves the Pharisee, who somehow has to be divided, to experience self-hatred, in order to accept love.

GENESIS 3: 9
But the Lord God called to the man and said to him, 'Where are you?'

So, after the first imperative and the first indicative in the word of God, now comes the first interrogative. And it too is typical. 'Where are you?' This suggests that God is ignorant and has to ask questions; and this is not so far from the truth.

This is the power of man; he can make God a searcher. The cross is the most potent example of man's freedom – freedom to reject God; but it also demonstrates God's refusal to take this as the last word; God will insist on pursuing man to the most ungodly places.

If this is so, the gospel makes it plainer than before that it is impossible to escape from God. In these days, when we hear a good deal about the inadequacy of the biblical cosmology,[41] it is worth noting that although the Hebrews did have a picture of the universe as a three-tier structure, they did not allow this deficient cosmology to overrule their truest insights about God. Ideas about God which are closely tied to the old cosmology are in fact deviations from the biblical idea of God. In this Genesis story, for example, God is unequivocally in the world. Psalm 139 testifies to the impossibility of getting away from God – there may be a heaven and earth and underworld, but God is not restricted to heaven as a divine group area.[42] The whole point of the book of Jonah is that God cares for his relationship with all people and it is impossible for his servant to escape from his demand.[43] 'God is inescapable. He is God only *because* he is inescapable. And only that which *is* inescapable is God . . . it is safe to say that a man who has never tried to flee God has never experienced the God who is really God. . . . A god whom we can easily bear, a god from whom we do not have to hide, a god whom we do not hate in moments, a god whose destruction we never desire, is not God at all, and has no reality.'[44]

This is the dilemma of Adam. The man and the woman recognize it. They recognize that God is God; if he were not, there would be no need to flee; but the flight is useless, and is known to be so as soon as the question comes. God may ask, but the question is scarcely needed, for the man makes no effort to delay answering. In ordinary circumstances a person pursued by one calling 'Where are you?' can move away out of range. Adam cannot. And so he is filled with fear. To be known by God is the most alarming thing, if our condition is such that this cannot be welcomed as supreme blessedness. To us who have developed such an efficient resistance to self-disclosure, the knowledge that our secrets are open can be the greatest incentive to the ultimate repudiation of our createdness – namely self-destruction.

The fall of man brings out a new aspect of the nature of God; he becomes less of a law-giver, more of a questioner. Jesus came as the new law-giver, certainly; but, particularly in his dealings with the individual children of Adam, he preferred to be a questioner. When people came to him inviting him to act as judge and legalist, he turned the questions back on the questioner, and himself acted as questioner.[45] When a lawyer attempted to use Jesus as a superior authority in law, Jesus answered not with a ruling but with a parable, and a question.[46] In its mission to the world, the Church is often wiser to stand as a questioner rather than as a know-all authority. The questioner stands alongside the man who is questioned, as Jesus stood along-side the lawyer and his own friends, as God walked about the garden looking for Adam and Eve. And the Church has to ask over and over the same question which was posed to the world in the person of Jesus, the question which is the question of God in the garden – 'Where are you?' Where are you in relationship to your surroundings, your neighbours, yourself? And this is a genuine question, a seeking; it is not asked as an examiner asks a question, knowing the answer himself full well. God is pictured here in Genesis as a searcher, as one who does *not* know the answer, who has to call to the man to cause the man to disclose himself. God is affected by our situation; throughout the prophets and the New Testament we hear of a God who experiences both joy and suffering in his relationship with his people; the scale of the estrangement from God is felt and expressed first by God, not by Adam; it is God who first asks 'Where are you?'

God has the humility to admit and express his ignorance. At certain moments, this is the attitude which can supremely convey to man a sense of security. Nothing is more offensive than to hear a false claim that we are entirely known and understood. The immigrant to Southern Africa often hears the white man's claim, 'Wait until you have been here longer, *you see, we know the Native*'. Howard Thurman's rejoinder is entirely justified: 'When the Southern white person says, "I understand the Negro", what he really means is that he has a knowledge of the Negro within the limitations of the boundaries which the white man has set up. The kind of Negro he understands has no existence except in his own mind.'[47]

God in Christ entered this alien world of sin and death, and sought for man; with his whole life, Christ asked 'Where are you?' He sought for man and found him in his isolation, and explained himself in the parable of the Lost Sheep.[48] The searcher with his questionings was rejected; there was no room at Bethlehem, no room in the temple; there was no room in the Holy City; he was crucified outside the city wall.[49]

Man has the power to make God a searcher. But God is known to be God by his power to follow man to wherever he goes, to make him turn and meet him. God is the one who draws me out of my isolation, who comes meeting me; God is the one who asks me this question so authoritatively that I am forced to do something about it. This was the supreme miracle in Christ; not that he did one particular act or another, but that he was *there*, available, meeting people, wearing a garment with a hem that could be touched.[50] And this again is what the Church is for, in the conventional residential parish and in any other grouping in which it may find itself; it is there as the Word of God meeting man, asking this question with a unique persistence and passion. Where the Church acts by coercion rather than by persuasion, where it represents God's grace as unanswerable force rather than as the love which seeks to evoke a response, it is betraying a vital aspect of its mission: it is misrepresenting the

God whose first word to man and woman is this searching question.

GENESIS 3: 10
He replied, 'I heard the sound as you were walking in the garden, and I was afraid because I was naked, and I hid myself.'

Up to this point, man has been able to make rational answers to the questions put to him from his environment; he has been giving appropriate names to the things which were put in front of him. But now his answering is completely irrational and inappropriate. God asks simply, 'Where are you?' But the man hears the question as 'Why have you been hiding?' God sends out a message which indicates that he is an inquirer, looking for a friend; the man receives the message as if coming from an alien and hostile authority. It is not God's speaking that has gone wrong, but man's hearing. Man's receiving equipment has become distorted; it filters off some of the genuine elements of the message and interpolates elements which are inappropriate and alien. His guilt makes him attribute an authority-role to God which God has not been asserting at all. Practically all the misunderstandings and strains which happen between people are the result of either distorted hearing or confusion about authority; and when, as so often, these two elements are present in one situation, it takes a power from outside the situation to bring understanding and reconciliation. And it is exactly this kind of healing which is promised as a gift of the Spirit. Jesus says that the Spirit 'will not speak on his own authority, but will tell only what he hears'.[51] He will not come injecting a whole stack of prefabricated answers into our situation; but he will enable a person to trust that he is *really* heard, that there is in the universe a reliability of hearing, and therefore a reliability of knowing, which can restore real trust. The Holy Spirit is known first of all as that ability in a person which enables him *really* to hear another person, which enables him to quieten his own anxieties so as to be free to listen to the other person's anxieties, and then to feed back to the other person what he has really been saying. How many of us are able, even in reporting a simple conversation, to speak only what we have heard? If only we could, how our lawyers would lose business!

The question 'Where are you?' is heard by Adam as a threat; he makes it to be a threat because of the recollection of his immediately preceding history. The question itself need not be threatening; it can be quite neutral; it can be loving. But a man who is improperly dressed, as Adam is, hears such a question as a threat, whatever the intention of the questioner may be. Jesus picks up the same theme even more clearly in his parable about the Wedding Garment.[52] Commentators note that it would be unreasonable to expect a man picked up off the street to be spruced up in a morning-suit ready for a wedding, and therefore suggest that Matthew has rather roughly tacked two parables together which were originally separate. This is no doubt correct; yet the word of God, as we now have it by the Spirit's providence, does give us this consecutive effect and, so arranged, it gives us a valuable understanding of God's judgement. The question, 'My *friend*, how did you enter here without a wedding garment?', is not in itself a loaded or threatening one; the man has a perfectly good reason; he has been invited off the street and has had no opportunity to prepare. But the man gags himself; he refuses to speak a word. He refuses to acknowledge that he is there only at the king's invitation; he refuses his role of a guest; this is tantamount to claiming an independence, an insistence on being there on his own terms. And it is because of this silence, not because of his being improperly dressed, that the man is cast out of the banquet. The teaching here, therefore, underlines that of the earlier part of the parable, where the guests who had been invited renounced their role of guest, and chose rather to remain in areas where they had rights; they had got for themselves farms and businesses to control, and preferred this role of independence to the un-protected dependence of existing at another person's invita-tion.[53] Christ's parable spells out in different words the core of this story in Genesis 3. Here, Adam is expelled from the garden not simply because he is improperly dressed but because he has refused this role of being a guest in the garden on God's terms. The woman is attracted to the fruit by the suggestion that through eating it she will get more status, more skills, more protection from the demand of being simply a *person*; the appeal of being 'as God' is the appeal of having for oneself a higher status, a stronger armoury of defence. This obviously implies a refusal of nakedness, and nakedness becomes a problem as soon as the fruit is eaten. The more clothed we become, the more farms and businesses and religious convictions and degrees and skills and whatnot we dress up in, the harder it becomes for us simply to meet as persons, as guests of each other. The gospel is a specimen answer to this problem at its extreme; God overcame the supreme disadvantage of being hampered by the most inescapable degree of status of all, the status of being God, and is seen characteristically and normatively in the man who was a guest everywhere, who had nowhere to lay his head, who ended up in the most conspicuous and cursed nakedness on the cross. And, if you have seen Jesus, you have seen God. Jung suggested that man could force God to become mature and that this was the cause of God becoming man in Christ.[54] However this may be from the strictly theological standpoint, it certainly is true that the Church, in continuance of Christ's activity, is called to help men to become free from the pressures that make them chase after Godlike status, so as to be able to meet each other as guests of each other.

The fear and flight in Adam are the result of the activity of conscience, which is an evidence of conflict and division. Conscience is that element in man which is conscious of himself over against God. 'It is the function of the conscience to put man to flight from God . . . it agrees with God, and on the other hand in this flight it allows man to feel secure in his hiding-place. . . . Here, distant from God, man plays the judge himself and just by this means he escapes God's judgement. Now man really lives by his own good and evil, from the innermost division within himself. . . . Conscience is not the voice of God to sinful man; it is man's defence against it, but as this defence it points towards it.'[55]

Conscience does indeed make cowards of us all. Conscience is the effect of the knowledge of good and evil, the effect of setting oneself in the position of judge. When Christ said 'Do not judge',[56] he was, among other things, meaning

'Don't let this habit of judging overrule you; be free of it, as a chosen disciple; be free of this inhibition on your activity, as you were designed to be; be free of the constant striving to justify yourself, which is the work of conscience in opposition to God, so that you spend all your time weighing up good and evil.' It is precisely this habit of getting satisfaction from exercising our knowledge of good and evil that leads us into the habit of passing judgement on other people.

GENESIS 3: 11–13

God answered, 'Who told you that you were naked? Have you eaten from the tree which I forbade you?' The man said, 'The woman you gave me for a companion, she gave me fruit from the tree and I ate it.' Then the Lord God said to the woman, 'What is this that you have done?' The woman said, 'The serpent tricked me, and I ate.'

The effect of all this is seen in the working of Adam's mind; knowing good and evil, in the sense we have been considering, his conscience leads him to seek exact justice for himself, at the cost of all his relationships; he is therefore led directly to blaming God – '*You* gave me this woman, it's her fault, and your fault'. Woman becomes an enemy, and God becomes an enemy. Where is the previous joy in the existence of woman, in the existence of the other? Adam's arguments are undeniable, and yet they are the arguments of death; the eating *has* led to death. The only way through is to accept death as Christ did, to forgive – which means refusing to take up the weapon which the enemy has, by his offence, put into your hand. But to blame God is the opposite, for it means that we must be establishing another standard over against God by which to judge God.

Previously, there has been reference to 'wife' and 'husband'. But these words do not apply now. Adam finds himself unable to say, 'It's all my wife's fault'. He is trying to undo the relationship. He refers to her as 'the woman whom you gave me', not as 'this wife of mine'. The elder son in Jesus' parable does the same; he cannot bring himself to call his junior 'this brother of mine'; he refers to him as 'this son of

yours'; and by so doing he disowns his relationship not only
with his brother but also with his father.[57] It is impossible
to disown the human brother without disowning the God
who has given us this brother. The same applies to this man
and this woman; they prove, in the first episode of the Bible,
that it is impossible to keep separate the two great commandments, to love God and to love the other person; the denial
of the second is automatically the denial of the first.

The woman follows the same technique; in accusing the
creature, the serpent, she accuses its maker. But this is a
word said, as we often speak, with the purpose not of seeking
truth but of finding a point of blame; it is said, like so many
of our words, with no reflection on the question 'What good
does it do to say this?' The serpent did nothing, except start
off a conversation, setting one truth against another. It gave
no command; it did not even suggest a course of action. The
degree of 'temptation' in the snake has been minimal. Responsibility for the trouble is firmly on the human actors.

Man sets himself up as prosecuting counsel; and the vigour
with which he plays this role is in proportion to his deeper
fear of finding himself the defendant. We seek our acceptance, not through the forgiveness of sins in Jesus Christ, but
in discovering a greater unacceptableness in persons who are
different to us. We identify evil as something which resides
most conspicuously in settings which are clearly different to
our own – in the communists, or the blacks, or the whites,
or in the World Council of Churches, or in homosexuals, or
pedestrians, or students, or presidents, and so on. This comes
as good news. Religion can be one of the best sanctions for
corporate hatred. The teaching of history, also, can be a
most effective method for instilling a lifelong habit of locating
evil outside one's self and outside one's group. Words and
formulae will not cure man of this habit; the only hope is
that someone may willingly be the victim of our prosecution,
be reckoned with the transgressors, and so pull out into
consciousness the latent guilt which makes us so keen on
establishing our innocence. And this is the policy of God in
Christ Jesus.

We find it easy to rest in the question 'Who is to blame?'
The legalistic theological attitude has stopped short of

blaming God, but it has become skilled in passing all the blame back to Adam; no matter how difficult it may be to imagine, it was Adam's sin which started it all off, long, long ago. And so our theology, in its popular form at least, has been providing for us precisely what it should have been removing, namely a system of 'fate', an inescapable force which we can blame for all our evils. But it should be obvious that the point of the story is not to give us a figure to blame but to show the uselessness of this whole kind of question; it shows that when we seek for an origin of evil we are running away from ourselves. 'Anybody who raises the question of how evil came into the world is turning the question away from himself. He wants to find an *original cause* of evil. But an evil which is caused is no longer an evil; it is only fate, an inevitable process.'[58] There is, therefore, an immensely strong pressure on us to treat this story as early history and not as myth. If we can treat it as history, we can happily intellectualize the discussion, we can withdraw into the safety of a general dissertation. If we dare to treat the story properly as myth, we cannot evade the fact that when God says 'Adam, where are you?' he is speaking to us.

This is not to deny that, in the proper analyses of the social scientists, acts are related to previous acts, and that connexions can be discovered which link acts in a chain of cause and effect. The scientist, standing outside the area which he is observing and looking at it in retrospect, can establish a statistical linkage between, for instance, premature parental deaths and juvenile delinquency. 'But none of these statistics will help in determining, before rather than after the event, whether the untimely death of a father will cause an adolescent boy to become a problem or will nerve him to achieve a premature maturity. To an external observer no conscious choice of evil is ever discernible. There is always a previous condition or the force of an antecedent impulse which seems to offer a complete explanation of the inevitability of the act.'[59] The social scientist works with tools which are of immense value within their range of operation; and it is possible to believe that there are no factors which are in principle outside this range of operation. But any person whose experience makes him feel obliged to attribute some

meaning to the concept of moral responsibility, and to the
learnings gained from introspection, must affirm that, while
descriptions of behaviour in terms of causative determinism
may be valid, these are not the only meaningful descriptions;
and in many circumstances they are not the most important
and personally helpful descriptions. To the man who insists
that the *only* valid account of things is in terms of the impersonal working-out of automatic pressures, we must ourselves insist on asking whether he attributes value to anything
himself, for instance whether he considers 'freedom' a 'better'
thing than slavery and, if so, where he gets his idea of
'betterness' from; and if he goes on to insist that the *only*
certain thing is a blind mechanism, he must face the question
of whether his own arguments in favour of this blind mechanism are themselves derived only from blind mechanism and
have therefore no basis in rationality.

So, if we accept that there is a valid sense in which we can
speak of guilt, and if we agree that the basic character of sin
is non-faith, how can this be dealt with? Not by argument,
persuasion, or intellectualizing. An idea which can be shifted
by argument is only an opinion, it is not a belief arising out
of a person's real being; and the shifting of such an opinion
is not going to change the person. People's real beliefs are
derived from deep social experience, as Marx saw so clearly,
and the way to change people is to face them with a new
social experience. We only increase guilt if we demand from
people behaviour for which, due to their social experience,
they have no capacity. Professional sociologists are often
far more sensitive than Christian preachers in realizing that
all sorts of forces may go to make up a person's behaviour,
and that first of all that person has to be given an experience
of acceptance. If a deaf child is given an experience of
rejection by a congregation, no words spoken to him about
the love of God can argue that experience out of him. It is
not just an explanation of the world that we need, but a
changing of it. However 'liberal' a person may be, on the
race issue for instance, at some point or other he will be
defensive, he will feel that the attack is getting too near the
bone, that it is unfair; and his defensiveness will take the
form of an explanation; which is precisely what is not

needed. How I can go on doing this! How I hate interruption when I start! I dare not really confess my faults because I do not deeply enough trust in the reality of a change *which has come*. For I do believe in a new social reality if I believe in Christ. I believe that the Kingdom of God has come, with all that that means. I am not going to repent, nor is anyone else, until we have seen and felt something of it. I may be told *about* things, and then I may be told to *be* what I have been told about; for specimens, see almost any Sunday-school lesson book; I will be told what I must be, but will I be helped to become what I have been told to be? Will I be given some sort of experience, and some help to reflect on that experience, which will enable me to become in response to this exposition, and thus to repent? The work of the first Christian preachers did not start with a moral demand to repent; it started with them giving people an experience of the Kingdom.[60] The procedures of sacramental confession are all very good and necessary; but the most significant confessions really take place *after* absolution, not before; for it is in the power of an experience of the Kingdom that we can be free to face each other without disguise. It is when we have been released from the inhibitions on self-disclosure that we can really confess to each other.

The man and woman in our story agree, in effect, that God is to blame. But the Hebrew writer could not say so in as many words, because he had no personal or social experience which could be interpreted as meaning that God had accepted the blame; he could offer only broad hints that the blameworthy event had come about through the things that God had made; he could have sympathized with the words of the penitent thief in 'Friday Morning':

> You can blame it on to Adam,
> You can blame it on to Eve,
> You can blame it on the apple,
> But that I can't believe.
> It was God that made the Devil
> And the Woman and the Man,
> And there wouldn't be an apple
> If it wasn't in the plan.

It's God they ought to crucify
Instead of you and me,
I said to the carpenter
A-hanging on the tree.[61]

It's God they *ought* to crucify; the witness of the New
Testament is that this is what *has* happened; the name of
God stands for the one who alone can take the blame and
has taken the blame, and this was spelt out in the death of
the Son of God.[62] God is the only one left free to accept the
disorder of the world and to take it upon himself and be
treated as a criminal. Jesus, Son of God, agent of creation,
was deprived of all his powers and abilities; he did not
merely die, but died empty and stripped. Nowhere is this
expressed more powerfully than in the Isenheim altarpiece
of Grünewald; there, Christ hangs as a great, lumpy, immobile weight, straining the crossbeam of the cross almost
to breaking; his skin is not only suffering from the wounds
of the scourging; it is also pock-marked all over with the
sores of the skin diseases which afflicted the patients of the
hospital for which Grünewald made his painting. And,
beyond this, the whole condition of his skin is that of a
plucked bird; elsewhere in the altarpiece, on all the angels
and on various kinds of creatures, it is obvious that Grünewald's great symbol for power is feathers; feathers stand for
mobility, strength and protection – and the figure of Christ
hangs with all his mobility, strength and protection removed.
And the whole being of John the Baptist is concentrated into
one long, curved, pointing finger which indicates the Crucified as if to say, 'That's the Son of God – believe it if you
dare'.

And the disciple-community of Christ has again to face
the question of which Adam it is representing, the first or
the second – the blame-passer or the blame-bearer. The first
Adam dissociates himself from the situation of guilt and disorder; when he sees a person in whom disorder is particularly
conspicuous, the best that he can say is, 'There, but for the
grace of God, go I'. For the second Adam, the grace of God
does not distinguish him from the person of disorder; on the
contrary, it draws him closer, so that his word is, 'There, by

the grace of God, *am* I' – I somehow share the character of the disorder, its blame and its guilt.[63] The Church and the Christian find that they are led more and more deeply into trouble the more closely they are identified with Christ.

Without making a great fuss about it, the Gospels show how Jesus' willingness to be blamed spread infectiously to his associates; repeatedly, we see evidence that the Apostles made no effort to conceal their stupidity, cowardice and faithlessness at the times of crisis; we read all about the impossibly shaky foundation the contemporary Church was built on; it is part of the actual propaganda for the Church that its top brass all ran away at the moment of need,[64] that Jesus called its archbishop 'Satan',[65] that there was so much rivalry and ambition among them that they missed all the main points which he was trying to get across to them.[66] These stories show what Jesus had done to these men; he had made them free to accept blame, free to see and acknowledge their share in the disorder of the world that crucifies its maker. If the Church does not have this freedom to speak the truth about itself, it has dropped out of the succession of the Apostles and cannot lead the rest of the world into honesty and truth.

CHAPTER EIGHT

Curse and Blessing

GENESIS 3: 14–15
Then the Lord God said to the serpent:
    'Because you have done this you are accursed
    more than all cattle and all wild creatures.
    On your belly you shall crawl, and dust you shall eat
    all the days of your life.
    I will put enmity between you and the woman,
    between your brood and hers.
    They shall strike at your head,
    and you shall strike at their heel.'

Now God passes sentence. He is in the role of judge, and his pronouncements combine justice and mercy, blessing and curse. We noted in our study of the first chapter that the rule of law is an essential part of the creation mandate. Here this principle is seen in practice. God does not act as arbitrary tyrant; he hears the evidence, and the defendant is not sentenced until he has first been charged and given an opportunity to plead. This is not as superficial as it may sound. God's own righteousness is denied when people are treated as guilty when they have been given no opportunity to face the charges against them. The South African Terrorism Act, for instance, which allows people to be held indefinitely in solitary confinement with no visitors except the police and without any recourse to the courts, is an offence against the nature of God himself. About 250 years ago the authorities of Cambridge University deprived a certain Dr Bentley of his degrees without charging him or hearing his defence; when the case was taken to court, this action was declared to be null; in giving judgement, Mr Justice Fortescue quoted the case of Adam, stating that even Adam had been called upon to meet the charge against him before being expelled from Paradise.[1] God's justice, therefore, can be seen as a first precedent in human law.

The snake is the first to be sentenced; but a major part of its sentence consists of its disordered relationship with man. Its offence has been trickery, expressed in the uniquely dangerous form of godless religious argument. This enemy attacks the heel of man in his upright manhood and brings him down when he least expects it. Man and snake are trapped henceforward in a permanent hostility, in which both sides will score points but neither side can win.

But the seed of the woman shall bruise the head of the serpent; this is the protevangelium – the first intimation of the gospel; the new Eve has been provided, whose seed, the second Adam, has overcome the serpent. The serpent is not the equal and opposite power to Christ; man is vulnerable, with his heel, an Achilles heel, planted on the earth, on the level of the serpent; but the head of the serpent is ultimately more vulnerable still. The last word in the Bible about the serpent does identify it with the Devil and Satan, and the serpent is cast out.[2] But in Genesis there is a curse and a blessing, to continue until the time of the end; Adam is permitted to live, but under these conditions of conflict; and the serpent is permitted to live.

GENESIS 3: 16
To the woman he said:
> *'I will increase your labour and your groaning,*
> *and in labour you shall bear children.*
> *You shall be eager[a] for your husband,*
> *and he shall be your master.'*

a) Or *feel an urge.*

God speaks to the man and woman separately; not only has he a separate message for each of them, but they are established in their distinctiveness as separate beings. In a real sense, they are back at the start. It is not good that man should be alone; but alone they are, in their guilt and in their curse. They have accused each other; and now each is against the other, in spite of their feeble attempt to disguise their differences. And this condition never quite leaves the man and woman. When a great experience of unity comes to them, to us, often there is a move, from one side or even from both, to withdraw into isolation again from the implications of the experience. We doubt whether we can still think of ourselves as being in possession of that which we have generously given, and we are unwilling to face life with this reduction of our armaments and secrets. We have a wide range of skills for this kind of tactic, and it is easy enough to pull in reasons of religion or morals, especially when the experience has been in terms of an encounter between the sexes. This is the pain of our situation; we cannot quite crawl into each other's skins and share each other's life-space, even when we feel we should be able to do so.

For the woman, good and evil, pleasure and pain, exist together. In Genesis 1, verse 28, childbirth was a simple blessing; this is not overruled here; but now it is also a curse. Man and woman are still together, which is a blessing, but their togetherness is also a curse; there is a threat that they will be rivals and enemies of each other, as well as being spouses. There is a threat that each will be a cause of division within the other; the presence and the power of the husband will lead to a struggle of motivations in the mind of the wife; and, by implication, the same will happen in the mind of the husband due to the presence and power of the wife.

Part of the curse is that childbirth does not come with the same ease and lack of strain that it usually does among animals. It seems to be part of the twistedness of the human mind that expectant mothers are made to feel that a tremendous amount of pain is the normal, proper thing. The way to natural childbirth is largely a matter of the mind, thinking of the event as a special kind of *work* ('labour' as the New English Bible translates it) rather than pain; there is no hard work that does not involve pain, if you look at it with a 'pain-ful' mind. But even 'natural childbirth' does not solve this difficulty; in the very period of history when its wisdom and techniques have been developed, so the pain of bringing up the born child is being increased; and this is an almost entirely mental pain, particularly the anxiety stimulated by psychological studies which indicate that mental disorders and psychological deviations are often caused by the most commonplace actions of parents. There seems to be no sure

means of avoiding such troubles; once again, our relationships are continually in need of healing. We tend to think
that the sacrificial system of the Old Testament, with its
stress on guilt offerings for sins unconsciously committed,
was a lot of superstition from which we are mercifully
delivered. But maybe they had some value after all. It is the
unintended, unconscious occasions of maladjustment that
most harass us. When all has been said about the unnecessary
apartheids which man devises for the oppression of his fellow-
men, the most universal, the most dangerous one, is that
between parent and child, for it is from failures in this
relationship that most mental and spiritual maladjustment
comes. Our situation needs salvation, and salvation has
come for it. It was due to no wild deviation, no improper
overriding of the value of the individual, that the apostolic
work of the first Church was directed at households rather
than at isolated persons. In these days, the members of our
families become much more scattered in different occupations; the Church is being stimulated to think in terms of
specialized chaplaincies so that the Church may be the
Church in the various non-domestic situations where man
finds his identity; but even so, the parish still remains the
basic form of the Church, because almost everyone is involved in the domestic situation to some extent. *But* if this
is to be more than an institutional relic, the Church has to
be far more directly related to its households than it usually
is now; if it is going to be an agency of healing in the domestic
situation it must be far more careful to hold families together
in its worship and its activities; too often, by accident or
design, it connives at the fragmentation of the family, instead
of making full use of its opportunities to bring households
together into the presence of the healing Christ.

In spite of the 'pains' of childbirth, the woman will be
eager for her man; she will be concerned to attract him;
there will be at least an element of insecurity and anxiety
on both sides. One will be trying to find in the other a
security and a valuing which has been missing elsewhere.
Because they come to each other from their two different
histories, they will have different needs. They may speak
similar languages, both verbally and sexually, and yet be

meaning different things by them. And so each will be carrying on a secret inner language, each will be nourishing unspoken private thoughts, hidden from the other, because neither is able completely to liberate the other to speak aloud.

St Paul is often thought to have had a rather low opinion of women and of the sex relationship as a whole. But he insists that in Christ's fellowship woman is as essential to man as man to woman[3] – which must have been a difficult teaching for many people to accept. He also reminds his readers of the actual primacy of woman.[4] Further, he insists on the husband's duty to love his wife, with the same kind of passion and sacrifice with which Christ has loved the Church.[5] He also requires that husband and wife be subject *to each other*.[6] All these considerations are ways in which Christ, in practical application, is drawing the sting of the curse of woman's subordination: he is defeating the irrational tyrannies which have for so long oppressed woman, so that the subordination which remains can be seen as a legitimate, but limited, aspect of a proper relationship according to God's design.[7] This is one implication of Christ's work as the healer of society. Even in our days, when the legal rights of women have been won in the State, and even to some extent in the Church, Paul's teaching may still be valuable. It is easy, now, for the husband to be subject to the wife, to fall in casually with her wishes, instead of really loving her: so he must be told firmly to *love* her. It is easy, also, for the wife to 'love' the husband, to fob him off with a bit of affection or sexual submission, instead of really respecting him, especially with regard to the work which he has to do to bring the family an income. So she must be told firmly to *respect* him, or be subject to him. The virtues which have to be taught are those which are difficult, not those which come naturally.

GENESIS 3: 17–19
And to the man he said:
  '*Because you have listened to your wife*
    and have eaten from the tree which I forbade you,
    accursed shall be the ground on your account.

With labour you shall win your food from it
all the days of your life.
It will grow thorns and thistles for you,
none but wild plants for you to eat.
You shall gain your bread by the sweat of your brow
until you return to the ground;
for from it you were taken.
Dust you are, to dust you shall return.'

A curse is placed on man which goes through him to the earth itself. Man is inseparable from the earth on which he stands. He is continuous with nature, and if he is to be saved, nature must be saved with him. If nature is to be saved, this must happen through man, for salvation as understood in the Bible involves some capacity for willed response, which man can make, and must make, on behalf of nature.

Man was made from dust, and to dust he returns. This is the tragedy of man. But we go on to say that this is the tragedy of dust itself; if man experiences futility and fragility, then, in some sense, the rest of nature experiences these things too, for it cannot be detached from man. 'The tragedy of nature is bound to the tragedy of man, as the salvation of nature is dependent on the salvation of man.'[8] If man needs saving, the rest of the world will need saving as well.[9] Theologically, we say little about what nature is; we have little to offer in the way of a static description of nature. We see it as we see ourselves, in terms of what it is becoming; we see it in terms of its hope, of its potential. We see it waiting, in the power of what is to come, but not yet in the possession of what is to come. The full assertion of our freedom as members of God's family is to be expressed in terms of an assertion of that which is natural – 'the redemption of our *bodies*'.[10] And so, even dust will have the character once again, as it did before the Fall, of being a symbol of hope rather than doom, of creation rather than death.

God's intention is to renew and to complete his creation through persons, complete persons who can offer a willed response and not merely an instinctive reaction. Therefore, the creation of what we call Creation, and the creation of this community of people, are not two events but one, and

231

belong together. The symbols of dread which appear in the creation of the heavens and the earth – darkness and chaos and the deep – appear in the story of the creation of the people of Israel in the Exodus narrative; and in the great songs celebrating God's mighty acts, Creation and Salvation are placed so close alongside each other that it is difficult sometimes to see which is meant.[11]

The subduing of the created order, and the bringing of it into co-operation with the createdness of man, underlie both Genesis and Exodus. So, in Exodus, the people are not saved without a significant difference being made to the natural creation too.[12] And in the new creation in Christ, there is the same pattern. Stars and animals have their place in the birth of the new community in the birth of Jesus.[13] The death of Jesus brings forward the primal darkness, the absence of sun;[14] the earth shakes, it loses its character as the foundation and security of all that is on it.[15] It shakes again at the new birth of Jesus and of Israel, at Easter, and the sun is saved.[16] Wind and flame represent nature's participation in the purpose of the sharing of God's Spirit.[17] All through, we are not being saved *from* the world, but we are sharing in the saving *of* the world. If our salvation is to come from a Saviour who would save us from the works of the Creator, we would be involved in a movement *from* the world. But the Bible, all through, speaks of a movement of God *towards* the world, towards the world in its very disorder. The badness of the world is the most potent reason for its attractiveness to its Lord and to his associates.

WORK

The effect of the Fall, therefore, is not to be seen in the fact that man is closely related to the things of the earth; this relationship is part of the good plan of creation, and to be saved from such a relationship is no part of the authentic Christian hope. On the contrary, the effect of the Fall is the dislocation between man and the rest of the natural creation, the weakening of the close relationship that there ought to be. The ground becomes an enemy to wrestle with; man is no longer just a gardener looking after an established park;

he is no longer just a worker. The friendly relationship between himself and the ground from which he was made has been spoiled, and so now there is a perpetual cause for resentment in the attitude of the ground to him. Man has become the peasant, whose lifelong battle with the soil seems to yield so little reward; he has become the hungry nomad, picking up the odd bits of nourishment from a mainly inedible vegetation.

There is no suggestion that work, in itself, is part of the curse; at the beginning of the story, God is pictured as a craftsman, and man was commissioned to be a caretaker. In the first chapter, man is commanded to subdue the earth, and this obviously implies the exercise of energy in a systematic and purposive manner. But the Fall has disorganized man's relationship to the rest of the creation, and this shows itself most immediately in the area of work. We might have expected that the main signs of this disorganization would be in the hostility between man and other animals, the danger to man from marauders and parasites, the threat of flood and earthquakes, and all that sort of disturbance. But, in fact, the primary sign of the disorganization is to be seen in the way that man's own efforts are hindered by nature. Man has the sense not that nature is always trying to kill him so much as that nature is always trying to discourage him, to make him feel that his efforts are not worthwhile. Nature is not an out-and-out enemy; she is just bloody uncooperative; and this is really more difficult to live with, because it means that I can have hopes and ambitions of producing something that will satisfy my pride and give me a sense of achievement, but *things* have such a way of going wrong.

The next chapter, the story of Cain and Abel, gives a specimen of how this works out. It is in the area of work that relationships first go wrong. Two workers, two producers, find themselves in conflict about the value of their products; and so one of them has to be eliminated.

Part of the curse of work is that it goes on non-stop until death, according to verse 19. Work is a natural part of man's life, but only a *part*, according to the original intention. This again corresponds with the mandates to man in chapter 1, where the command to subdue the earth is significantly modified by the establishing of the Sabbath. Man is not supposed to be so 'dedicated to' his work that he has no energies left for anything else, for this means that he has yielded his authority, and his work has 'subdued' him. Even in societies where the genuine wisdom and skill of man has resulted in a general easing of the hardships of life, there are many who restlessly hammer away at the work to which they have *given themselves*, as if it were immoral to be stopped by anything less than death. In this case the fall of man is shown by his willingness to live under a curse and pretend that it is no curse – to elevate it, indeed, to the status of a religion. The doctrine of justification by works, so articulately rejected by the Reformation, comes back in the form of justification by work. 'The job' is the godlike factor which will restore our credit balance, when we see how carelessly we have treated our commitments to God and our neighbour; 'the job' becomes a major item of moral currency to be used to buy us out of our debts in our personal relationships; it is worshipped as a divine factor because it is credited with the power to forgive us. Religion does not save us from this; in fact, the more closely a man's work takes him to the recognized 'things of God', the more dangerous is this matter, because the work then seems to be all the more surrounded with divine approval. This is the problem of the full-time minister, who may feel that his job is to keep God in business and to furnish him with daily guidance; but it can equally be the problem of the devoted layman who wants to 'work for God' in his spare time. The Church, as we know it, would have died without the work of ministers and devoted laymen; but as we look forward to the coming of the Kingdom we are looking forward to the death of the Church, at least in the form in which we know it; we are wanting our work to fall away. Nonetheless, some of us may feel, it would be tactful if our Lord, when fixing the date for the Second Coming, could avoid the first Tuesday of the month, so as not to disturb our church council meeting.

There is an element of curse and an element of blessing in work; and the curse is most effective at those points where it is least perceived, where it disguises its enslaving character and sets itself up as a god. Jesus did not speak of 'giving himself' to his work or employment or vocation; he was conscious that he had a work to do which had been *given to him* to do by God,[18] and that this work, mighty and demanding though it might be, had very definite limits.[19] His work was blessed, in so far as it was not done for its own sake; his achievement was the result, the by-product, of his relationship with the Father; he went out from his communion with the Father into effective activity in the world. Work comes to have the character of curse when it is a substitute for this communion with the Father, or when it is used as a means of earning this communion with the Father – or with anyone else, or with oneself. For then it becomes impossible to handle failure, because the failure in work means a loss of currency with which to purchase one's admission to communion; the curse of the things that go wrong, the obstructions, the thorns and thistles, this curse becomes overemphasized in its effectiveness, because it not merely obstructs the job, but also devalues the currency by which one is hoping to gain admission. Jesus' handling of the curse is shown in his refusal to be harassed by the obstructions which faced him, the limitations on his activities and abilities. He was able to take the obstructions when they had been woven together in the most concentrated form by his opponents, and to accept them as a crown; he converted the thorns into a symbol of genuine mastery by accepting them and carrying them on his head as kingly insignia.[20]

The proper work of Jesus, and of all who are called by him, is the fulfilment of the will and purpose of God.[21] This includes the whole concern for renewing and reconciling and healing the world in all its sectors and communities. It includes the responsible use of the whole range of human ability and power, economic and spiritual, political and physical. But, while this is the proper work of Jesus and his associates, and while this is the only commitment which can properly be called 'vocation', there is significance in the fact that Jesus was skilled in a particular trade. It is part of legitimate Christian symbolism that our Saviour was a man who knew the principles involved in manufacture, that he was experienced in the process of converting nature into culture, that he had been disciplined by the procedures relating to the purchase of raw materials and the distribution of the product. Whereas, in the Old Testament, the bread of God was just found on the ground as manna in the desert, now, under the gospel, the bread of God comes to us through the medium of that which man has manufactured. This does not mean that we can in any way organize the grace of God, which still comes to us as that which is beyond us; it does mean that the ways by which God chooses to communicate grace are directly related to the work by which man exercises his power in the world. Manna, being 'direct from God', can have nothing of the political significance which is properly to be found in the eucharistic bread. The latter affirms to us that nature depends on man for its character of glory or shame, in so far as nature has been brought into relationship with man. 'Bread for myself is a material problem: bread for other people is a spiritual problem.'[22] The bread that man makes can be a most potent weapon in his fight against his fellow-men; it can be the object of manipulations which put it beyond the buying power of the poor; as we have seen, it can represent even more universally than money the division between man and man, the contest for what there is not enough of: or it can be the eucharistic bread of brotherhood, a miniature version of what all creation can be when man brings it to participate in the offertory. The eucharist is given to us to teach us the truth not only about God and about man, but also about bread. We can too easily wrap up the bread of the eucharist in such a lot of specialized piety that we fail to see the connexion between it and the bread of the tea-room, the crust in the gutter. The symbol can go sour. The salvation is for the *world*, and to concentrate on the stewardship of things in the *church* context only, without extending the same critique to the way we use things in the world, is the most basic misrepresentation of what the Church is for. The whole of nature is to participate in Christ's reconciliation. And on behalf of the created order, man (not only Christian man) sings Benedicite, crediting the whales and the lightning with attitudes of praise.

DEATH

As a curse, work is to continue until man returns to the ground from which he came. Work leads to death, and death is the doom on work. Within the order of living things, we see a development towards greater order and complexity, in the comparison between the amoeba and the primate, in the growth from the acorn to the oak. In his work, man consciously contributes to the imposition of order and to the development of complexity – whether the particular work be that of controlling the forces of nature in a hydro-electric scheme, or of devising a political instrument to bring about a more just society, or of bringing up little children in a secure and educative setting. And death is the curse, because then the orderly arrangement of the living thing decomposes into disorder; then, our ability to impose order ceases, and we lose our control. All the time, we seem to have been trapped in a losing battle against the tendency of the whole universe to disintegrate. This is the curse of death, that it is a doom on fellowship and community, and on all the central things that a man feels are most worth striving for. And yet, it is also a blessing, for it is an end; and in being an end it is a reconciliation, for it is a return to the earth from which man was made.

Man is doomed to return to dust. This is not to say that dust itself is cursed. It is part of the creation, which is good; and the creation itself is designed to be changing, to be in time, and therefore to be finite. The finiteness itself is not evil, nor is it in itself an evidence of evil. The return to dust is not a distinct curse; it is taken for granted as part of man's condition as a creature of time. Life could not be if there were not a continual passing of things into the past. No new point can be reached unless something is left behind.[23] Unless things are allowed to return to dust, to become past, to be forgotten, they become a burden, a bondage, a superstition. In the lives of churches, societies, nations and individuals, it is only too easy for policies to be maintained this year because they were maintained last year, and not because there is a positive motivation for them out of the circumstances of this year. If we postpone our forgetting, if we allow our forgetting ability to atrophy, we are insulating ourselves against renewal and isolating ourselves from grace.

Yet it is not only our policies which are to return to dust; it is ourselves. *We* are returning to dust; we are going to be buried; we are going to be only a memory in the mind of a few people who themselves are going to be buried soon after. *We* are going to be forgotten. And all the most costly enterprises that we have spent ourselves on, they are going to be forgotten also; for, even in the case of men who leave great architectural monuments behind them, the greatest energies of men are usually spent in the painful and time-consuming areas of personal relationships, and the memories of all this work move into the past more ruthlessly than any physical structures. Time takes the links and bonds that we have tried so hard to make by our patience and understanding, our forbearance and charity, and grinds them into dust; and what we do preserve and save from the process is so often the occasions of failure, the guilts and hurts; these get left as sore chips amid the general facelessness of dust. In that case, what on earth is the point of praying for God's Kingdom to come on earth, into this area of impermanence? What on earth is the point of acting in accordance with this prayer, in the search for justice or beauty or truth, in the effort to make love alive? If all is vanity, there is not much point in trying to be either good or wise.[24]

Jesus was involved, as all men are, in the processes of time. Most of what he did and said was forgotten; only a handful of his activities have been recorded; and even these are strangely disconnected – a sermon here, a healing there, but no apparent strategy. Most of his activities seem to have been unplanned, immediate responses to immediate situations. The relationships that he took most trouble with, the building up of the disciple-community, fell completely apart in the crisis. He ended up a rather interesting failure. 'Sent into the world to rescue the millions of mankind, to bring the whole earth back to God, his work in the end amounted to a number of separated bits and pieces – each thing in itself of course worthwhile, but without any apparent co-

238

hesion, a number of individual works performed on a number of different days in a number of different places, scattered and divided by time and distance, without any perfection of wholeness or integration. But in the Resurrection of Jesus, God took these bits and pieces of a disjointed ministry and wove from them a single garment of salvation for the whole world. The many and various things which Jesus did in Galilee and Judaea were not lost. They were raised with him on the first Easter morning. . . . They were recovered and secured for ever. . . . Christians have been partakers of Christ's resurrection and this means that for them, as for him, nothing in human life is lost or left behind.'[25]

Dust stands for the wastage of substance, the breaking down of things by the effects of time. The Resurrection stands for the victory over dust and wastage. This is part of what Jesus means by saying that God's will is 'that I should lose nothing of all that he has given me, but raise it up at the last day'.[26] This is part of what St Augustine means by saying that those who love God 'will never lose those who are dear to them, for they love them in one who is never lost'.[27] What is past is safe; it can be allowed to be put into the past. At the Last Judgement that which is truly dust in us will be consigned to destruction and its proper oblivion, and what is valid about us will be disclosed in its proper durability.

For many of us the most immediate importance of the victory over death is in this sense of the victory over wastage. We can feel and know that it is worth while trying to retain an integrity in a world of lies and false compromises: it is worth while trying to stand for justice and righteousness in a situation where all the initiatives seem to be with the forces of injustice and prejudice. Death and all its satellites are doomed: even though one dies, righteousness and freedom are ultimately stronger, and the battle for them is not merely a noble, futile demonstration. In the Bible's most systematic account of the meaning of resurrection, after all the sublime language about man's glorious destiny and the victory over death, St Paul can end by saying: 'So, stick to what you are doing for the Lord, and don't be discouraged by anything:

give yourself entirely to it, because your work for the Lord's purposes cannot be wasted.'[28]

For Christians, the blessing and curse of death remain, with a much stronger accent than before. Death remains the destroyer, the last enemy, the wages of sin.[29] If this were not so, there would be need of a better victory than the victory over death. It was in the form of death that all the forces of evil combined against the Son of God. Death is the worst thing. And yet, it is a blessing; it is a supreme means of association with Christ, as the entrance to eternal life, as the central symbol of our vocation. 'When Christ calls a man, he bids him come and die.'[30] But this immensely widens the range of what 'death' can mean; the 'death' which is this blessing is not just the death of the body. We are not brought nearer to Christ, or transformed automatically into saints, by the accident of physical death. The entry into eternal life is in the midst of this life. The moment of crisis is not the moment of physical death but the moment of commitment to Christ, which is symbolized by baptism. It is through being born again, not through physically dying, that we enter the Kingdom;[31] and it is this newly-born person that Christ can raise and keep with permanent durability. At this point, death is not a curse, it is a necessity, for baptism is a death, a burial.[32] Baptism is the point at which man accepts death, accepts the fact that the controls are outside himself; it is the sign that all that one has is on loan, and that not even our highest possessions or closest relationships are ours to grasp at and hang on to by our own efforts. Every day after baptism is a day of dying, of being willing to let go, of being stripped as Christ was in his dying. The Church is supposed to be the practice-ground for dying; but very often it is much worse than its members in the actual disciplines involved; it is possible, only too often, for Christians who individually are humble, charitable and un-grasping, to work off their hidden prides and hatreds and acquisitivenesses through the Church, so that the Church becomes far less satisfactory than, for instance, an ordinary household, as a training-ground in the disciplines that are necessary for dying. But, for people who have had this practice in dying daily, the eventual death at the end of this life can come with its sting drawn and its terrors stilled and its curse tamed. It can be the welcome sister, as it was for St Francis,[33] or the last station on the road to freedom, as it was for Bonhoeffer.[34]

GENESIS 3: 20
The man called his wife Eve[b] because she was the mother of all who live.

b) That is *Life*.

The man has no response to make to God after hearing all the words of the curse. Instead, he turns to the woman, and sees in her the point at which a change is needed. Her previous name 'Woman' has spoken about their relationship to each other in the present; she has been the one who has enabled him to be. Now the man picks up the theme of motherhood which has been so important in her curse; the new name which he gives to her diverts attention from her relationship to himself; she becomes characterized as a functionary, as mother to her future offspring. 'Mother' is a powerful name; in this context, it is a word of great hope; it is a word which has to be built into the fabric of the story at the earliest possible moment, for it is more primal and basic than even the word 'Father'. Nonetheless, in this context, 'Mother' is a far poorer name than 'Woman': there is no ecstasy in it, no passionate recognition; in giving the woman this name, the man is pushing her identity away from himself. 'Woman' is a uniquely human word; 'Mother', for all its power and value, is not.

The name 'Mother' asserts the call to mankind to be fruitful and to increase. There is obedience and wonder and hope in this call. But it is also a preparation for one's own disappearance. From this point onwards in the biblical narrative, Adam's only recorded activity until his death is to inseminate his wife. He gives her the name 'Eve' immediately after his own condemnation to return to dust. 'Mother' is a name of promise: but also it stands for one from whom there is a movement away. For Adam at this particular moment, it is a word of the future; but for all of us who read the story, 'Mother' inevitably stands for the receding past.

Some rabbis have taught that the most important word of the whole Hebrew scriptures is, 'This is the book of the generations of Adam'.[35] The whole of mankind is one family, one race, and no man can say, 'I am of better or earlier stock than you'. Those who belong to the family of the second Adam may also see themselves in relation to the new Eve. She is willing to be the means by which a whole new race is brought to birth, a race which can include all people regardless of their physical ancestry. Whereas the first Eve reached out for and grasped a status for herself, Mary was simply willing to accept the incredible role to which she had been called.[36] Her son gives her as Mother to the disciple whom he loved, and through him to the whole disciple-community which he loves, the whole new family of his adopted brothers.[37]

GENESIS 3: 21
The Lord God made tunics of skins for Adam and his wife and clothed them.

God gives clothes. He accepts man as he is; he recognizes that man feels this need for covering. These clothes are not a disguise; but they do show that man feels that he is disunited and that he therefore has to be concealed. When he seeks to overcome this disunity he exposes himself, as he does in such activities as sex and prayer; and such seeking, he feels, requires a proper privacy. Truthfulness does not mean that everything must be publicized: if we publicize something which is properly private, we are liars, however accurate our words; by our publicity, we have proclaimed something to be public which is not properly public. The provision of concealment is part of preservation – preservation only for death, maybe, but still a blessing. God does not allow our stupidity to limit his mercy.

This is the end of the story of shame. Shame has entered the situation as a result of the original action; the two people have done their feeble best to conceal themselves, from God

and from each other, and have failed. They have treated
lightly their relationship with God, and they have come to
disown each other. Their misery is complete. The logical
punishment would be for God to deprive them of even their
own wretched attempts to clothe themselves, so that they
might feel to the full the shame which they have brought on
themselves. But God is, even at this stage, the source of
salvation and forgiveness. He does for them what they have
been unable to do for themselves. By supplying them with
equipment for their preservation, he shows that his attitude
is not bound to the past; his own concern is stronger than
their lack of concern, and he is not prepared to allow their
offence to be the last word about them. This is forgiveness:
it looks all wrong; it looks as if one is turning one's back on
all principles of justice and fair dealing; it looks as if one is
treating the guilty as innocent. And this is indeed the case,
for this is what God's justifying of the guilty is about; it is
not a legal pretence that the guilty are not guilty: it is the
refusal to treat a person's guiltiness as being the supremely
significant fact about him; it brings a new set of priorities
into the customary sequence of offence, guilt and penalty.
This is the gift of Christ, for whom this whole procedure did
not merely *feel* like death; for him, it *was* death, death to
social and moral status, death to the normal rules of common
sense and personal security, death on a cross. The Christian
mandate to forgive is not just an instruction to be virtuous;
it depends on us recognizing that a vital new factor has
intervened which puts the original offence in a completely
new perspective. To fail to forgive is not just bad; it is failure
to act in accordance with the facts; it is pointless. It is as if I
lend my neighbour a bucket of water for his garden in the
middle of the drought and then ask for it back for my own
garden just after a soaking thunderstorm.[38]

GENESIS 3: 22
*He said, 'The man has become like one of us, knowing good and evil;
what if he now reaches out his hand and takes fruit from the tree of
life also, eats it and lives for ever?'*

In making the world as a whole, God was simply acting according to his nature as the creative being; but in making man God took a calculated risk, the risk of failure. Maybe he acted on Chesterton's remark that if a thing is worth doing it is worth doing badly. Certainly the experiment with man involves much disappointment. The story of Noah speaks to us of our sense of not merely being disappointing but of being a disappointment *to* someone. God suffers first, and to a profounder degree than man. Only God *can* suffer to that extent, and this is the heart of the meaning of the story of the Passion, the passion in the heart of God. Only one who is totally unclouded by guilt in his mind and conscience can weigh the significance of sin and evaluate its seriousness. So God says that he is sorry that he has made man, and the reader accepts that this is a just judgement upon his community, that it does not deserve to survive, that the earth cannot be relied on as an accepting home for men who hate the earth's creator.

The pain of the risk which God has taken afflicts him at all the crises of the history of the People of God; the majority of the community is continually found to have separated itself from the truth, in the Flood, in the Exodus, in the division of the kingdoms, in the Exile, and in all the lesser crises. Yet in all these moments, there is a community which is a creative minority of success; there is a remnant which does not allow the forces of conformity, anxiety and sloth to have unrestricted influence. Christians say that in spite of everything, the creation of man has been a success, because they say that the Crucified, rather than the crucifiers, is the norm of man: his obedience has ultimately more to say about human nature than has all the disobedience of the rest of mankind. Earth is spoiled by man; but in man also it is healed. 'Since by man came death, by man came also the resurrection of the dead.'[39] Each of us must again face the question: Which Adam do you accept as characteristic of your hope, the first or the second?

If man has been unwise enough to eat of the tree of knowledge, he may miss the blessing of death by eating of the tree of life. The idea of an elixir of life has had at least an occasional attraction for very many people, although a standard objection to the idea of eternity is that unceasing existence is a horrible thought. Sartre suggests that the unbroken company of other people is the main characteristic of hell.[40] But it is the atheist, who is committed to despair, who sees this; the believer, knowing some relationship to God, and having some hope, may not be so wise; he may be tempted to devise means of getting back into the garden and of making sure of his own security and immortality. So, in his mercy, God makes this impossible. Life is not to be grasped like this; the blessing of death cannot be avoided by either the selfish virtue of the good or the misplaced skill of the clever. Even though it appeared to him in its worst form, death could not be finally avoided by the Son of God himself. But he has made a way to the tree of life by another path, not by the avoidance of death, but by its acceptance. The life we might hope for by avoidance of death is the life of the old. The life we do hope for through association with Christ is the new, and it comes, not through the prolongation of the old, not by the selection of the best of the old, but by the death of the old. The way to the tree of life is through death in association with Christ.

GENESIS 3: 23
So the Lord God drove him out of the garden of Eden to till the ground from which he had been taken.

So Adam is sent out from the garden, into the area where death is characteristic and unavoidable. Our normal shorthand word for this area is 'history'. Whatever else may or may not happen, the most basic shaper of history is the fact of death; without it, history as we know and understand it simply could not be. Earlier, we sensed a problem; on the one hand the story of Adam and Eve is universal, it is about the way things *are* now if it is about anything at all: but on the other hand it is presented as a story of the beginning, and it is *needed* as a story of the beginning, at least by the kind of people who need a clearly marked pattern in history to enable them to cope with a situation of oppression. Perhaps a solution to this problem can be approached in this way: the garden situation is indeed our contemporary situation, it is *our* situation, and has been so for every generation of man. It was so for the first generation of man, in the first generation when a creature emerged that was capable of bearing the responsibility for his choices, right or wrong. But this Adam, 'man' with a universal name, moves out of this universal setting into history; he almost immediately passes out of the story, and into the centre of the stage steps the first individually named person, Cain. This is the name of the first creature to add a moral dimension to that basic feature of history which is called death. Cain has the moral ability to make a death murder. If it is allowed that at some stage such a being must have appeared on earth, the name we give to this being is Cain. The story of Cain and Abel is part of our past *history*; the story of Adam and Eve is part of our present *experience*. The two stories are not of the same type, although it would be wrong to make the distinction absolute. In the same way (although, again, the parallel is not complete) the whole gospel, including especially the Crucifixion and Resurrection, is primarily something which is true about us now; rooted in history though it is, it is contemporary to all history. The primary Easter message is not that Jesus Christ rose from the dead in A.D. 32 but that Jesus Christ is risen today; and similarly with the rest of the gospel episodes. The same is not quite true of Abel's successor, St Stephen. The second Abel is part of our past *history*; the story of the second Adam is part of our present *experience*. We can meet God *in the company of* Abel and Cain, Stephen and Saul of Tarsus; but we meet God in so far as we ourselves *are* Adam, in so far as we ourselves *are* the Body of Christ. The Apostles are our ancestors, Christ is our contemporary.

In one sense, Adam's expulsion from Eden is a return; he was made outside Paradise, and he goes back to the area outside Paradise. He was made of the earth outside Paradise, and he goes back to look after that earth out of which he was made. In looking after the soil, man is looking after himself; his hopes and his future are inextricably bound up with the soil, and if he fails to care for the soil, he is doomed himself. The implication is that if man will care for the soil, the crops will virtually look after themselves; man's mandate is to till the ground, not to grow things. This is to put the point into an exaggerated form, but the emphasis remains true. It is not just the fault of a few greedy farmers, but of a whole epoch of society, when wrong agricultural and forestry methods can turn huge tracts of good land into dust-bowls. The three biggest single things in the world which are due to man's work are probably dust-bowls, polluted rivers, and smog; these represent man's failure to care for the three primary states of matter in which man finds himself and of which he is made. The complex processes of motivation which lead to this despoiling of land, water and air may be a better guide to the meaning of the Fall than even Belsen and Hiroshima.

However, in another way, the move out of Eden is more than a return. We see in the next verse that it is a move in a specific direction – eastwards. It is the eastern border of the garden that has to be defended against man. The author, therefore, had a general impression that man had come from the East; and this appears to be accurate, at least with regard to the man whose movements we can to some extent trace, namely civilized man. It seems to be clear that Africa has a good claim to be called the cradle of mankind – some of the most significant evidence for this has been discovered only a few miles from Johannesburg. But, for the most part, we do not have a great *feeling* that we derive our humanity from a mysterious creature who went around Southern Africa cracking open the skulls of baboons with the humerus of an antelope. The factors which we think are significantly human come to us from man of the East, in the very recent history of man, in the last 15,000 years or so. Southern Africa has been isolated from the East until recently, by a variety of factors, such as the fact that its only two navigable rivers flow into the Atlantic, the lack of harbours in its very smooth coastline, the prevalence of the tsetse-fly, which has virtually prevented the use of animal transport, and the great barriers of jungle in the south and desert in the north. These are the reasons, rather than some innate biological deficiency, that have caused the people of Africa to have been, on the whole, backward in the development of techno-

247

logical civilization. But the people of the West, who pride themselves on having taken civilization to Africa, have to remember that until a very few centuries ago the technological gap between Europe and Africa was insignificant; the food-producing revolution took place in the river valleys of what we call 'the East', and initiated the process which we call civilization. The people of north-western Europe took over all the basic elements of civilization from others; they did not have to invent letters or numbers, agriculture or husbandry, fire or wheels, arches, ships, mathematics, medicine, metaphysics, navigation or money, or the use of metals, wind, water and oil.

There are about seventy departments at our University in Johannesburg. Of these, a few are concerned with the contemporary languages of north-western Europe and Africa. Of the others, it is very difficult to discover a discipline which has originated entirely within the culture of the modern West, with no kind of debt to other cultures. Radiology appears to be the best candidate; electrical engineering, anaesthesia, sociology and some of the disciplines of dentistry could also perhaps qualify. But the overwhelming majority of modern studies have been taken over from areas east of western Europe. For us, even more than for the people of the Bible, man has come from the East. Above all, our Christ is from the East; and it will do us no harm to bear all this in mind as we face the situation of the south.

God shows himself, from the start, as a God who sends. He sends Adam; he sends Abraham; he sends Amos, Jeremiah, Ezekiel. He sends his Son. He sends the Body of his Son, the apostolic community, the sent brotherhood. The Good Shepherd is a driving as well as a gathering figure. He 'casts out' his own sheep (the verb is the same one that is used in the previous paragraph of St John's Gospel, concerning the man who was cast out of the synagogue).[41] The mission of Christ is a deliberate expulsion, a thrusting out of the nest.

Later in Genesis, we read how Abraham, with great care, cost and precision, bought a grave for himself and his wife.[42] This was his family's only territorial possession, a place for not-being-in; a person does not enter his grave until he dies, and then he no longer is. This is all that the new Israel of God can possess, a grave and a cross, of which the one certain thing is that they are empty; they are points *from* which there has been mission and movement. In this sense, the cross stands for the very potent absence of Christ, not for his presence. The cross on the altar, the cross on the church tower, the cross on the bishop's chest, these are not to hold our gaze. The cross stands out in its emptiness. Our orders are, as it were, to come and glance at this cross and see that Christ is not there. Come and glance at this grave, says the angel, and see that it is empty; he is risen and gone before you into Galilee. The only command to 'come' is a command to come and see where Jesus *was*, to see the one place on earth where he assuredly is not. You are not to come and stay; you are to go tell people that Jesus has *gone*. Jesus himself has the same message, he will be going to Galilee, and his friends will have to race to keep up with him. Just as the first Adam and his sons were sent into history, so the second Adam and his brothers are sent into history, into Galilee, the place of unbelief, of sickness, of disorder, the place on the boundaries of God's people. Only there will you find him; and when you do find him, it will be only to hear that your journey has scarcely begun; again he will say 'Go'. He will promise to be with us always, but we cannot separate the promise from the command; the presence of Christ is promised only to the mobile Church, the disciple-community that is apostolic. [43] If we want to be in the succession of the Apostles, we have to take part in the mission of the Apostles: without the mission, the succession is a mere badge or formula.

But the scene into which Adam is sent is still part of God's creation. The world into which Christ calls his associates is the world over which he has been given all authority. [44] The Good Shepherd is no absentee manager: after casting out his sheep he goes before them. [45] The eagle that thrusts its young out of the nest hovers over them as they learn to fly; it spreads out its pinions to catch them as their strength fails, and carries them along on its wings. [46]

We are not taking Christ to any place, or to people who

would otherwise not have him. We go to meet a Christ who is already Lord of the place to which we go; we go to help people to meet the Christ who is already their Lord as well as ours. 'In Assam, where a discussion of the missionary task was going on, a young minister got up and said: "When we think of our missionary task, we imagine our Lord saying to us, 'Go there or there or to the other place.' That is all wrong. What he is saying to us is not 'Go there', but 'Come here', for he is already there." '[47]

For it was Adam who was first sent out, and we are sent in his company, to discover our unity with all his descendants. The fact that we are 'in Christ' does not isolate us from the rest of humanity. A characteristic word spoken about Christ was 'Behold, the Man'.[48] The more we are 'in Christ' the more we are 'in man'. We are man becoming man, discovering man, talking to man, helping man to be man; we are sent to meet man who, in history, is bent on being less than he really is. We are the gift of Christ to *men*, to enable each other to grow to mature Adam-hood, to the measure of the stature of the fullness of Christ.[49] We betray this mission of Christ if we present the Church as yet another kind of segregation, another kind of dissociation through which men can sanctify their lust for isolation and differentness; we shall be offering just another kind of circumcision, instead of the new creation which puts the question of both circumcision and uncircumcision into the background.[50] Christ has come asserting the value of man, and the Resurrection shows that this valuing is true, that its validity cannot be thwarted by death or any other lesser separation. 'Nothing . . . can separate us from the love of God in Christ Jesus our Lord.'[51] If God is power or beauty or goodness, separation is unfortunate but not absolutely disastrous. But if God is love, if God's basic characteristic is that he values me and by that valuation releases me to be truly me, if the nature of God is to draw me out from my self-imposed banning order, then separation is the one totally destructive threat, the will to be separate is the most complete refusal of what is true, the life of separation is the most complete lie. The will to live in isolation, the habit of expecting that the

other man will act towards us in accordance with his unlovedness, the straining to assert a value to ourselves in terms
of our distinctness from others, this is to refuse the gospel, to
call good evil; it is another example of blasphemy against
the Holy Spirit.[52]

We can spend a lifetime discovering what this solidarity
in Adam means – that our value lies, not in our distinctness
from, but in our association with, the rest of humanity. It is
the hardest lesson for most of us. We may find it reasonably
possible to see ourselves in association with the reckless
prodigal son; it may be more difficult to be alongside the
inhuman, rejecting, elder son; yet the father goes out to
them both, overruling the protests of both; he calls them
both his sons.[53] It is not for us to make this true, or to try to
preserve it. Preservatives are wasted on the living truth of
the risen Christ, as Joseph of Arimathaea discovered. We
can no more make this truth than we can break it; what is
given to us is the opportunity either to conceal it or to reveal
it; and it is on this question that we all have to examine
ourselves. The truth itself is stronger than our lovelessness
and confusion; it is stronger than the superhuman forces
which seem to make our thinking and deciding so feeble; it
is stronger than the dilution which weakens our love and
the relativisms that weaken our will. It is stronger than both
death and life; it is stronger than the angels and princi-
palities and powers. And so it is stronger than the cherubim
standing outside the garden.

GENESIS 3: 24
*He cast him out, and to the east of the garden of Eden he stationed
the cherubim and a sword whirling and flashing to guard the way to
the tree of life.*

In the seventeenth century it grieved Dr Thomas Burnet to
think of these angels having to stand outside the garden, at
least until the Deluge, i.e. more than 1500 years. 'How easy',
he suggests, 'would it have been, in a well-watered place
like Paradise, to have surrounded the garden with a stream
or a river, which would have been an abundantly sufficient

obstacle to Adam and Eve, who knew nothing as yet of the use and construction of boats or ships!'[54]

But our story tells that the garden was guarded by the flaming sword, turning every way, to protect man from invading the area of immortality; and it speaks of these cherubim, which are the 'living creatures' of Ezekiel.[55] 'Living-ness' is their essential characteristic: they are the ideal defenders of the tree of life. Having the quality of life in full measure, they discourage those who are insecure, who have this quality incompletely. They stand for that fear and inhibiting sense of inferiority which comes to us in the presence of someone who is more thoroughly alive than we are.

ANGELS

Language about angels and cherubs is so diseased, after several centuries of misuse, that it serves now to stimulate unbelief. Especially in the graphic arts, we have copy after copy of a physical *thing*, which at first was drawn or carved to express a transcendent reality but now exists as a detached image for its own sake. A. C. Bridge alleges, for instance, that a woodcarver, commissioned to make the figures of four angels for an altar, will not concentrate on any transcendent reality in which he believes, but upon the accepted conventional manner of producing this particular piece of church furniture. 'He will not be interested in angels. He will be interested in the particular ecclesiastical *bric-à-brac* which purports to represent angels. Thus, he will produce neither a symbol nor a work of art but a meaningless object which will stand in the church as a perpetual monument to the unbelief of its maker and as a permanent deterrent to belief in angels.'[56] And so, every Michaelmas, we have sermons preached which seem to be fighting a rearguard action on behalf of some incredible physical being, belief in which is reckoned to be of a piece with believing in Christ.

But here, in the first appearance of an angel in the Bible, we have the corrective. The angel is not introduced for its own sake; it is a way of representing the human experience of being excluded. This experience is one of the most grievous kinds of distress, and so it is here characterized in as frighten-

252

ing and personal a manner as possible. We need some terms with which to express this sort of overwhelming influence; in the Bible the imagery of 'angels' is used, where we might nowadays use more abstract terms. So angels are usually perceived as alarming, even where they stand for realities which are creative and good. Gabriel, for instance, stands for the comprehension and communication of truth; but it is still alarming to be confronted by such a power, as Mary found.[57]

There is not much point in preaching belief in the existence of angels for their own sakes, just as we have no mandate to preach the existence of nationalism or race prejudice; what we have to preach is the gospel, the good news that these things, whatever language we use for them, need no longer tyrannize us. St Paul, for instance, knew only too well that the angel of religious exclusiveness and enthusiasm could threaten to destroy a man; but Christ has met and mastered these powers on his cross and brought them into subjection to himself.[58] The great angel of exclusion no longer has absolute power, and my sense of having been excluded is no longer the primary truth about me. Further, not only have these powers been deprived of their ability to separate me finally; some of them at least have been drawn into a community of obedience to Christ. It can be a most liberating experience to realize that a force in oneself which has seemed to be most disordered and hostile – such as sexuality or aggressiveness – can be taken out of this hostility and brought into one's obedience, in the community of service shared by the rest of one's abilities. We could even specify the roles of the three traditional archangels, corresponding to the three styles of behaviour which are present in differing proportions in everyone. Raphael, who carries prayers to heaven, is the compassionate-helper type: Gabriel, who conveys or interprets messages, is the logical-thinker type: Michael, the leader of the hosts of God, is the aggressive-battler type. In most of us, one or other of these 'angels' is suppressed: the aggressive person is afraid of showing his 'helper' side, because it will look like weakness: the thinker pretends that everything can be solved by 'being correct', regardless of the emotions flying around: the helper is afraid of speaking the truth, because it might hurt. But the archangels are, in Christ, an integrated team; in Christ, a person can use every faculty. And it may be significant that the leadership of the team goes to the 'angel' who can most obviously do most damage, Michael, the aggressor. So much harm has been done by the wrong use of power, and it is today caught up in so many ambiguities and puzzles, that good people are more scared of this aspect of their nature than of any other; but Martin Luther King is not alone in pointing out that the sources of oppression and injustice are to be found not only in the activity of the bad people but even more in the inactivity of the good;[59] there is, maybe, a special booby-prize in heaven, or a special place in hell, for the man who is so 'good' that he has forgotten how to be angry; and our areas of strain and oppression have called out, and could use many more, people whose predominant gift is consecrated aggressiveness. Christ draws these 'angels' into his kingdom, and overcomes their threat of separating us from the love of God and from the truth about ourselves.

THE SWORD

The sword is an independent thing, moving by its own power and not because of any hand holding it. The cherubim seem to be static, but the sword moves in all directions, flaming and unpredictable. Here the writer may be taking into his story the experience of lightning, which, especially in the less temperate areas of the world, is a most powerful force for keeping a person immobile and insecure; we think that the storm has shifted, that it is safe to make a move, when suddenly the lightning jumps back and attacks a place it had left quite a long time ago, as if to say, 'Get back behind the line; you can't play tricks with me'. Lightning is the roving guardian of heavenly authority, the supreme demonstrator of deterrent force.

The barring of the way to the tree of life is a blessing and a deliverance. But we would be missing one of the elements of the text if we refused to admit that there is also something here of retribution. God is perceived as one who can get fed up with the whole situation, who can break off a sentence in sheer desperation. His speech is left half-finished; the creating Word finds himself wordless, like an angry child. Unless this is in some way true, we are just playing with words when we talk about the 'wrath' of God. Wrath cannot be wrath unless there is emotion in it. What is special about the wrath of God is that it results from love and not, as it does usually in us, from unlovedness. 'The wrath of God is his refusal to allow us to rest until we have become fully what we are.'[60] The wrath of God erects obstructions to us when we seek to get the fruit of the tree of life by *trying*, by searching for it, working for it, earning it, by attempting to make it part of a bargain with God. As children, we get so much teaching about goodness and heaven which is based on a bargain system that we often take this into adulthood and marriage also; and in the first years of marriage, especially, there may be plenty of very godly wrath as we learn together that the basic things can be received only as gifts and not as counters in a commercial system.

When we are aware of being excluded, the first reaction of many of us is to attempt to pay the entrance fee ourselves. And so we try to be good. The 'bad' anger of the child brings 'just' punishment from the poor old insecure threatened parent; and so it becomes a 'Christian duty' to spend lots of energy in holding down our anger so that neither Dad nor God can see it. But this detail in Genesis shows that God is no stranger to the mechanisms of anger. The Christian does not have to wear himself out in trying to conceal his anger from God; on the contrary, he can take Archbishop Leighton's advice and vent all that is in his soul into the bosom of God.[61] And if he doesn't care to use his own words, he will find plenty of verses in the Psalms with which to express his feelings.

The wrath of God is the last word in this story of Genesis; it is the last word of the Old Testament.[62] But within the covenant of the gospel, it is only the last word of the beginning. There is a judgement of man which is directly brought about by the presence of Christ in the world. The associates of Jesus found themselves under judgement all the time. Peter's first encounter with Jesus stimulated all Peter's latent hostilities towards himself, it brought out the self-hatred which was preventing him from being willing to face the possibility of his own mature goodness. Jesus' judgement on him was to present a more powerful motive which would overrule the self-hatred; and the effect was that Peter came to accept and value and love the future self which was being disclosed, on the far side of the disclosure of his inadequacy.[63] This is the manner in which judgement is made by the one who is both creator and saviour, who is known as the one who saves what he creates. The judge is the same as the one who is victor over evil; he is the one who has most decisively disclosed the horror of evil; but he is also the one who has shown most characteristically that evil is the corrupted form of good. The supreme good of love can become distorted into the supreme evil of hatred; and Christ's victory is able to reverse this distortion and to vindicate the durable character of that which has been created for love. Creator, saviour and judge are all one. 'At every stage of creation God confronts what is actual in the world with what is possible for it.'[64] Precisely the same procedure applies when God is in the role of saviour and judge. By saving us, the judge puts the destiny for which we were created alongside the disorder of our history; our potential judges our past, our destiny judges our disobedience. This is happening every day, in communities and individuals. And the work of the Spirit of God is continually to be making this judgement accessible and effective, with both its pain and its promise.[65]

This contemporary judgement of the disciple-community appears most vividly in the Letters to the Seven Churches.[66] And it is in the case of the most morally confused of all these churches that the most specific promise is given concerning the rectifying of the fall of man; Ephesus is the church which has had the highest consciousness of its destiny, and has experienced the most profound fall; it has stood out rightly for all the correct principles, but in doing so it has rejected the only gift which the Church ultimately has to offer, love. The person who 'overcomes' through this situation – in other words, the person who retains his association with Christ to the point of martyrdom – will find that the entrance to Paradise has at last been unbarred and that access to the tree of life is at last open.[67]

THE WAY TO THE TREE OF LIFE

So we look from the beginning of the Bible to its end. The Bible begins in a garden but ends in a city. Our hope is not to return to the womb, to the joys of a fabulous golden age of the past. Our hope is not for a reversal of history or for a removal of experience. The city is the ultimate community, to which each citizen brings the wealth of his experience and the benefit of his acquired skills. The origin of man is in natural imagery, his destiny is in political imagery. Political action will not, of itself, bring about the Kingdom of Heaven on earth; but it is in terms of political rather than biological science that we assess the degree to which man is approximating to or deviating from his destiny.

In the city of God, as in the garden, the tree of life is in the middle.[68] In fact, its meaning and blessing are made doubly secure by the vision that there are two trees, one on each side of the river, drawing sustenance from the water of life and making it available to the nations. They do not only bear fruit for the maintenance of life: they bear medicinal leaves for the restoring of life and for the rectifying of the disorder of the nations. They represent the purpose of God to make man whole, to make all groups of men whole, and to make all the universe whole.[69] The river is in between the trees, and runs down the middle street of the city which is God's gift to his people. This double image of the tree of life in the city of God can, therefore, represent the point of convergence of the whole creation, human and non-human.[70] In this view God is worshipped by the innumerable throng of people who are moving *out of* their nations, their groups of ancestral and cultural origins, *into* the single community of adoration.[71] But, as in the Pentecost experience, their true diversity is not overruled; the image of the city, the complex community, is there to safeguard the precious individuality of each person: each person in the final community has a specific identity as a son of God.[72]

For Adam and for the whole of mankind, the way to the tree of life is not opened by acts of individual heroism in battle against the sword and the cherubim, but by sharing in the community of Christ, who has overcome death and all that separates man from man. 'The words, "In Adam all . . ." included the whole family of man in death; the promise, "In Christ all . . ." cannot include less than that in life. The genealogies of the gospel linking Christ himself with the unknown myriads of the past are a symbol of the unbroken cord with which God will finally draw Adam to Paradise.'[73]

The vision of the heavenly Jerusalem is beyond space or history. There remains the earthly Jerusalem, very much in space and history. Adam died. A tradition developed that his skull was buried at 'a place called the place of a skull, which is called in the Hebrew Golgotha'.[74] And there was set up another tree, outside the walls of that city, which is in space and history. '*Lignum crucis arbor scientiae*' – 'the wood of the cross is the tree of knowledge'. Set in the middle of space and history, the cross is for us the tree of truth and of life; it is the sign that we can be associated with the Lord of life only through death; but it is also the sign of healing, for he who is lifted up on the tree is drawing all men to himself and so to each other.[75]

This whole story has been about me, for I am Adam. I am in the middle of space and history, for I measure things in space in terms of their distance from me, and I measure things in history in terms of the interval of time which separates them from the moment which I now experience. If Adam is not me, he is not, his story is an idle diversion. If Christ has come to take us and break us and make us his body, must we not say the same also of him, the second Adam? If Christ also is not me, he is not; his story also is an idle diversion to me if I am not identified with him, not because I am good, but because he is man.

> We thinke that Paradise and Calvarie,
>   Christ's Crosse, and Adam's tree, stood in one place;
> Looke Lord, and finde both Adams met in me;
>   As the first Adam's sweat surrounds my face,
>   May the last Adam's blood my soule embrace.[76]

Notes

CHAPTER 1

1. Augustine, *Confessions*, trans. R. S. Pine-Coffin (Penguin, Harmondsworth, 1961).
2. Dietrich Bonhoeffer, *Creation and Fall*, trans. John C. Fletcher (SCM Press, London, 1959).
3. John 14: 9.
4. Revised Standard Version, Preface.
5. Revelation 7: 9 14.
6. Colossians 1: 20.
7. Matthew 27: 57—28: 7; Luke 24: 5.
8. G. A. F. Knight, *A Christian Theology of the Old Testament* (SCM Press, London, 1959), p. 109.
9. Gerhard von Rad, *Old Testament Theology*, trans. D. M. G. Stalker (Oliver & Boyd, Edinburgh, 1962, 1965), Vol. I, p. 148.
10. Ibid., Vol. II, p. 338.
11. Gerardus van der Leeuw, *Sacred and Profane Beauty*, trans. David E. Green (Weidenfeld & Nicolson, London, 1963), p. 280.
12. William Wordsworth, *Ode: Intimations of Immortality from Recollections of Early Childhood*, l. 18.
13. Hebrews 11: 14–16 (R.S.V.).

CHAPTER 2

1. John 1: 1, 2, 14; Chrysostom, quoted in Thomas Aquinas, *Catena Aurea* (E.T., Parker, Oxford, 1845), Vol. IV, pt. 1, p. 7.
2. D. Bonhoeffer, *Creation and Fall*, p. 13.
3. Augustine, *Confessions*, p. 262.
4. Ibid., p. 263.
5. Jeremiah 23: 7–8.
6. Luke 3: 8.
7. Psalm 24: 1.
8. Isaiah 44: 28—45: 7.
9. Exodus 32: 4.
10. 2 Samuel 6: 6.
11. Genesis 28: 16 ff.
12. Exodus 3: 5.

13. Deuteronomy 16: 2.
14. Acts 7: 47; Revelation 21: 3.
15. Colossians 1: 20.
16. Colossians 1: 15.
17. L. S. Thornton, *The Common Life in the Body of Christ* (Dacre Press, London, 1942), p. 293.
18. Colossians 1: 20.
19. E. L. Mascall, *Christian Theology and Natural Science* (Longmans, Green, London, 1956), p. 155.
20. Augustine, op. cit., p. 283.
21. Ephesians 3: 19.
22. Job 3: 21.
23. *The Book of Common Prayer*, Collect for the Fourth Sunday after Trinity.
24. C. S. Lewis, *Screwtape Letters* (Geoffrey Bles, London, 1942), p. 64.
25. G. K. Chesterton, *The Innocence of Father Brown* (Penguin, Harmondsworth, 1950), p. 140.
26. Mark 15: 33–34.
27. Quoted by Helmut Thielike, *How the World Began*, trans. John W. Doberstein (James Clarke, London, 1964), p. 25.
28. 2 Maccabees 7: 28.
29. Hebrews 11: 3.
30. Romans 4: 17; 1 Corinthians 1: 28.
31. J. E. Fison, *The Blessing of the Holy Spirit* (Longmans, Green, London, 1950), p. 211.
32. Carl G. Jung, *The Integration of the Personality*, trans. Stanley Dell (Kegan Paul, Trench, Trubner, London, 1940), p. 295.
33. 2 Corinthians 5: 21.
34. G. A. F. Knight, *A Christian Theology of the Old Testament*, p. 111.
35. Exodus 10: 21.
36. Jonah 2: 3.
37. 1 Kings 19.
38. G. von Rad, *Genesis*, trans. John H. Marks (SCM Press, London, 1961), p. 47.
39. J. E. Fison, op. cit., p. 186.
40. Matthew 8: 18 ff.
41. Acts 2: 2.
42. Matthew 3: 13–17.
43. John 16: 7; 14: 12.
44. H. A. Williams, *Jesus and the Resurrection* (Longmans, Green, London, 1951), p. 7.
45. Psalm 33: 6, 9.

46. Psalm 119: 32.
47. D. Bonhoeffer, *Ethics*, trans. Neville Horton Smith (SCM Press, London, 1955), p. 248.
48. The Koran, trans. J. Rodwell (Dent, London, 1909), sura 3, v. 42, p. 390.
49. John 1: 4.
50. Psalm 148: 5.
51. Paul Tournier, *A Doctor's Casebook in the Light of the Bible*, trans. Edwin Hudson (SCM Press, London, 1954), p. 143.
52. John 1: 5.
53. J. E. Fison, *The Christian Hope* (Longmans, Green, London, 1954), p. 95.
54. John 2: 4; 7: 30; 12: 27–31; Galatians 4: 4.
55. T. R. Milford, *Foolishness to the Greeks* (SCM Press, London, 1953), p. 24.
56. Pierre Teilhard de Chardin, *The Phenomenon of Man* (Collins, London, 1959), p. 68.
57. Genesis 22.
58. See D. Bonhoeffer, *The Cost of Discipleship* (SCM Press, London, 1959), p. 85.
59. 2 Corinthians 6: 14–18; Revelation 2: 20; 3: 16.
60. Ephesians 3: 17.
61. Mark 4: 3–8, 26–32; 13: 28–29; Matthew 13: 24–30.
62. Matthew 2: 1–12.
63. Acts 13: 6.
64. Ignatius of Antioch, *Letter to the Ephesians*, 19, in *Early Christian Writings*, trans. Maxwell Staniforth (Penguin, Harmondsworth, 1968), p. 81.
65. Augustine, *Contra Faustum Manichaeum*, II, 5, quoted in M. F. Toal, *Patristic Homilies on the Gospels* (Mercier Press, Cork, 1955), Vol. I, p. 233.
66. *The Cloud of Unknowing*, trans. Clifton Wolters (Penguin, Harmondsworth, 1961), pp. 128–9.
67. Teilhard de Chardin, op. cit., p. 100.
68. John 12: 23 ff.
69. Mark 8: 34–35.
70. Revelation 13; 19: 11–21.
71. Erich Fromm, *The Art of Loving* (Allen & Unwin, London, 1962), p. 40.
72. Romans 8: 38–39; Galatians 2: 20.
73. John 19: 30.

CHAPTER 3

1. Deuteronomy 6: 4; Isaiah 42: 8.

2. Genesis 11 : 7; Isaiah 6 : 8.
3. J. W. Colenso, *The Pentateuch and the Book of Joshua Critically Examined* (Longman, Green, Longman, Roberts & Green, London, 1863), Vol. IV, p. 106.
4. John 20: 22–23.
5. Erich Fromm, *The Art of Loving*, p. 38.
6. N. Berdyaev, *Freedom and the Spirit* (Geoffrey Bles, London, 1935), p. 70.
7. Teilhard de Chardin, *The Phenomenon of Man*, Introduction by Sir Julian Huxley, p. 20.
8. John Burnaby, *Darwin and the Human Situation* (Heffer, Cambridge, 1959), p. 6.
9. Teilhard de Chardin, op. cit., p. 184.
10. G. van der Leeuw, *Sacred and Profane Beauty*, p. 158.
11. Colossians 1 : 15.
12. M. Luther, *Ein' feste Burg*, trans. T. Carlyle: *The English Hymnal*, no. 362 (Oxford University Press, London, 1933).
13. See J. E. Fison, *The Blessing of the Holy Spirit*, pp. 189 ff.
14. Werner Pelz, *Irreligious Reflections on the Christian Church* (SCM Press, London, 1959), pp. 77 ff.
15. J.-P. Sartre, *Nausea*, trans. Robert Baldick (Penguin, Harmondsworth, 1965), p. 180.
16. G. van der Leeuw, op. cit., p. 160.
17. C. Cavarnos, 'Iconographic Decoration in the Orthodox Church', in *The Orthodox Ethos*, ed. A. J. Philippou (Faith Press, London, 1964), p. 182.
18. Philippians 2: 6–8.
19. Konrad Lorenz, *On Aggression* (Methuen, London, 1967), p. 196.
20. Quoted in Frank Lake, *Clinical Theology* (Darton, Longman & Todd, London, 1966), p. 138.
21. Theodosius Dobzhansky, *The Biological Basis of Human Freedom* (Columbia University Press, New York, 1954), pp. 56 f.
22. Genesis 11 : 1–9.
23. Acts 2: 5, 41.
24. Acts 2: 8–10, 42–47.
25. Matthew 28: 19.
26. Acts 2: 17–18.
27. John 11 : 50.
28. John 8: 39.
29. Mark 11 : 18.
30. John 12: 9–19.
31. John 7: 41–52.

32. 1 Corinthians 13: 12.
33. Exodus 3.
34. See Genesis 6: 1–4, for an example in the Hebrew scriptures.
35. Galatians 4: 5.
36. Matthew 27: 17.
37. 2 Samuel 23: 20.
38. T. H. White, *The Sword in the Stone* (Collins, London, 1950), p. 314.
39. Ephesians 4: 10.
40. Reinhold Niebuhr, *An Interpretation of Christian Ethics* (Meridian Books, New York, 1956), p. 167.
41. John 13: 13–17.
42. 1 Corinthians 12: 4–30.
43. John 18: 23.
44. Robert Bolt, *A Man for All Seasons*, in *New English Dramatists 6* (Penguin, Harmondsworth, 1963), p. 97.
45. Acts 22: 25.
46. Matthew 28: 18.
47. Mark 12: 13–17.
48. e.g. Psalm 10.
49. Matthew 28: 19.
50. Galatians 3: 27–28.
51. Judges 12: 6.
52. Ephesians 1: 10.
53. Ephesians 3: 1–11.
54. Psalm 8.
55. Matthew 6: 19–21.
56. Galatians 1: 8–11.
57. 1 Corinthians 3: 3–5.
58. Harvey Cox, *The Secular City* (SCM Press, London, 1965), p. 130.
59. Psalm 24: 1.
60. Psalm 115: 16.
61. Leviticus 25: 23.
62. Colossians 3: 5.
63. Deuteronomy 26: 1–4.
64. e.g. Judges 8: 23.
65. 1 Samuel 8: 10–20.
66. Deuteronomy 19: 14.
67. 1 Kings 21.
68. Numbers 18: 24.
69. F. Verinder, *My Neighbour's Landmark* (Land and Liberty Press, London, 1950), p. 58.
70. H. A. Williams, *Jesus and the Resurrection*, pp. 19 ff.

263

71. Denis de Rougemont, *Lettres sur la bombe atomique*, quoted in P. Tournier, *A Doctor's Casebook in the Light of the Bible*, p. 27.
72. Matthew 4: 1–11.
73. Matthew 11: 4–5.
74. Michael Frayn, *The Book of Fub* (Collins, Fontana, London, 1965), p. 136.
75. Luke 24: 16; John 20: 14; 21: 4.
76. John 12: 24; 1 Corinthians 15: 36–44.
77. Genesis 9: 3.
78. Isaiah 11: 1–9.
79. G. von Rad, *Genesis*, p. 60.
80. Exodus 18.
81. Hebrews 3: 5–6.
82. F. Lake, op. cit., pp. 353 ff.
83. Ibid., p. 340.
84. Julian of Norwich, *Revelations of Divine Love*, ed. G. Warrack (Methuen, London, 1923), p. 10.
85. Nehemiah 9: 6.
86. Psalm 104: 14, 20, 22.
87. Augustine, *Confessions*, p. 21.
88. Exodus 20: 8–11.
89. Deuteronomy 31: 10–13.
90. Julius K. Nyerere, 'Education for Self-Reliance', in *The Ecumenical Review*, Vol. XIX, No. 4 (World Council of Churches, Geneva, October 1967), pp. 382 ff.
91. Exodus 23: 11; Leviticus 25: 1–7.
92. Leviticus 25: 8–17.
93. Leviticus 25: 29–31.
94. Psalm 115: 16.
95. Philippians 3: 20.
96. Revelation 21: 1.
97. Romans 8: 38–39.
98. 1 Kings 8: 30.
99. 1 Kings 8: 27.
100. Psalm 8: 5–6.

CHAPTER 4

1. Ian G. Barbour, *Issues in Science and Religion* (SCM Press, London, 1968), pp. 419 ff.
2. For a detailed exposition of the nature of apostasy and idolatry, see J. E. Fison, *The Blessing of the Holy Spirit*, Chapters 8 and 9.
3. Erich Fromm, *The Art of Loving*, p. 59.
4. Herbert Butterfield, *The Origins of Modern Science* (Bell,

London, 1957), p. 1. For an extended study of the implications of this paragraph, especially with reference to the principle of 'bisociation', see Arthur Koestler, *The Act of Creation* (Hutchinson, London, 1964). For a theoretical and practical study of the educational processes which can train minds for creative thinking, see Edward de Bono, *Lateral Thinking: A Textbook of Creativity* (Ward Lock, London, 1970). Both these books are full of provocative insights which are relevant to the theme of the present chapter.

5. Augustine, *Confessions*, pp. 295, 308.
6. Quoted by C. A. Coulson, *Science and Christian Belief* (Collins, Fontana, London, 1958), p. 80.
7. Teilhard de Chardin, *The Phenomenon of Man*, p. 211.
8. Letter signed 'Speckled' in *The Star*, Johannesburg, 20 May 1963.
9. C. A. Coulson, op. cit., p. 122.
10. L. C. Birch, *Nature and God* (SCM Press, London, 1965), p. 60.
11. Robert L. Short, *The Gospel According to Peanuts* (Collins, Fontana, London, 1966), pp. 69 f.
12. Teilhard de Chardin, op. cit., pp. 189 f.

CHAPTER 5

1. Exodus 3.
2. 1 Kings 18: 39.
3. 1 Kings 18: 21.
4. John 20: 28.
5. Paul Tillich, *The New Being* (SCM Press, London, 1956), p. 109.
6. Mark 5: 21–43.
7. Helmut Gollwitzer, *The Demands of Freedom* (SCM Press, London, 1965), p. 80.
8. James Thurber, *The Thirteen Clocks* (Hamish Hamilton, London, 1951), p. 106.
9. Michel Quoist, *Prayers of Life* (Gill, Dublin, 1963), p. 111.
10. John 14: 28.
11. John 20: 17.
12. Françoise Gilot and Carlton Lake, *Life with Picasso* (Nelson, London, 1965), pp. 214–19.
13. John 4: 10, 14; 7: 37–38.
14. G. A. F. Knight, *A Christian Theology of the Old Testament*, p. 33.
15. Ezekiel 37: 1–10.
16. 1 Corinthians 12: 12.
17. Theodosius Dobzhansky, *The Biological Basis of Human Freedom*, p. 13.

18. Teilhard de Chardin, *The Phenomenon of Man*, p. 121.
19. G. van der Leeuw, *Sacred and Profane Beauty*, p. 210 (see also p. 204).
20. Revelation 21: 1, 23; 22: 1–2.
21. G. von Rad, *Genesis*, p. 77.
22. Luke 23: 39–43.
23. 1 Peter 3: 19.
24. John V. Taylor, *The Primal Vision* (SCM Press, London, 1963), pp. 164 ff.
25. John 20: 15.
26. 1 Samuel 10: 8. Augustine, seventh homily on 1 John, para. 8, in Augustine, *Later Works*, selected and translated by John Burnaby (SCM Press, London, 1955), p. 316.
27. D. Bonhoeffer, *Ethics*, p. 248.
28. Isaiah 14: 12–14.
29. John Milton, *Paradise Lost*, Book 1, l. 263.
30. Reinhold Niebuhr, *An Interpretation of Christian Ethics*, p. 83. 2 Corinthians 11: 14.
31. Philippians 2: 1–8.
32. Luke 10: 18.
33. Isaiah 45: 7; Amos 3: 6.
34. John 15: 16.
35. 1 John 4: 8. See Ian G. Barbour, *Issues in Science and Religion*, p. 445.
36. Genesis 3: 5, 22.
37. Matthew 4: 1–11.
38. See H. A. Williams, *God's Wisdom in Christ's Cross* (Mowbray, Oxford, 1960), pp. 21 ff.
39. Luke 23: 39–43.
40. Mark 15: 34.
41. Luther, quoted in D. Bonhoeffer, *Life Together*, trans. John W. Doberstein (SCM Press, London, 1954), p. 7.
42. Acts 8: 26–40.
43. Erich Fromm, *The Art of Loving*, p. 81.
44. Luke 6: 12; Matthew 11: 27; John 14: 10.
45. John 16: 32–33.
46. J. E. Fison, *The Blessing of the Holy Spirit*, pp. 197 f.
47. H. Butterfield, *The Origins of Modern Science*, p. 221.
48. C. A. Coulson, *Science and Christian Belief*, p. 50.
49. Matthew 22: 42.
50. Exodus 3: 14. Martin Buber, *Moses* (Harper & Row, New York, 1958), p. 52. (The version Buber gives is actually, 'I shall be present as which I shall be present'.)
51. Ibid., p. 50.

52. John 20: 28.
53. John 11: 50.
54. Howard Thurman, *Jesus and the Disinherited* (Abingdon, Nashville, 1949), p. 19.
55. John 3: 3–5.
56. John 1: 12–13.
57. Mark 3: 28–30.
58. e.g. Judges 5.
59. H. A. Williams, *The True Wilderness* (Constable, London, 1965), p. 52.
60. H. Butterfield, op. cit., p. 73.
61. Harvey Cox, *The Secular City*, p. 24.
62. Quoted by H. Butterfield, op. cit., p. 98.
63. Teilhard de Chardin, op. cit., p. 230.
64. Hebrews 11: 8–10.
65. A. N. Whitehead, *Process and Reality*, quoted in L. C. Birch, *Nature and God*, p. 59.
66. Matthew 24: 23.
67. *The Cloud of Unknowing*, pp. 59–60.
68. H. Thielike, *How the World Began*, p. 100.
69. J.-P. Sartre, *L'être et le Néant*, quoted in Paul Tournier, *The Meaning of Persons*, trans. Edwin Hudson (SCM Press, London, 1957), p. 130.
70. 1 Corinthians 13: 6.
71. Genesis 5: 2.
72. Revelation 2: 17.
73. Victor White, *God and the Unconscious* (Collins, Fontana, London, 1960), p. 44.
74. Peter Abrahams, *Return to Goli* (Faber & Faber, London, 1953), p. 97.
75. 2 Samuel 13.
76. Erich Fromm, op. cit., p. 43.
77. James Thurber and E. B. White, *Is Sex Necessary?* (Penguin, Harmondsworth, 1960), p. 88.
78. D. H. Lawrence, *A Propos of Lady Chatterley*, pp. 246 f., quoted in *The Trial of Lady Chatterley*, ed. C. H. Rolfe (Penguin, Harmondsworth, 1961), p. 160.
79. Ephesians 5: 31–33.
80. e.g. Judges 14: 20.
81. Luke 2: 41–51.
82. Mark 3: 31–35; Luke 11: 27–28.
83. Luke 2: 35.

CHAPTER 6

1. Bengt Sundkler, *The Christian Ministry in Africa* (SCM Press, London, 1960), p. 284.
2. See Marie-Louise Martin, *The Biblical Concept of Messianism and Messianism in Southern Africa* (Morija, Basutoland, 1964), p. 109.
3. Reinhold Niebuhr, *The Nature and Destiny of Man* (Nisbet, London, 1943), Vol. II, p. 5.
4. J. E. Fison, *The Christian Hope*, p. 27.
5. M.-L. Martin, op. cit., p. 106.
6. B. Sundkler, op. cit., pp. 283 f.
7. G. von Rad, *Old Testament Theology*, Vol. I, pp. 141, 154.
8. See note 6 of chapter 3, p. 68.
9. Ezekiel 28: 11–15.
10. John Osborne, *A Subject of Scandal and Concern* (Faber & Faber, London, 1961), p. 46.

CHAPTER 7

1. e.g. S. R. Driver, *The Book of Genesis* (Methuen, London, 1904), p. 36.
2. 2 Corinthians 11: 3. See R. H. Strachan, *The Second Epistle of Paul to the Corinthians* (Hodder & Stoughton, London, 1935), p. 18.
3. Numbers 21: 6.
4. Numbers 21: 9.
5. Isaiah 6: 2.
6. 2 Kings 18: 4.
7. John 3: 14.
8. Revelation 12: 9.
9. Stephen Potter, *Supermanship* (Rupert Hart-Davis, London, 1958), p. 28.
10. Isaiah 40: 25.
11. Roger Tennant, *Theology*, Vol. LXIV (S.P.C.K., London, December 1961), p. 504.
12. Matthew 7: 24.
13. Matthew 23: 4–22.
14. Philippians 2: 6.
15. H. A. Williams, 'Theology and Self-Awareness', in *Soundings*, ed. A. R. Vidler (Cambridge University Press, London, 1962), pp. 83 f.
16. Jeremiah 7: 4.
17. Exodus 32: 8.
18. 1 Corinthians 15: 10.

19. Ephesians 3: 12.
20. e.g. *The Orthodox Liturgy* (S.P.C.K., London, 1939), p. 53.
21. H. A. Williams, *The True Wilderness*, p. 141.
22. K. Lorenz, *On Aggression*, p. 205.
23. Mark 2: 7.
24. Luke 15: 2.
25. E. L. Mascall, *Christian Theology and Natural Science*, p. 34.
26. T. Dobzhansky, *The Biological Basis of Human Freedom*, p. 132.
27. Ibid., p. 118.
28. J. Burnaby, *Darwin and the Human Situation*, p. 8.
29. T. H. Huxley, *Evolution and Ethics* (Macmillan, London, 1903), p. 83. For a fuller discussion of this question, see Ian G. Barbour, *Issues in Science and Religion*, pp. 408–14.
30. Luke 24: 31; 2 Corinthians 5: 4.
31. Luke 23: 12.
32. Mark 12: 13.
33. John 18: 3.
34. Paul van Buren, *The Secular Meaning of the Gospel* (SCM Press, London, 1963), p. 179.
35. T. E. Hulme, *Speculations*, ed. Herbert Read (Kegan Paul, Trench, Trubner, London, 1936), pp. 13, 71, etc.
36. Paul van Buren, op. cit., p. 180.
37. E. W. Southcott, *The Parish Comes Alive* (Mowbray, Oxford, 1956), p. 43.
38. Matthew 7: 23.
39. Matthew 5: 20–48.
40. John 8: 1–11.
41. e.g. J. A. T. Robinson, *Honest to God* (SCM Press, London, 1963), pp. 11 ff.
42. Psalm 139: 7–10.
43. Jonah 1: 3–4.
44. Paul Tillich, *The Shaking of the Foundations* (Penguin, Harmondsworth, 1962), pp. 47 ff.
45. Mark 10: 17; Luke 12: 14.
46. Luke 10: 25–37.
47. Howard Thurman, *Jesus and the Disinherited*, p. 77.
48. Luke 15: 4–10.
49. John 1: 11.
50. Matthew 14: 36.
51. John 16: 13.
52. Matthew 22: 11–14.
53. Matthew 22: 1–10.
54. Carl G. Jung, *Answer to Job*, trans. R. F. C. Hull (Routledge & Kegan Paul, London, 1954), p. 70.

55. D. Bonhoeffer, *Creation and Fall*, pp. 82 f.
56. Luke 6: 37.
57. Luke 15: 30.
58. H. Thielike, *How the World Began*, p. 166.
59. Reinhold Niebuhr, *An Interpretation of Christian Ethics*, p. 78.
60. Luke 9: 2.
61. Sydney Carter, 'Friday Morning', v. 2: full text in *Risk*, Vol. II, No. 3 (World Council of Churches and World Council of Christian Education, Geneva, 1966), p. 43.
62. 1 Peter 2: 24.
63. Luke 22: 37.
64. Mark 14: 50.
65. Mark 8: 33.
66. Mark 9: 32–33.

CHAPTER 8

1. *English Reports*, Vol. XCIII, King's Bench Division, XXII (William Green, London, 1909), I Strange 557. I owe this observation to an allusion to the case in *Practical Motorist*, April 1970 (IPC Magazines, London, 1970).
2. Revelation 12: 9.
3. 1 Corinthians 11: 11.
4. 1 Corinthians 11: 12.
5. Ephesians 5: 25.
6. Ephesians 5: 21.
7. Ephesians 5: 22.
8. P. Tillich, *The Shaking of the Foundations*, p. 89.
9. Romans 8: 19–22.
10. Romans 8: 23.
11. Psalms 89; 135; 136; Habakkuk 3.
12. Exodus 14: 21–22.
13. Matthew 2: 9; Luke 2: 7.
14. Mark 15: 33.
15. Matthew 27: 51.
16. Matthew 28: 2.
17. Acts 2: 2–3.
18. John 17: 4.
19. Matthew 15: 24.
20. John 19: 5.
21. John 4: 34.
22. N. Berdyaev, quoted by J. A. T. Robinson, *On Being the Church in the World* (SCM Press, London, 1960), p. 35.
23. Philippians 3: 13.
24. Ecclesiastes 7: 16.

25. H. A. Williams, *Jesus and the Resurrection*, pp. 66 f.
26. John 6: 39.
27. Augustine, *Confessions*, p. 79.
28. 1 Corinthians 15: 58.
29. 1 Corinthians 15: 26; Romans 6: 23.
30. D. Bonhoeffer, *The Cost of Discipleship*, p. 79.
31. John 3: 5.
32. Romans 6: 4.
33. *The Little Flowers of Saint Francis*, trans. L. Sherley-Price (Penguin, Harmondsworth, 1959), p. 200.
34. D. Bonhoeffer, *Letters and Papers from Prison* (E.T., SCM Press, London, 1967), p. 203.
35. Genesis 5: 1.
36. Luke 1: 38.
37. John 19: 27.
38. Matthew 18: 21–35; Ephesians 4: 32.
39. 1 Corinthians 15: 21.
40. J.-P. Sartre, *Huis Clos*, E.T. *In Camera*, in *Three European Plays* (Penguin, Harmondsworth, 1958).
41. John 10: 4.
42. Genesis 23.
43. Matthew 28: 5–20.
44. Matthew 28: 18.
45. John 10: 4.
46. Deuteronomy 32: 11.
47. The Bishop of Nagpur at the Anglican Congress, Toronto, in *Anglican Congress 1963* (S.P.C.K., London, and Seabury, New York, 1963), p. 126.
48. John 19: 5.
49. Ephesians 4: 8, 11–13.
50. Galatians 6: 15.
51. Romans 8: 38–39.
52. Mark 3: 29–30.
53. Luke 15: 20, 24, 28, 31.
54. J. W. Colenso, *The Pentateuch and the Book of Joshua Critically Examined*, Vol. IV, p. 151.
55. Ezekiel 1: 5; 10: 1, etc.
56. A. C. Bridge, *Images of God* (Hodder & Stoughton, London, 1960), p. 29.
57. Luke 1: 29.
58. Colossians 2: 15.
59. Martin Luther King, Jnr., *Stride Toward Freedom* (Gollancz, London, 1959), p. 192.
60. H. A. Williams, *The True Wilderness*, p. 144.

61. Frank Lake, *Clinical Theology*, p. 369.
62. Malachi 4: 6.
63. Luke 5: 1–11.
64. L. C. Birch, *Nature and God*, p. 101.
65. John 16: 8–11. See H. A. Williams, *The Four Last Things* (Mowbray, Oxford, 1960), p. 18.
66. Revelation 2: 3.
67. Revelation 2: 1–7.
68. Revelation 22: 2.
69. Ephesians 1: 10.
70. See Teilhard de Chardin, *The Phenomenon of Man*, pp. 293 f.
71. Revelation 7: 9–10.
72. Revelation 21: 7.
73. John V. Taylor, *The Primal Vision*, p. 171. 1 Corinthians 15: 22.
74. Mark 15: 22. A. E. J. Rawlinson, *The Gospel According to Saint Mark* (Methuen, London, 1925), p. 233.
75. John 12: 32.
76. John Donne, 'Hymne to GOD my GOD, in my sicknesse'.

Acknowledgments

The author and publishers wish to acknowledge their indebtedness for permission to reproduce copyright material as follows: from the New English Bible, Old Testament, © 1970, by permission of Oxford and Cambridge University Presses; from *Confessions* of St Augustine, translated by R. S. Pine-Coffin and published by Penguin Books, Harmondsworth, 1961; from *Creation and Fall* by Dietrich Bonhoeffer, translated by John C. Fletcher, and published by SCM Press, London, and Macmillan, New York, 1959; from *The Origins of Modern Science* by H. Butterfield, published by G. Bell, London, 1951; from 'Friday Morning' by Sydney Carter, published in *Songs of Sydney Carter in the Present Tense*, Book 2, © 1960 Galliard Ltd, published in Great Britain by Galliard Ltd and distributed in the United States by Galaxy Music Corporation; from *The Biological Basis of Human Freedom* by Theodosius Dobzhansky, published by Columbia University Press, New York, 1954; from *The Blessing of the Holy Spirit* by J. E. Fison, published by Longmans, Green, London, 1950; from *The Christian Hope* by J. E. Fison, published by Longmans, Green, London, 1954; from *The Art of Loving* by Eric Fromm, published by Allen & Unwin, London, and Harper & Row, New York, 1957; from *A Christian Theology of the Old Testament* by G. A. F. Knight, published by SCM Press, London, and John Knox Press, Richmond, 1959; from *An Interpretation of Christian Ethics* by Reinhold Niebuhr, published by Meridian Books, Cleveland, 1956; from *Irreligious Reflections on the Christian Church* by Werner Pelz, published by SCM Press, London, 1959; from a letter signed 'Speckled', published in *The Star*, Johannesburg, South Africa, 20 May 1963; from *Jesus and the Disinherited* by Howard Thurman, published by Abingdon Press, Nashville, 1949; from *Jesus and the Resurrection* by H. A. Williams, published by Longmans, Green, London, 1951; from *Theology and Self-Awareness* by H. A. Williams, published by Cambridge University Press, London, 1962.

Index of Names and Subjects

A figure in brackets after a reference to one of the 'Notes' pages (pp. 259-72) indicates the related page in the main text.

Aaron, 28

Abel, 233, 246

Abraham, 13 f., 24, 49, 82, 248

Abrahams, Peter, 172, 267

Adam, 13, 127, 140, 145, 147, 151, 153, 163 f., 166 f., 175, 183 f., 194, 208 ff., 213 f., 217 f., 219, 221, 224, 226 f., 241 f., 245 f., 248 ff., 257 f.

Africa, African, 20, 81, 97, 99, 117, 125, 134, 139, 142, 171, 176, 179 ff., 186, 210, 247 f.

Afrikaner, 181

Ahab, 98

Amos, 248

Angels (cherubim, seraphim), 187, 249, 251 ff., 254, 257

Antichrist, 159, 161

Aquinas, Thomas, 259 (21)

Aristotle, 119, 122, 163, 184

Augustine, 14, 22 f., 32, 56, 124, 140, 146, 239, 259, 260, 261, 264 (110), 265, 266, 271 (239)

Babel, 80

Babylon, Babylonian, 17 ff., 54, 107, 147

Bacon, Francis, 163

Baptism, 15, 93, 136, 154, 161, 199, 240

Barabbas, 83

Barbour, Ian G., 9, 120, 264, 266, 269 (206)

Beckett, Samuel, 185

Bentley, Dr, 226

Berdyaev, Nicholas, 68, 184, 262, 270 (236)

Birch, L. C., 126, 265, 267 (165), 272 (256)

Bolt, Robert, 263 (92)

Bonhoeffer, Dietrich, 14, 241, 259 (22), 261 (42), 261 (49), 266 (146), 266 (154), 270 (218), 271 (240), 271 (241)

Bono, Edward de, 265 (124)

Book of Common Prayer, The, 34, 146, 260

Book of Common Prayer (South Africa), 110

Breughel, Pieter, 117, 188

Bridge, A. C. 252, 271

Bridges, Robert, 117

Britten, Benjamin, 189

Buber, Martin, 158 f., 266

Burnaby, John, 69, 205, 262, 269

Burnet, Thomas, 251

Butterfield, Herbert, 162, 264 (123), 266 (157), 267 (163)

Caiaphas, 159

Cain, 233, 246

Carter, Sydney, 270 (224)

Cavarnos, C., 262 (74)

Chesterton, G. K., 35, 244, 260

Chrysostom, St John, 22, 259

Church, 15, 16, 25, 55, 71 f., 81, 90, 92 f., 100, 103 f., 120 ff., 136, 148, 153, 164 f., 194 f., 199, 204, 209 f., 214 f., 218, 224 f., 229, 230, 234, 240, 249

Civilization, 140, 248

Cleopas, 206

Cloud of Unknowing, The, 261 (57), 267 (166)

Colenso, J. W., 54, 67, 262, 271 (252)

Commandment, 26, 42, 84, 110, 145 ff.

Cosmology, 18, 30 f., 42, 213
Coulson, C. A., 126, 265 (125), 265, 266 (157)
Cox, Harvey, 96, 163, 263, 267
Curse, 95, 153, 185, 226 ff., 233 ff., 237
Cyrus, 149

Damascene, St John, 74
Darwin, Charles, 133
Death, 55, 59, 152, 164, 219, 237 ff., 243, 244 f., 250 f., 258
de Rougemont, Denis, 102, 264
Devil, 147 f., 185, 188, 192, 227
Dobzhansky, Theodosius, 79, 136, 205, 262, 265, 269
Donne, John, 117, 272 (258)
Doubt, 162 ff., 187 f., 212
Driver, S. R., 268 (186)
Duns Scotus, J., 147

Eden, Paradise, 139 ff., 173, 183 f., 226, 246, 251, 256, 258
Education, 20, 56, 84, 90 f., 97, 103, 111, 123, 163, 169
Egypt, 19, 37, 70, 74
Elijah, 38 f.
English, 39, 156, 167, 171, 180 f.
English Reports, 270 (226)
Ethiopian eunuch, 154
Eucharist, 15, 25, 81, 100, 110, 113, 136, 143, 146, 169, 199, 206, 236
Europe, Europeans, 20, 81, 99, 142, 176, 181, 248
Eve, the woman, 80, 165, 170 f., 186, 192, 193 f., 197 ff., 208, 211, 217 f., 228, 229, 241 f.
Evil, 63, 66, 147 ff., 184, 220 f., 237, 240, 256
Evolution, 17, 59, 68, 85, 101, 110, 125, 136, 157, 205 f.
Exile, 82, 119, 244
Exodus, 13 ff., 24 f., 232, 244
Ezekiel, 248

Faith, 73, 86, 131, 164 f., 191
Fison, J. E., 10, 40, 182, 260 (36),

260, 261 (45), 262 (71), 264 (121), 266 (155), 268
Forgiveness, 67, 200, 203 f., 206, 219 f., 234, 243
Fortescue, J., 226
Francis of Assisi, 241; Little Flowers of, 271
Frayn, Michael, 264 (104)
Freedom, 23, 56, 71 f., 95, 117, 133, 241
Freud, Sigmund, 133
Fromm, Erich, 64, 68, 122, 154, 173, 261, 262, 264, 266, 267

Gabriel, 253
Galileo, 123
Gilot, F., 265 (134)
God; as Father, 14, 17, 20, 21, 40, 63, 83, 83, 130 f.; image of (see also Jesus Christ), 67, 69, 70 ff., 78, 169, 193; nature, character of, 34, 35, 41, 42, 48, 49, 66, 79, 120, 121, 131, 133, 150, 153, 158, 161, 168, 170, 188, 213, 214, 215, 233, 248, 255
'God', meaning of, 24, 25, 27, 30, 31, 39, 69, 115, 129, 151, 191, 196, 218
Gollwitzer, Helmut, 132, 265
Grace, 194 f., 212, 224
Graves, Robert, 104
Greek, 39, 141, 180
Grünewald, Matthias, 224
Guilt, 185, 212, 222

Hamlet, 133
Handel, G. F., 117
Haydn, Joseph, 10, 33, 39, 61, 108
Hebrew, Hebrews, Israel, 14, 15, 17, 21, 24, 26, 28, 37, 39, 45, 54, 67, 82, 83, 98, 111, 117, 133, 134 ff., 167, 171, 175, 180, 194, 201, 213, 223, 232
Herod Antipas, 207
Herod the Great, 29, 55
History, 14, 15 ff., 29, 37 f., 129, 158, 180 f., 245, 258
Hollis, Christopher, 182

Hope, 16, 110, 241, 257
Hulme, T. E., 209, 269
Huxley, Sir Julian, 68, 262
Huxley, T. H., 206, 269

Ignatius of Antioch, 56, 261
India, Indian, 35, 46, 124, 140
Isaac, 49
Israel, Israelite, *see* Hebrew
Iwand, H. J., 132

Jacob, 28
Jairus's daughter, 131
Jehovah's Witnesses, 130
Jeremiah, 248
Jerusalem, 28, 154, 258
Jerusalem Bible, 130
Jesus Christ, 14, 24, 25, 27, 46, 61,
    81, 93, 104, 115, 129, 151, 152,
    158 ff., 171, 175, 176, 199, 208,
    212, 215, 225, 230, 235, 248,
    254; arrest, trials of, 91 f., 207;
    ascension of, 41, 88, 133, 136;
    baptism of, 15, 36 f.; Body of,
    100, 135 f., 194, 209, 246, 248;
    in Creation, 19, 53, 232; cross,
    crucifixion, death of, 15, 17, 29,
    35, 36, 37, 40, 47, 59, 65, 71, 82,
    92, 112, 120, 142, 151, 155, 187,
    189, 195, 200, 213, 215, 218, 219,
    224, 232, 240, 243, 244 f., 246,
    253, 258; descent into Hades by,
    38, 142; Epiphany of, 55 ff.;
    foot-washing by, 91; future
    coming of, 114, 234; as Good
    Shepherd, 248 f.; healing work
    of, 131, 179, 238; an image of
    God, 71 f., 102, 106, 156, 193;
    incarnation, birth of, 44, 74, 87,
    106, 189, 232; judgement of, 48,
    239, 255 f.; as man, 134, 161,
    250; as Messiah, 181 f.; nature-
    miracles of, 102; parables of
    (*see also* Prodigal Son), 41, 52,
    179, 203 f., 214, 215, 217, 219;
    resurrection of, Easter, 15, 17,
    35, 36, 41, 67, 71 f., 92 f., 105,
    112, 120, 136, 142 f., 183, 206,

232, 239, 246, 249, 250 f.; as
    second Adam, 13, 141, 143, 154,
    193, 200, 206, 208 ff., 224, 227,
    242, 244, 246, 249, 258; Sermon
    on the Mount of, 42, 190, 211
    ff.; as servant, slave, 75, 137,
    148, 193; as son of David, 159
    ff.; as Son of God, 20, 35, 67,
    83, 106, 107, 130, 133, 148,
    159 ff., 193; stilling of storm by,
    40, 103; teaching of, 94, 216,
    218, 239; temptation of, 102,
    151, 152; two natures of, 122;
    virgin conception of, 23, 34, 87,
    160
Joel, 82
Johannesburg, 94, 125, 130, 141,
    247, 248
John the Baptist, 24, 36, 224
Jordan, 15, 36, 40, 181
Joseph of Arimathaea, 251
Jubilee, year of, 112
Julian of Norwich, 109, 264
Jung, C. G., 37, 218, 260, 269
Justice, 27, 89, 91 ff., 112, 226
Justification, 34, 71, 196, 234, 243

Kekulé, F. A. von, 123
King James Version, 135
King, Martin Luther, 254, 271
Kingdom of God, 15, 26, 55, 63,
    154, 161, 211, 223, 234, 257
Knight, G. A. F., 259 (18), 260
    (37), 265 (135)
Koestler, Arthur, 265 (124)
Koran, The, 42, 261

Lake, Carlton, 265 (134)
Lake, Frank, 107 f., 262 (77), 264,
    272 (255)
Land, 97 ff., 111 f., 180
Law, 28, 40, 91 f., 111, 120 f., 145,
    149, 157, 195, 197, 214
Lawrence, D. H., 267 (174)
Leighton, R., 255
Lenin, V., 182
Levites, 98
Lewis, C. S., 34, 260

Locke, John, 156
Lorenz, Konrad, 77, 198, 262, 269
Love, 51, 64 f., 67 f., 93, 131, 133, 150, 154, 155, 160, 168, 170, 220, 230, 250
Luther, Martin, 22, 35 f., 71, 154, 262, 266

Mann, Thomas, 132
Maoris, 99, 125
Marriage, 78, 84, 111, 146, 168, 170, 172 ff., 180, 255
Martin, M.-L., 268 (180, 183)
Marx, Karl, 182, 222
Mary, 178, 253; as new Eve, 227, 242
Mary Magdalene, 143
Mascall, E. L., 32, 260, 269 (205)
Messiah, 25, 106, 181, 189, 206. See also Jesus Christ
Mgijima, Enoch, 180
Michael, 147, 253 f.
Michelangelo, 132
Michigan, University of, 86
Milford, T. R., 261 (48)
Milton, John, 147, 201, 266
More, Thomas, 92
Moses, 14 f., 25, 107, 124, 158, 195
Myth, 18, 37, 40, 68, 121, 123, 179 f., 183 f., 221
Mzobe, Michael, 183

Naboth, 98
Nagpur, Bishop of, 271 (250)
New English Bible, 39, 40, 135, 167, 228
Newton, Sir Isaac, 184
Niebuhr, Reinhold, 181, 263 (90), 266 (148), 268, 270 (221)
Niemöller, Martin, 77
Noah, 244
Nongqause, 182
Nyerere, Mwalimu Julius K., 111, 264

Okavango, 139
Original Sin, 84, 204 f., 208 f.

Orthodox Churches, Eastern, 74, 182, 196
Orthodox Liturgy, The, 269 (196)
Osborne, John, 185, 268
Owen, Wilfred, 189

Paradise, see Eden
Paschasius, 67
Pasteur, Louis, 59
Paul, 13, 36, 92, 152. See also Index of Scriptural References
Pelz, Werner, 71, 262
Penitent thief, 141, 154
Pentecost, 40, 80 ff., 93, 153, 155, 257
Peter, 255
Philip, 154
Picasso, Pablo, 134
Pilate, Pontius, 29, 38, 47, 152, 207
Pinter, Harold, 185
Plato, 35
Pluto, 156
Politics, 27, 54, 55, 84, 88 ff., 114, 182, 235 f., 257
Potter, Stephen, 190, 268
Power, 88 f., 91 f., 103 f., 254
Practical Motorist, 270 (226)
Prodigal Son, 179, 203, 219, 251
Proudhon, P. J., 94

Quoist, Michel, 132, 265

Race, Racialism, 15, 44, 49, 73, 79, 80, 81, 82, 85, 86, 159 ff., 174, 175 f., 196, 199, 242
Raphael, archangel, 253
Raphael Santi, 117
Rawlinson, A. E. J., 272 (258)
Revised Standard Version, 14, 130, 259
Robinson, J. A. T., 269 (213), 270 (236)
Rolfe, C. H., 267 (174)
Ryle, Sir Martin, 31

Sabbath, 107 f., 110 ff., 180, 234
Sanchez, F., 163

Sartre, Jean-Paul, 73, 169, 245, 262, 267, 271
Satan, see Devil
Saul, King, 146
Saul of Tarsus, 246
Schönberg, A., 117
Schopenhauer, A., 137
Science, 18 f., 30 f., 33, 45 f., 54, 60, 96, 118 f., 122 f., 126, 157, 162
Separation, apartheid, 48 f., 80, 94, 95, 154, 210, 258
Serpent, snake, 148, 185, 186 ff., 197 f., 201, 220, 227
Sex, sexuality, 78 f., 87, 143 f., 166 f., 172 f., 174, 178, 201 f.
Shembe, Isaiah, 182
Short, R. L., 265 (127)
Simeon, 178
Sin, 77, 93, 194 ff., 197 f., 208 f., 222, 244
Social sciences, 221
Socrates, 188
South Africa, Southern Africa, 9 f., 25, 56, 81, 90, 98, 99, 110, 117, 139, 144, 159, 164, 174, 176, 187, 196, 215, 226, 247
Southcott, E. W., 269 (211)
Spirit of God, Holy Spirit, 36, 39, 40 f., 67, 82, 130, 153, 154, 155, 161, 216, 232, 251, 256
Star, The, 265
Stephen, 246
Strachan, R. H., 268 (187)
Sundkler, Bengt, 183, 268 (180)
Symbol, symbolism, 70, 121, 157 f., 179, 187

Tanzania, 97, 111
Taylor, John V., 142, 266, 272 (258)
Teilhard de Chardin, P., 69, 124, 127 f., 137, 163, 261 (48), 261 (58), 262 (68), 262, 265, 266, 267, 272 (257)
Temple, William, 124

Tennant, Roger, 190, 268
Theology, 190, 268
Thielike, Helmut, 260 (35), 267 (169), 270 (221)
Thomas, 159
Thornton, L. S., 260 (29)
Thurber, James, 132, 265, 267 (174)
Thurman, Howard, 160, 215, 267, 269
Tillich, Paul, 130, 265, 269 (213), 270 (231)
Tippett, Michael, 23
Tournier, Paul, 43, 261, 264 (102)
Toynbee, Arnold, 16
Trinity, 67, 74, 122, 155, 199, 208
Tutankhamen, 70

Uzzah, 28

van Buren, Paul, 208, 269
van der Leeuw, Gerardus, 259 (19), 262 (70), 262 (74), 266 (137)
Verinder, F., 263 (99)
von Rad, Gerhard, 19, 40, 107, 141, 184, 259, 260, 264, 266, 268

Water, 15, 36, 38, 40, 47, 48, 60, 134, 139, 141
White, E. B., 267 (174)
White, T. H., 88, 263
White, Victor, 172, 267
Whitehead, A. N., 165, 267
Williams, H. A., 10, 100, 197, 260 (44), 263, 266 (152), 267 (162), 268 (194), 269, 271 (239), 271 (255), 272 (256)
Woman, see Eve
Wordsworth, William, 259 (21)
Work, 88, 110 f., 143, 232 ff.

Zion, 182, 187
Zulu, 39, 156, 186

Index of Scriptural References

A figure in brackets after a reference to one of the 'Notes' pages (pp. 259-72) indicates the related page in the main text.

GENESIS

1—3, pp. 9, 13 f., 120, 124, 125, 126

1: 1—2: 4 (*also referred to as* Genesis 1), pp. 18, 19, 20, 24, 31, 42, 76, 82, 116, 119, 121, 126, 129, 139, 150, 163, 205, 226, 233

1: 1-2, p. 22

1: 3-5, p. 41

1: 6-8, p. 47

1: 9-10, p. 50

1: 11-13, p. 52

1: 14-19, p. 53

1: 20-23, p. 58

1: 24-25, p. 62

1: 26-28, p. 66

1: 28, p. 228

1: 29-31, p. 105

2: 1-4, p. 106

2: 2-7, p. 129

2: 5—3: 24 (*also referred to as* Genesis 2 and 3), pp. 120, 121, 125, 205

2: 5-25 (*also referred to as* Genesis 2), pp. 42, 126, 139, 150, 163, 184, 205

2: 5, p. 140

2: 8-9, p. 137

2: 10-15, p. 138

2: 16-17, p. 145

2: 18, p. 153

2: 19-20, p. 155

2: 21-22, p. 165

2: 23, p. 167

2: 24, p. 173

2: 25, p. 178

3: p. 204

3: 1, p. 186

3: 2-3, p. 192

3: 4-5, p. 193

3: 5, p. 266 (151)

3: 6, p. 196

3: 7, p. 201

3: 8, p. 210

3: 9, p. 213

3: 10, p. 216

3: 11-13, p. 219

3: 14-19, p. 186

3: 14-15, p. 226

3: 16, p. 227

3: 17-19, pp. 230 f.

3: 19, p. 233

3: 20, p. 241

3: 21, p. 242

3: 22, pp. 243, 266 (151)

3: 23, p. 245

3: 24, p. 251

5: 1, p. 271 (242)

5: 2, p. 267 (171)

6: 1-4, p. 263 (83)

9: 3, p. 264 (106)

11: 1-9, p. 262 (80)

11: 7, p. 262 (67)

22: p. 261 (49)

23: p. 271 (248)

28: 16 ff., p. 259 (28)

EXODUS

3: pp. 263 (83), 265 (129)

3: 5, p. 259 (28)

3: 14, p. 266 (158)

10: 21, p. 260 (37)

14: 21-22, p. 270 (232)

18: p. 264 (107)

20: 8-11, p. 264 (110)

23: 11, p. 264 (111)

32: 4, p. 259 (28)

32: 8, p. 268 (195)

LEVITICUS, p. 99
25: 1–7, p. 264 (111)
25: 8–17, p. 264 (112)
25: 23, p. 263 (97)
25: 29–31, p. 264 (112)

NUMBERS
18: 24, p. 263 (98)
21: 6, p. 268 (187)
21: 9, p. 268 (187)

DEUTERONOMY
6: 4, p. 261 (66)
16: 2, p. 260 (28)
19: 14, p. 263 (98)
26: 1–4, p, 263 (98)
31: 10–13, p. 264 (111)
32: 11, p. 271 (249)

JUDGES
5: p. 267 (162)
8: 23, p. 263 (98)
12: 6, p. 263 (93)
14: 20, p. 267 (176)

I SAMUEL
8: 10–20, p. 263 (98)
10: 8, p. 266 (146)

2 SAMUEL
6: 6, p. 259 (28)
13: p. 267 (173)
23: 20, p. 263 (88)

I KINGS
8: 27, p. 264 (115)
8: 30, p. 264 (115)
18: 21, p. 265 (129)
18: 39, p. 265 (129)
19: p. 260 (38)
21: p. 263 (98)

2 KINGS
18: 4, p. 268 (187)

NEHEMIAH
9: 6, p. 264 (109)

JOB
3: 21, p. 260 (33)
40—41, p. 61

PSALMS, pp. 117, 255
8: pp. 116, 263 (94)
8: 5–6, p. 264 (116)
10: p. 263 (92)
24: 1, pp. 259 (26), 263 (97)
33: 6, 9, p. 260 (42)
89: p. 270 (232)
104: 14, 20, 22, p. 264 (109)
115: 16, pp. 263 (97), 264 (113)
119: 32, p. 261 (42)
135: p. 270 (232)
136: p. 270 (232)
139: 7–10, p. 269 (213)
148: 5, p. 261 (42)

ECCLESIASTES
7: 16, p. 270 (238)

THE SONG OF SONGS, p. 173

ISAIAH
6: 2, p. 268 (187)
6: 8, p. 262 (67)
11: 1–9, p. 264 (106)
14: 12–14, p. 266 (147)
40: 25, p. 268 (190)
42: 8, p. 262 (66)
44: 28—45: 7, p. 259 (26)
45: 7, p. 266 (148)

JEREMIAH
7: 4, p. 268 (194)
23: 7–8, p. 259 (24)

EZEKIEL
1: 5, p. 271 (252)
10: 1, p. 271 (252)
28: 1–15, p. 268 (184)
37: 1–10, p. 265 (135)

AMOS
3: 6, p. 266 (148)

JONAH
1: 3–4, p. 269 (213)
2: 3, p. 260 (38)

HABAKKUK
3, p. 270 (232)

MALACHI
4: 6, p. 272 (255)

2 MACCABEES
7: 28, p. 260 (35)

MATTHEW
2: 1–12, p. 261 (55)
2: 9, p. 270 (232)
3: 13–17, p. 260 (40)
4: 1–11, pp. 264 (103), 266 (151)
5: 20–48, p. 269 (212)
6: 19–21, p. 263 (94)
7: 23, p. 269 (212)
7: 24, p. 268 (190)
8: 18 ff., p. 260 (40)
11: 4–5, p. 264 (103)
11: 27, p. 266 (155)
13: 24–30, p. 261 (53)
14: 36, p. 269 (215)
15: 24, p. 270 (235)
18: 21–35, p. 271 (243)
22: 1–10, p. 269 (217)
22: 11–14, p. 269 (217)
22: 42, p. 266 (158)
23: 4–22, p. 268 (192)
24: 23, p. 267 (166)
27: 17, p. 263 (83)
27: 51, p. 270 (232)
27: 57—28: 7, p. 259 (17)
28: 2, p. 270 (232)
28: 5–20, p. 271 (249)
28: 18, pp. 263 (92), 271 (249)
28: 19, pp. 262 (82), 263 (93)

MARK
2: 7, p. 269 (200)
3: 28–30, p. 271 (251)

3: 29–30, p. 267 (161)
3: 31–35, p. 267 (178)
4: 3–8, 26–32, p. 261 (53)
5: 21–43, p. 265 (131)
8: 33, p. 270 (225)
8: 34–35, p. 261 (60)
9: 32–33, p. 270 (225)
10: 17, p. 269 (214)
11: 18, p. 262 (82)
12: 13, p. 269 (207)
12: 13–17, p. 263 (92)
13: 28–29, p. 261 (53)
14: 50, p. 270 (225)
15: 22, p. 272 (258)
15: 33, p. 270 (232)
15: 33–34, p. 260 (34)
15: 34, p. 266 (154)

LUKE
1: 29, p. 271 (253)
1: 38, p. 271 (242)
2: 7, p. 270 (232)
2: 35, p. 267 (178)
2: 41–51, p. 267 (178)
3: 8, p. 259 (24)
5: 1–11, p. 272 (256)
6: 12, p. 266 (155)
6: 37, p. 270 (218)
9: 2, p. 270 (223)
10: 18, p. 266 (148)
10: 25–37, p. 269 (214)
11: 27–28, p. 267 (178)
12: 14, p. 269 (214)
15: 2, p. 269 (204)
15: 4–10, p. 269 (215)
15: 20, 24, 28, 31, p. 271 (251)
15: 30, p. 270 (220)
22: 37, p. 270 (225)
23: 12, p. 269 (207)
23: 39–43, pp. 266 (142), 266 (154)
24: 5, p. 259 (17)
24: 16, p. 264 (105)
24: 31, p. 269 (206)

JOHN
1: 1, 2, 14, p. 259 (22)
1: 4, p. 261 (42)

1: 5, p. 261 (45)
1: 11, p. 269 (215)
1: 12–13, p. 267 (161)
2: 4, p. 261 (46)
3: 3–5, p. 267 (161)
3: 5, p. 271 (340)
3: 14, p. 268 (187)
4: 10, p. 265 (134)
4: 14, p. 265 (134)
4: 34, p. 270 (235)
6: 39, p. 271 (239)
7: 30, p. 261 (46)
7: 37–38, p. 265 (134)
7: 41–52, p. 262 (82)
8: 1–11, p. 269 (212)
8: 39, p. 262 (82)
10: 4, pp. 248, 271 (249)
11: 50, pp. 262 (82), 266 (159)
12: 9–19, p. 262 (82)
12: 23 ff., p. 261 (60)
12: 24, p. 264 (105)
12: 27–31, p. 261 (46)
12: 32, p. 272 (258)
13: 13–17, p. 263 (91)
14: 9, p. 259 (14)
14: 10, p. 266 (155)
14: 12, p. 260 (41)
14: 28, p. 265 (133)
15: 16, p. 266 (149)
16: 7, p. 260 (41)
16: 8–11, p. 272 (256)
16: 13, p. 269 (216)
16: 32–33, p. 266 (155)
17: 4, p. 270 (235)
18: 3, pp. 207, 269
18: 23, p. 263 (92)
19: 5, pp. 270 (235), 271 (250)
19: 27, p. 271 (242)
19: 30, p. 261 (65)
20: 14, p. 264 (105)
20: 15, p. 266 (143)
20: 17, p. 265 (134)
20: 22–23, p. 262 (67)
20: 28, pp. 265 (130), 266 (159)
21: 4, p. 264 (105)

ACTS
2: 2, p. 260 (40)

2: 2–3, p. 270 (232)
2: 5, p. 262 (81)
2: 8–10, p. 262 (81)
2: 17–18, p. 262 (82)
2: 41, p. 262 (81)
2: 42–47, p. 262 (81)
7: 47, p. 260 (29)
8: 26–40, p. 266 (154)
13: 6, p. 261 (55)
22: 25, p. 263 (92)

ROMANS
4: 17, p. 260 (35)
6: 4, p. 271 (240)
6: 23, p. 271 (240)
8: 19–22, p. 270 (231)
8: 23, p. 270 (231)
8: 38–39, pp. 261 (65), 264 (115), 271 (250)

I CORINTHIANS
1: 28, p. 260 (35)
3: 3–5, p. 263 (96)
11: 11, p. 270 (230)
11: 12, p. 270 (230)
12: 4–30, pp. 91, 263 (91)
12: 12, p. 265 (135)
13: 6, p. 267 (170)
13: 12, p. 263 (83)
15: 10, p. 268 (196)
15: 21, p. 271 (244)
15: 22, p. 272 (258)
15: 26, p. 271 (240)
15: 36–44, p. 264 (105)
15: 42 ff., p. 53
15: 58, p. 271 (239 f.)

2 CORINTHIANS
5: 4, p. 269 (206)
5: 21, p. 260 (37)
6: 14–18, p. 261 (49)
11: 3, pp. 186, 268

GALATIANS
1: 8–11, p. 263 (95)
2: 20, p. 261 (65)
3: 27–28, p. 263 (93)
4: 4, p. 261 (46)

4: 5, p. 265 (83)
6: 15, p. 271 (250)

EPHESIANS
1: 10, pp. 263 (93), 272 (257)
3: 1–11, p. 263 (94)
3: 12, p. 269 (196)
3: 17, p. 261 (51)
3: 19, p. 260 (33)
4: 8, p. 271 (250)
4: 10, p. 263 (88)
4: 11–13, p. 271 (250)
4: 32, p. 271 (243)
5: 21, p. 270 (230)
5: 22, p. 270 (230)
5: 25, p. 270 (230)
5: 31–33, p. 267 (175)

PHILIPPIANS
2: 1–8, p. 266 (148)
2: 6, p. 268 (193)
2: 6–8, p. 262 (75)
3: 13, p. 270 (237)
3: 20, p. 264 (114)

COLOSSIANS
1: 15, pp. 260 (29), 262 (70)
1: 20, pp. 259 (15), 260 (29)
2: 15, p. 271 (253)
3: 5, p. 263 (97)

HEBREWS
3: 5–6, p. 264 (107)
11: 3, p. 260 (35)
11: 8-10, p. 267 (165)
11: 14–16, p. 259 (21)

I PETER
2: 24, p. 270 (224)
3: 19, p. 266 (142)

I JOHN
4: 9, p. 266 (150)

REVELATION
2—3, p. 272 (256)
2: 1–7, p. 272 (256)
2: 17, p. 267 (171)
2: 20, p. 261 (49)
3: 16, p. 261 (49)
7: 9–10, p. 272 (257)
7: 9–14, p. 259 (15)
12: 9, pp. 268 (187), 270 (227)
13: p. 261 (61)
19: 11–21, p. 261 (61)
21—22, p. 139
21: 1, pp. 264 (114), 266 (139)
21: 3, p. 260 (29)
21: 7, p. 272 (257)
21: 23, p. 266 (139)
22: 1–2, p. 266 (139)
22: 2, p. 272 (257)